D1357781

German Buenos Aires, 1900–1933

Social Change and Cultural Crisis

The Texas Pan American Series

German Buenos Aires, 1900–1933
Social Change and Cultural Crisis

By Ronald C. Newton

University of Texas Press, Austin & London

The Texas Pan American Series is published with the
assistance of a revolving publication fund established
by the Pan American Sulphur Company.

The publication of this book was assisted by a grant
from the Andrew W. Mellon Foundation.

Library of Congress Cataloging in Publication Data
Newton, Ronald C   1933–
    German Buenos Aires, 1900–1933.
    (Texas Pan American series)
    Bibliography: p.
    Includes index.
    1. Germans in Buenos Aires. 2. Buenos Aires—Social
conditions. I. Title.
F3001.9.G3N48   301.45'13'10821   77-7206
ISBN 0-292-72714-3

To the memory of my friend

JOHN HUNTER ARMSTRONG

Contents

Acknowledgments

For their aid and encouragement at the outset of this study, I am especially indebted to Dr. Ricardo Caillet-Bois; the Alemann family of the *Argentinisches Tageblatt*; Herr Müller of the *Freie Presse*; Pfarrer Heuser and Frau Heuser; and Dr. K. W. Körner and Frau Körner; all of Buenos Aires. My thanks go also to the officials and staffs of the Verein Deutscher Ingenieure in Argentinien; Club Alemán "Vorwärts"; Federación de Asociaciones Argentino-Germanas; Cámara de Comercio Argentino-Alemana; Deutscher Klub Buenos Aires; Goethe Institut Buenos Aires; Dirección de Inmigración; Biblioteca del Ministerio de Agricultura; Biblioteca Nacional; Biblioteca del Congreso; Biblioteca del Banco Tornquist; Biblioteca de Ciencias Sociales, Instituto di Tella; Institut für Auslandsbeziehungen (Stuttgart); Bundesarchiv-Militärarchiv (Freiburg i.B.); and the Friedrich-Ebert-Stiftung (Bonn/Bad Godesberg). For helpful suggestions and criticisms I owe thanks to Professors Karl J. R. Arndt, L. E. Hill, Carl Solberg, Morton Winsberg, and Alberto Ciria. The study was begun as a pastime in Buenos Aires while I was engaged upon another project funded by the Social Science Research Council; it was continued with financial assistance from Canada Council and the President's Research Fund of Simon Fraser University—thanks are due to all of them. I am especially thankful to Jo Cook, who typed the manuscript, and to my wife Ortrud, who saw it through.

West Vancouver, British Columbia
December 1976

Preface

In the three decades before World War I, the grasslands of Argentina, the Humid Pampa, were transformed into one of the world's major foodstuff-producing and exporting regions. Simultaneously, the economy of the Argentine republic was closely meshed into the world trading system whose motor and chief beneficiary was industrialized Western Europe. The facts of geography dictated that the port of Buenos Aires would be the funnel through which would flow the bulk of the Pampa's foodstuffs and fibers in one direction, and of Europe's manufactures, capital, technology, and surplus labor power in the other. It was only in 1880 that civil strife abated sufficiently to permit the city's confirmation as both the political capital of Argentina and the nation's economic metropolis. Nevertheless, its population had been rising steadily since midcentury; growth accelerated with the economic boom of the years 1882–1889, and from the mid-1880s to 1914 population quintupled to one and one half million. The secondary cities of the eastern Littoral—Rosario, Santa Fe, La Plata, Bahía Blanca—also experienced great increases, though in smaller absolute numbers. Hence the curious fact that at the outbreak of the First World War, of the nearly eight million inhabitants of this eminently agricultural and pastoral land, just over half were classified as city dwellers. And urban preponderance would, of course, continue to increase.

The principal source of population increase was European immigration. Between 1857 and the beginning of the Great Depression of the 1930s (when the Argentine government for the first time restricted the entry of foreign workers), some 6.4 million immigrants entered the country; and their greatest demographic impact was felt in the eastern cities. By the 1880s four-fifths of the adult male population of Buenos Aires was foreign born; in 1914 the proportion was three-quarters. It entered upon a steady decline thereafter; however, as late as 1936 (by which time the city's population had risen to 2.4 million) 49 percent of the adult population had been born outside the republic. The immigrant avalanche markedly altered the genetic and cultural character of the original *criollo* population of Argentina, which had been little more than a million at the middle of the nineteenth century. Its effects would presumably have been greater still were it not for the fact that fully four-fifths of the immigrants were of the kindred, easily assimilable, Latin peoples of Southern Europe—and for the fact, also, that nearly half of *all* immigrants to Argentina left the country again.

The textbook explanation of these twin phenomena—the agglomeration of immigrants in the gateway cities of the east, and the high incidence of reemigration—is that the promise of the thinly settled interior proved largely illusory to peasants forced out of zones of rural overpopulation in Western Europe. The vision of prosperous settlements of independent smallholders on the Pampa was precluded from the 1870s onward by the expansion of extensive, heavily capitalized, and export-oriented *estancias*. Would-be peasants unable to obtain property confronted the meagre alternatives of short-term, exploitative, rental agreements on the land or removal to the city. From either place it was but a short step to reemigration or continuation of the search elsewhere in the Americas.

This explanation, however, is valid only in a general way, and it is serviceable for only a relatively limited period of time—the two decades or so prior to the crash of 1889, during which the competition for the republic's remaining prime agricultural land was at its most intense. During the decade of the 1880s 70 percent of the economically active immigrants had declared themselves to be agriculturalists (the same percentage, in fact, had held since the beginning of immigration records). In the following decade, however, the figure fell sharply to 45.7 percent; it was 42 percent in the first decade of the new century, and less than 25 percent in the second. Peasants, in other words, were increasingly replaced by immigrants in commercial, industrial, professional, artisan, and service occupations—that is, urban occupations. They brought with them the skills and habits of Europe's high urban tradition. With few exceptions they had no intention of starting a new life on the Argentine land. Many, in fact, reversed what is sometimes proffered as the typical immigrant experience: having achieved a modest prosperity in urban pursuits, they might well follow the path of bourgeois entrepreneurship most appropriate to time and place, the purchase of rural property for productive or speculative purposes.

If unavailability of land was not the principal determinant of reemigration from Argentina—after the 1890s, at any rate—it is nevertheless true that possession of land was a powerful inducement to stay to a migrant whose mind was not otherwise made up, and there were many of these. The fact is that with the preemption of much of the Pampa by the *estancieros* and the coeval development of Argentina's investment, extractive, processing, transport, and utility structures as extensions of the European system, the definition of immigrant itself became elusive. There was a spectrum of types. At one extreme were those who knew that, barring accident, they would return to their European homelands. They were the managers and technicians of the installations pertaining to the several informal empires that shared Argentina: the British, the French, the German, and, after World War I, the North American. Though relatively few in number, they were highly influential in directing both the development of the Argentine economy and the formation of attitudes among their own immigrant countrymen. Farther along the spectrum, in vastly greater numbers, were the immigrant workers, artisans, professionals, and small business owners who sought to "make America." For them Argentina was a temporary expedient; the goal was an honored and comfortable old age in the natal village in Swabia or Galicia or the Ticino. The archetypes were the *golondrinas*, the Spanish and Italian field laborers who in their thousands first followed the European harvest northward and then, on the approach of autumn, took steerage passage to Argentina to perform identical labor during the Southern Hemisphere summer. Similar motives, however, were equally compelling to British bank tellers and German engineers, Yugoslav stone masons and Catalan *almaceneros*, French *pâtissiers* and Italian architects. The range of possibilities among this great mass was of course almost infinite. Such persons could become "immigrants" at the end of an intricate skein of choice and accident, when the ties that held them to Argentina came to seem stronger than those that drew them away. Or, it was sometimes the children who were the true "immigrants," those who remained in the New World when their parents demanded to return to the Old to die. At the far end of the spectrum were those who had little choice but to stay, either because (before the steamships) they were unable to face the rigors of a return voyage to Europe, or because—like the East European Jews, the Armenians, the Volga-Germans—they had no homeland to which to return.

With the foregoing I mean to suggest a number of points. First, that great numbers of immigrants originated in European urban environments and were fully capable of functioning well in a similar Argentine milieu. Second, that our detailed knowledge of their experience there is even more rudimentary than of the rural settlements; we know virtually nothing of the processes that made Argentines of a portion of them, and returnees of the remainder. Third, that especially given the reevaluation of "ethnicity" and "the melting pot" that is at present taking place among students of the immigrant experience in

North America, it would seem consummate folly to translate North American concepts indiscriminately to the Argentine context. Hence my purposes in the study of the German-speaking community of Buenos Aires which follows are twofold: to find out what happened to one well-demarcated cultural group during a period of rapid demographic growth and apparent increase of pressures on foreigners to become Argentinized; and having done so more or less satisfactorily, to attempt to extract working hypotheses to be applied and refined in further investigations.

It scarcely need be said that German speakers made up one of the smaller Western European communities within the Argentine metropolis. They numbered some four thousand in the early 1880s, thirty thousand on the eve of World War I, and perhaps forty-five thousand on the eve of World War II. But it scarcely need be said either that the influence of German merchants, industrialists, academics, professionals, military men, and artisans was far out of proportion to their numbers. The German community's relatively small size makes it a more manageable object of study than, for example, the vast Italian or Spanish collectivities. By the 1920s it came to comprise all social levels, although its center of gravity was a large and occupationally diverse middle class; the community therefore serves in some ways as a litmus paper of social changes taking place in the larger urban society. One could anticipate, finally, that the surviving documentation would be ample and of high quality. This expectation was met in general, although time and a turbulent political history have left vast unfillable *lacunae.*

Precisely this political history, moreover, has created a problem which I do not feel that I have dealt with satisfactorily: the situation of German-speaking Jews within the community before and after 1933. Any historian or social scientist who has encountered in Buenos Aires the pervasive *desconfianza* toward anyone investigating anything will appreciate the difficulties inherent in the study of foreign communities. In the matter of two communities as sensitive toward the ambiguities and sufferings of their past as the German and the Jewish, the problems are greater still. A Germanic background and *bona fides* have made the one accessible to me. I regret that the other is not; I have no remedy. Also, in only a few places do the sources give voice to women among the immigrants. This too is regrettable, for it would surely be instructive to know something of the experience of this sizable minority of immigrants—particularly those who came unaccompanied. But again there is no obvious remedy.

North American scholars have considered the principal function of the urban immigrant community to be that of a sort of halfway house: a social environment in which the newly arrived migrant can find respite from the shocks of the new land and in which he may learn, as painlessly as possible, the techniques of adaptation. At some indeterminate point he may then, from a position of strength, pass from adaptation to assimilation. The community would thus last only as long as the flow of new immigrants; should the flow dry up the community would disappear once the last sizable immigrant generation had been assimilated. In Argentina, however, particularly among the Germans and other peoples who held themselves biologically or culturally superior to the *criollos*, the community's function could not be defined in such unequivocally teleological terms. Just as often it has resembled the extraterritorial quarter in which foreign merchants customarily lived and did business in the classic trading cities of the Mediterranean world and the Orient. At times it has been a citadel, occasionally a political bridgehead (as the German communities certainly were for the nazi activists of the 1930s). It is true, of course, that in Buenos Aires the German-speaking community has been swallowed up by the surrounding Argentine society since 1945, just as the comparable English-speaking community is undergoing the same process at the present time. But these developments are explicable in terms of specific historical events—chiefly the failure of the European mother countries to sustain their informal dependencies with emigrants, economic opportunity, and the intangible trappings of imperial prestige— and it does not seem necessary to consider them the foredoomed consequences of inexorable processes.

The communal conviction of superiority to the surrounding culture profoundly affected the ways in which individuals experienced adaptation and assimilation (or behavioral and structural assimilation). Although spokesmen of the German community claimed special gifts of adaptation for the Germans, all the evidence to be presented indicates this was far from the case. At best, German business owners were quick to adapt sales and manufacturing practices to Argentine conditions. But as individuals the Germans throve only when there was little competition. Neither artisans nor farmers nor small business owners adapted themselves sufficiently well to meet the challenges of the more austere folk of Southern and Eastern Europe. From the *criollos* themselves, middle-class German professional and white-collar workers encountered increasing competition after World War I; they were thus forced to adapt themselves much more extensively to the usages of Argentine nationalism. It is worth noting, however, that middle-class business owners did not encounter the same upward thrust on the part of the *criollos* and had consequently less need to alter their behavior.

As to integration into the familial and primary group structures of the receiving society, or structural assimilation, it is well to remember the predominance of sheer numbers that the immigrants brought to the processes of social change. In the cities especially, *lo criollo* was not the core to which all others had to attach themselves; rather, in the decades around the turn of the century, urban society was in a process of fusion, a process of becoming. Hence it was quite possible for ethnic groups to maintain their existence over several generations, though not necessarily by remaining hermetically closed. In the German population the relative scarcity and low fecundity of German women caused concern, but the cultural subsystem was maintained nevertheless. Marriages tended to follow religious and socioeconomic class lines as much as ethnic lines. Germanic culture could be preserved and transmitted so long as the spouse (normally the wife) of an exogamous marriage could be induced to learn the language, keep a German household, and work for a German education for the children. This process of transmitting and preserving Germanic culture through non-Germanic media could only exist with the local reinforcement of a structure of voluntary associations which provided a nearly complete Germanic social environment; it was reinforced also, more distantly, by the prestige of German art and industry, science and military might. This was of course facilitated by the fluidity of urban immigrant society at the time, and the self-deprecation that *criollos* were wont to assume when confronted by European bearers of culture. Two world wars would be required to alter the latter.

The study is also meant to serve as the necessary preliminary to an understanding of the virulent nazism of the years from 1933 to 1945. In this regard, a number of points emerge from the following pages. After 1918 Argentina served as a bolt-hole for German political fugitives as well as capitalists unable to tolerate postwar instability in Europe. They were welcomed by the community's business leadership, which emerged from the war prosperous, arrogant, and utterly hostile to the new, postarmistice, Germany. These men apparently supported anti-Weimar causes in Germany with lavish donations. They also gained control of the community's schools and associations and worked to suppress dissent. Authoritarian and vestigially monarchist, they acceded to the coming of nazism in 1931 and sought to turn the movement to their own purposes. Insofar as nazism engaged mass sentiment, however, its appeal was essentially of the moralistic, antielite, anticapitalist, "left-wing" variety. The nazi period, in other words, began amidst social class conflict and contradictions between appearance and reality. The further elaboration of these themes and examination of the mechanisms by which nazism entered Argentine public life are the substance of a second volume which will, I hope, appear in due course.

German Buenos Aires, 1900–1933

Social Change and Cultural Crisis

1. Before 1914: the Old Colony

Ernst Bachmann of Bielefeld was a restless spirit who migrated to Argentina after seeing duty as a Prussian officer during the campaigns of 1866 and 1870. In the New World he turned his hand to many ventures. He was a free-lance journalist; he coauthored (with one Van Gelderen) a *Nuevo método para aprender alemán*, worked as editor-in-chief of the *Deutsche La-Plata Zeitung*, and lectured at the Escuela de Guerra. In 1882 he figured among the founders of the Association for the Protection of Germanic Immigrants (Verein zum Schutze germanischer Einwanderer), and in 1884 he had to reply (satisfactorily, by his own account) to sharp questioning within the association concerning his personal activities on behalf of certain Basel colonizing firms. He returned to Germany in 1889 to head up the Argentine Information Bureau in Berlin. The office was closed in 1891, and Bachmann died there the following year in his mid-forties. In 1884, in his capacity as editor of *Kunz' Yearbook and Address Calendar of the German Colony in Buenos Aires*, he wrote:

> Is the history of the German-speaking collectivity in South America any less instructive, any less inspiring, than that of North America? Have, for example, German striving, German intellect, German education, German efficiency and accomplishment received less recognition on the shores of La Plata than those of the Hudson or Mississippi? By comparison, certainly not! Quite the contrary! There [in North America], all that has been accomplished in fully two centuries by several million German immigrants and their descendants stands neither materially nor morally in any relationship to that which in South America—and especially in Argentina—has been achieved within a few decades by some thousands of our countrymen—achieved for themselves and for the whole of the Germanic peoples.
>
> *Materially*, certainly not, for one may assert with full confidence that here, a far higher percentage of the immigrant Germans have risen to affluence, prestige, high position, and influence, than in North America.
>
> Nor *morally* either, because here the immigrant German, in the midst of an overwhelmingly Latin population, runs far less danger

of giving up his nationality, customs, language, habits—in short, of being *de*nationalized—than in North America. There, through almost constant interaction with members of the racially related Anglo-Saxons, his Germanic form and being are soon enough swallowed up in the sea of Americanism. Precisely for that reason it is impossible for those Germans settled in the northern half of the New World—in the midst of that gigantically developed, all-absorbing industrial people—ever to fulfill the high cultural mission that has been assigned to the German people.

Nor can the hundreds of thousands streaming yearly to the ports of the American Union turn Germany's emigration to the advantage of the Fatherland—its industry, trade, and economic well-being. Such a purpose can much better be accomplished through a partial redirection of the great stream of German emigration toward the lands of the South American East Coast. Here, a virtually untouched, highly rewarding field of activity awaits German energy, German intelligence, and German industriousness; moreover, a broad new market could be won for the export trade, industry, and productive strength of the mother country. [Finally, there is room here for the colonization projects] in which modern German national economists see the salvation of the nation's social future....

[Although the German community of Buenos Aires, some four thousand strong, is smaller than the French or English, not to mention the Italian or Spanish], in terms of prestige and influence in public and social life it undoubtedly occupies one of the leading places. The explanation lies basically in the German colony's unique composition, made up as it is of [socially] better, better-educated, and more prosperous elements.... The majority ... occupy relatively important positions in the business, official, and artisan classes. Because of their solid knowledge and economic well-being, indeed affluence, they are well received in better circles.

In *commerce*, this decisive aspect of American life, the great German trading firms are on top. One may well say that the leadership which the English once exercised in this area is today in the hands of the Germans on La Plata.... The heads and partners of the first-class firms have achieved not only a brilliant social standing, but their influence also reaches in a certain sense into public life. Many of them have voice and vote in the directories of the great state banks ... others are closely related through intimate social or familial connections to the first families of the land;

still others hold influential posts of honor in various branches of public administration.

[At a lower level], German *clerical employees* also have an excellent reputation. [As to German *academics*], the educated Argentine has long understood that the true light of science beams upon him more brightly and purely from the treasure houses of the German intellect than from the trumpery baubles of the Gallic spirit. [Superficial aspects of culture stem from French, Spanish, or Italian sources]: the quintessence of all knowledge from the Germans. *Artisans* [are also highly respected]; most are successful owners of their own businesses.

On the other hand, very few among the Germans in Buenos Aires are day laborers occupied in the most menial jobs. . . . True poverty [is] also very rare.[1]

The variety of Bachmann's promotional ventures epitomizes the probing dynamism of the German entrepreneurial community of the 1880s, just as his aggressive nationalism and celebration of material and social success catch up its dominant ethos. But, like Bachmann himself, these qualities were relatively new to the community. They went back no further than the political unification of the German Reich in 1871, the beginnings of regular steam navigation between the two countries in the late 1870s, and the boom in Argentina's export trade that set in at the start of the following decade. The community itself was by then more than half a century old; its earlier years had been rather more modest.

Its founders were merchants, artisans, free-lance soldiers, and failed agricultural colonists who drifted into Buenos Aires in the 1820s and 1830s. The early merchants were mostly of Hanse origins, a few of Rhenish. In the main, given the scant industrialization and the political fragmentation of the German hinterland, the merchants of necessity sought their trade goods, working capital, and ship bottoms wherever they could find them; their mercantile activity was consequently conducted along networks of commercial and familial connections among all the trading peoples of the North Atlantic Basin. Bearers of a cosmopolitan culture, in Buenos Aires they moved easily within the international trading community that formed in those years. In 1831 the traveler *Freiherr* von Weech reported that most of the young Germans who had received him with open-handed hospitality at the Deutscher Club of the time were employed by English-owned trading houses. German-speaking traders were active in the transactions of the "commercial rooms" established by the English in 1811; later, in the

1840s, they formed the second-largest contingent, after the English, in the Club de Residentes Extranjeros, which served the foreign merchant community as a bourse. International partnerships and working agreements were common and were often reinforced by judicious marriages; already by the second generation the structure of informal axes and alignments in Buenos Aires' commercial world had grown highly complex.[2]

This merchant community was, morever, in constant flux and transformation. By 1840, some five hundred German-speaking merchants had done business at one time or another on La Plata. In the following decade, however, the German trading community began to acquire a measure of stability. Between 1843 and 1845, Hamburg, Bremen, and Prussia established permanent diplomatic relations with the government of Juan Manuel de Rosas (at a most advantageous time for all concerned, of course, for they came during the deep estrangement between Rosas and the British and French governments). Although many important German trading families remained birds of passage, a number of them now began to identify themselves with the new country, either by acquiring extensive landed property or by marrying into prominent *criollo* clans, or often both.

One representative career is that of Klaus Stegmann, who got his start in the English firm of Jas. Brittain & Co., then became a partner of Brownell-Stegmann & Co. He married Narcisa Pérez Millán, widow of the flamboyant Indian fighter Friedrich Rauch (later the Stegmann line would also be joined to that of the eminent Martínez de Hoz family). By 1830 he had acquired land and was importing high grade German sheep-breeding stock. His stock-raising enterprises prospered and served by example to stimulate the enthusiasm for sheep raising that set in in the 1840s; by 1847 he was able to withdraw from commerce altogether. His sons Claudio Federico and Jorge were among the founders of the Sociedad Rural in 1866; Claudio's *estancia*, Los Poronguitos, on the Río Salado, became one of the showplace rural estates of Buenos Aires Province. Others of the early merchants who followed a similar course were the brothers Karl August and Hugo Bunge, Louis de Chapeaurouge, Franz Halbach (whom German writers credit with being among the first to use imported wire fencing), Eduard Gerding, Franz Mohr, Louis Vernet, and the Lahusens.[3]

The German merchant caste—or *Handelsstand*, as it was commonly called—in Buenos Aires grew slowly but steadily through the middle decades of the century. By 1865 there were thirty-four identifiably German import-export houses in the city, and by 1873, forty-three. They traded extensively with North German ports; almost all, however, also had family branches or working arrangements in Antwerp, Rouen, London, New York, Rio de Janeiro, Montevideo, and other ports in Europe and the Western Hemisphere. Among their owners and partners figured names that would continue to carry weight within the German-Argentine merchant patriciate well into the twentieth century: Altgelt, Arning, Bemberg, Bracht, Bunge, de Bary, Fels, Heimendahl, Lahusen, Mallmann, Mantels, Tornquist, von Eicken, Zimmermann. The three most important German houses of the later nineteenth century were founded in these years: Joseph Mallmann & Co. (1848), Otto Bemberg (1856; it became Bemberg, Heimendahl in 1864), and Ernesto Tornquist (which, although it took its definitive name only in 1872, was a direct descendant of earlier firms controlled by the Bunge, Altgelt, and Ferber families). All three financed their operations through family-controlled European banking houses—located not in Germany but in Brussels and Paris. Mallmann & Co. eventually concentrated exclusively on banking operations; after 1889 its mercantile functions were taken over by Bracht and the important Berlin firm of Staudt. The Bemberg and Tornquist firms, however, diversified broadly from their import-export origins; Casa Tornquist, in particular, became one of the prodigies of Argentine business. It built its fortune upon the negotiations of public loans in the money marts of Europe and its reputation upon the sub rosa diplomacy this entailed. It also came to be involved in a remarkable array of investment banking, commercial, agricultural, stock-raising, fishing, and colonization projects. It served for a time as the Argentine agent of Krupp and was represented in the management of firms engaged in the development of sugar growing and refining, tobacco, beer brewing, meatpacking, tannin extracting (from quebracho wood), engineering, and the fabrication of imported metals. By 1908 its total investments were calculated to be worth a quarter of a billion pesos.[4]

But the merchants and their employees formed at most a large minority of the city's growing German-speaking community, whose numbers rose from an estimated two hundred in the early 1830s to six hundred in 1855 and to twenty-one hundred or more in 1869. Like Rauch, numerous free-lance German officers left colorful traces in Argentina's nineteenth-century military history: Holmberg, Brandsen, and Kessler of the post-independence armies; Reich (or Reichert), alias Iwanowski, who rose to general before he was killed in a revolt in Mendoza in 1874; Schneider and Kleine, who, like Iwanowski, fought in the Paraguayan War; Rohde, who was seconded from the Prussian army to serve on Roca's staff during the Campaign to the Desert and who later led mapping expeditions up the Río Negro to the region of Nahuel

Huapí; Rohde's protégé, Wermelskirch, whose Argentine career extended well into the twentieth century. Especially in the early years, biographical data on these nomadic men are necessarily fragmentary.

Nor is much known of the common soldiers who served as mercenaries with the British, Brazilians, or Argentines (for example, the German Company of the San Martín Regiment in Rosas' time) or otherwise fetched up on La Plata. One remarkable career, however, that of ex-Sergeant Adolph Bullrich from Teupitz, near Berlin, has been preserved from historical oblivion. Bullrich was one of the many Germans serving in the Brazilian army who were captured by the Argentines at Ituzaingó in 1827. Taken to Buenos Aires and released there, he rapidly made his fortune as keeper of a general store and founder of a brewery. In the second generation his son Adolfo was owner of a major auction house, a director of the State Mortgage Bank, and, in the 1880s, *intendente* of the city. The statistician Friedrich Latzina and the self-made businessman, bank director, and railroad president Moritz Mayer were former Austro-Hungarian officers, as were Ferdinand Czetz, who rose to a post in the Ministry of War in which he was influential in reorganizing officer training, and Eugen Bachmann, sometime director of the Naval School and commander of the Trieste-built training ship *Argentina*.[5]

But the majority of newcomers were of civilian urban or small-town origins—skilled artisans, in the main, with smaller complements of retail merchants and innkeepers and a scattering of physicians, journalists, architects, schoolteachers, and other professionals. A high proportion of them proved capable of exploiting the city's manifold possibilities; a few would rise, or see their children rise, into the bureaucratic and landowning classes. The first Seebers, for example, arrived from the Odenwald in 1826 and established themselves as sausagemakers, then slaughterhouse operators; a descendant, Franz Seeber, gained fame as an army reformer and as the *intendente berlinés*, the Berlin-style mayor, of Buenos Aires. The son of the immigrant tailor Anton Winter was the General Lorenzo Winter of some distinction in the Campaign to the Desert. Two other tailors, Ulrich and Bechstedt, prospered sufficiently to become *estancieros*, proprietors of the Tailors' Ranch (*Estancia de los Sastres*) near Luján. The Holsteiner Johann Gotthilf Frers gained a footing in Buenos Aires as the first schoolmaster of the new Evangelical Congregational School (as well as organist and choirmaster) in the 1840s. He married into the Lynch Zavaleta clan, who were opposed to Rosas; after Rosas' fall he was named administrator of the Escuela Normal of the province of Buenos Aires and head of the Department of Schools, over the vehement protests of

Catholic factions. He acquired extensive property in the vicinity of Baradero and was the promoter of the Swiss colony founded there in the late 1850s. His son Emilio would have a most active public career: among other things, he was twice president of the Sociedad Rural and Argentina's first minister of agriculture when the position was created in 1898. One of the few authentic industrial entrepreneurs among the early immigrants was Philip Schwarz of Berlin, who arrived in 1855. By the time of his death forty years later he had established machine shops and a metal foundry which were among the few local sources of windmills, safes, oil presses, pasta-making equipment, and other light industrial machinery. What became of these enterprises after his death is not clear.[6]

The Ruhland-Reinhardt *Deutsche La-Plata Kalender* of 1873 offers the first comprehensive listing of German language business firms in the city. In that year, in addition to forty-three import-export houses, there were in the commercial sector eighteen warehousing operations (principally for the forwarding of hides and wool) and a miscellany of brokers, shipping and insurance agents, bill collectors, and so on. Nineteen firms were engaged in *Gastwirtschaft* (restaurants, bars, cafes, casinos, hotels, or combinations thereof); forty-five concentrated on retail sales (mostly of imports); and approximately one hundred are identifiable as small or medium-sized craft workshops. These independent artisans carried on a broad range of crafts but were represented especially strongly in those catering to the small luxury market: watchmaking and jewelry, the book trades (publishing, printing, lithography, bookbinding), and bespoke furniture making, upholstering, carriage building, leather working, hat making, and tailoring. At this time also, brewers such as Westermayr, Schellenschläger, Hammer, Rothenburger, and Bieckert—the last two of whom were Alsatians— were driving imported English beer from the local market (the important Quilmes and Palermo breweries would be founded only in 1889 and 1897, respectively, with the heavy backing of European capital). The *Kalender* also listed the 249 German-speaking residents who had died in the yellow fever epidemic of 1871. Of those whose occupations were recorded, thirty-one were in commerce, seventeen (including four professors and the secretary of the Sociedad Rural) were professionals, and more than eighty were artisans (not all independent) or shopkeepers. Only one individual—an unfortunate identified merely as "Ratje"—was recorded as a workman (*Arbeiter*).[7]

Thus by the 1870s the community's largest social element was a comfortably prosperous middle class; its mainstay was an independent artisanate, sometimes identified as the *Handwerkerstand*. These petty professionals, shopkeepers, and independent artisans remained socially distinct from the merchant class, or *Handelsstand*, and, in terms of status and the assumption of leadership roles, subordinate to it. Nevertheless, as the representative careers sketched above suggest, money making and upward social mobility in the American environment had done much to blur distinctions and call assumptions of hierarchy into question.

Nor do social distinctions appear to have greatly affected the development of a thriving associational life, or *Vereinsleben*—indeed, from the beginning, generous financial contributions to communal institutions were the surest means of confirming socially the status that had been gained, tentatively, through material success. Like other immigrant collectivities confronted by the inadequacy or absence of appropriate *criollo* institutions, the Germans united to create, in time, a comprehensive system through which virtually all social wants could be met within their own cultural context. This process began early. A mutual aid society (*Unterstützungsverein*) existed in the 1820s, and the early Deutscher Club, which went out of existence in 1838, served a similar function. A male choral society and an athletic club (*Turnverein*) are reported from the 1840s. The most important early social nucleus, however, was the Evangelical congregation, which was founded in 1843 and which began construction of its church building in Calle Esmeralda in 1851. The congregation administered the community's Protestant cemetery, shared with the English and North Americans, and supported its first school (which was in fact the first German school in South America), also begun in 1843. Except for ephemera, such as the secular Vorwärts School of the late 1860s, which closed as a result of the yellow fever epidemic of 1871, the Congregational School would remain the community's only school for half a century.

Specialized secular associations (*Vereine*) began to be founded in the 1850s and multiplied rapidly thereafter: another mutual aid society, two sickness insurance funds, the German Hospital (1878), and ultimately an orphanage (1909); a second athletic club (1855; it would evolve into the Deutscher Klub Buenos Aires after the turn of the century and be replaced by the New German Athletic Club); musical and social clubs such as Germania, Teutonia, Concordia, Eintracht, Heimath, and the Singakademie; and two Masonic lodges. As social nuclei, the clubs were supplemented by the German restaurants, beer halls, and casinos noted above; their number would increase. A German language periodical press began to emerge in the 1860s but became stable only with the founding of the *Deutsche La-Plata Zeitung* in 1878 and the *Argentinisches Tageblatt* in 1889. Each of these dailies also put out a weekly edition directed primarily toward a rural readership. The former remained under the ownership of the Tjarks family, originally of Hannover, almost from its beginnings until its closure in 1945; the latter, which still exists, has always been identified with the Alemann (originally "Allemann") family from Bern in German Switzerland.[8]

Nineteenth-century associational life was notable for its intensity, which at times expressed itself in remarkably bitter internecine feuding. The musical and social societies were especially given to factional disputes and frequent secessions and recombinations. Much earlier, the failed European revolutions of 1848 had sent dissenters, including Republicans and Socialists, to La Plata. They formed a loose anticlerical party which remained in a running feud with the Lutheran congregation for decades. The congregation itself was convulsed between 1862 and 1864 by the statute revision dispute within the Presbyterium. One session in January 1864 grew so acrimonious that the doors and windows of the church had to be sealed—in Buenos Aires' midsummer!—lest *criollos* outside learn of the disharmony at the heart of the German community, for the community's leaders were highly sensitive of the Germans' reputation for orderliness and of the need to keep up appearances in the eyes of the *criollos*.[9]

Still, the dominant impression of nineteenth-century *Vereinsleben* is that of egalitarian conviviality. The clubs and societies were hyperactively occupied with the yearly round of masked *Fasching* balls, concerts, "beer evenings," theater, founding-anniversary celebrations, and, in the sweltering summer months, mass expeditions to Palermo and Saavedra, then the leafy semirural outskirts of the city. At the end of April 1865, the combined musical societies of Buenos Aires descended by steamer upon their comrades in Montevideo for the First German Musical Festival on La Plata, a bibulous three days of parades, choral and band competitions, and banquets. The following year the Montevideo societies returned the visit, which began and ended in spirited parades of blaring brass bands and tossing banners between the landingbridge at waterside and the Hotel Louvre. One of the largest of the social clubs, Germania, founded in 1855, had become well known by the 1880s for its amateur theater and for its elaborate annual ball on the anniversary of the Prussian victory at Sedan in 1870. Its quarters in Calle Tucumán embraced, in the *criollo* style, a spacious central patio shaded by gnarled eucalyptus trees; inside, in addition to several reading rooms and a pair of bowling alleys (named "Moltke" and "Bismarck"), the largest space was given over to a banquet hall seating three hundred persons. The hall was dominated by a vast watercolor mural allegory of "Germania" striding above the formidable motto: *Das ganze Deutschland soll es sein!* ("There shall be a single Germany!")[10]

The bellicose touches in the foregoing description are not misleading, for things *had*, of course, begun to change with the events in Europe that culminated in the proclamation of the German Empire at Versailles in January 1871.

Already in late 1868, the flag of the North German Bund had been raised over the house of the Prussian consul, F. W. Nordenholz. Simultaneously, the consular offices of Hamburg, Bremen, Lübeck, Frankfurt, Oldenburg, Mecklenburg, Hannover, and Saxony were closed; and their coats of arms were retired to hang as historical curiosities in the gymnasium of the Turnverein. In 1869, the newly arrived resident minister of the bund (and later of the empire), R. Le Maistre, protested to the Argentine authorities that, although the first general census, taken that year, had recorded 217 "Prussians" as residents of Buenos Aires, all the remaining Germans had been lumped under the indiscriminate head "other nationalities." His representations were heeded, and the census results were duly amended to show a total of 2,139 "German" subjects in the city. The Austro-Prussian War of 1866 had caused, for a short time, dissension within the community; the war against France four years later was met, however, with a display of unified support. The support took two principal forms, which would be seen again in the twentieth century. One was a propaganda campaign, mounted through hastily created Spanish language journals, to counter the preponderant French intellectual influences in the capital. The other was the founding of a central committee to collect funds for wounded, widows, and orphans in the Fatherland.[11]

One of the principal consequences of these events was a marked decline in the cosmopolitanism that had characterized the community's early years. This was perhaps least true of the older merchant patriciate, whose high internationalism would remain largely intact until World War I, and in some cases even thereafter. Even at this level, however, the rapid industrial growth of imperial Germany and its thrust for export, and ultimately capital, outlets greatly increased the volume of interchange between the established houses of Buenos Aires and their correspondents, suppliers, and financiers in Germany; by the same token, the simultaneous increase in Argentina's capacity to supply Germany's demand for industrial raw materials (especially wool and hides) and foodstuffs also strengthened these relationships. The expansion of bilateral trade during and after the boom of the 1880s led to the founding in Buenos Aires of many new German trading houses and outlets of manufacturing firms. The heads of these newer establishments possessed fewer international connections than their predecessors in the Buenos Aires *Handelsstand* and less of their international culture. Naturally enough, the middle class, for its part, had never been as cosmopolitan in its outlook as the merchants; and it was precisely these independent artisans, tradesmen, and petty professionals who were most overcome by the perfervid nationalism of the new Reich of Bismarck and the Hohenzollerns. One measurable effect in Buenos Aires was the secession of the Swiss from the city's German language voluntary associations. The majority of the Swiss were not German-speaking in any case but, rather, Italian-speaking Ticinese, but hitherto the two collectivities had collaborated in numerous ventures. After 1871, however, the republican Swiss strengthened their own voluntary associations in the city.[12]

But, if vestiges of the earlier cosmopolitanism remained, virtually all trace of the rough egalitarianism of the community's beginnings was extinguished before the century was out. Toward 1900 it had been replaced by a social hierarchy of increasingly fine gradations among levels and of increasingly gross distances between extremes. The overriding cause of this change was the differential effect of Argentina's integration into the Western European trading system upon urban class and occupational structure. Briefly stated, the once modest merchant class evolved by the pre–World War I decade into a tight circle of powerful trading entrepreneurs who were represented in the directorates of the two German banks of the city and of the German-owned utilities, and who profited handsomely in their own right as agents of German trading and industrial firms, capital consortia, and steamship lines. But, in the same span of years, the position of the independent artisan class deteriorated rapidly in the face of the price competition of European manufactures and the wage competition of newer waves of immigrants from Southern and Eastern Europe, above all the Italians.

Between 1872 and 1876, steamers of the Hamburg-Süd, Kosmos, and North German Lloyd Lines began regular sailings between German and Argentine ports; later the HAPAG, Hansa, and Hamburg-Amerika Lines joined the South Atlantic run. The volume of shipping increased steadily, until by the year 1913 315 German-flag steamers (as well as a handful of sailing ships) touched at Buenos Aires. In 1894 the shipping agency of Antonio Delfino began a longtime association with the principal German lines. Delfino was reportedly instrumental in promoting the luxury passenger trade, of which the crack German liners had gained the lion's share by the outbreak of war in 1914. Under his aegis, Hamburg-Süd also took over between 1899 and 1902 the

Argentine-flag Linea Nacional del Sur, which operated coastal shipping to Patagonia; he and German colleagues also operated the La Porteña lighterage firm and the Argentine-flag river traffic between Buenos Aires and Montevideo.[13]

German banking facilities also increased with the growth of bilateral trade, although more slowly. In the depression year of 1875 the first direct German capital outlet, the German-Belgian La-Plata Bank, backed by the Berlin Diskonto-Gesellschaft, the Oppenheim Bank of Cologne, and private Belgian and Austrian houses, failed after three years; and there were transatlantic recriminations. For the time being, credit remained available through private and mostly non-German sources (although Casa Tornquist continued to represent the Diskonto-Gesellschaft and was by now in partnership with de Bary's of Bremen). Amidst the booming trade of the 1880s, however, the Banco Alemán Transatlántico (BAT) opened in 1887 as a branch of the Deutsche Übersee Bank of Berlin; its first head was the Argentine-born Carlos Maschwitz. In 1906 a second German branch bank, the Banco Germánico de la América del Sur (BGAS), was founded by a consortium headed by the Dresdner Bank. In these years, experienced and well-connected German and German-Argentine bankers moved easily in the financial circles—private and public (or "mixed")—of Buenos Aires: Mallmann and Diehl in the National Bank; Bullrich in the Mortgage Bank; Bunge, Tornquist, Heimendahl, Paats, and Moritz Mayer in the Bank of the Province of Buenos Aires. Gustav Frederking, who had immigrated in 1870 and had risen to a partnership in the Carabassa Bank, succeeded Maschwitz as director of the BAT in 1903.[14]

Shipping and banking facilities were indispensable to the steady growth of the German position in Argentine economic life, a position which by 1914 was second—although a distant second—only to that of Great Britain. Bilateral commerce led the way in this growth and was its most obvious manifestation. The Argentine trade statistics are by no means satisfactory, as will be indicated below. They show, however, that with the recovery from the depression of the late 1870s, German exports to Argentina quadrupled in value between 1876 and 1885; by the latter year they represented 8 percent of Argentina's total imports. They surpassed 10 percent in 1887 and 1888; after a three-year decline, they rose above 11 percent in 1892 and remained above that annual level until the beginning of World War I. From 1910 through early 1914, in fact, they took a sharp upswing: the German share of Argentina's total import reached its maximum, 18 percent, in 1911, and its greatest absolute value, 71.3 million gold pesos, in 1913. During the first part of this cycle, the bulk of Argentine purchases had been of light consumer goods; increasingly after the 1890s, however, they came to be concentrated in textiles, dyes, heavy electrical and railway equipment, and other capital goods. No figures are available on the sale of armaments.[15]

Correspondingly, German purchases of Argentine commodities—wool and hides, linseed, wheat and other cereals above all—rose from 2.4 percent of Argentina's gross export in 1875 to a maximum of 15.9 percent in 1899; in 1913 it was 12 percent. But, as the volume of Argentina's total export rose, approximately tenfold between 1871 and 1914, so also did the absolute value. By 1914 Argentina had surpassed Brazil as Germany's chief trading partner (on both import and export sides) in Latin America and was second only to the United States among all its non-European trading partners. In the last years before the war, the competition for the lucrative Argentine market grew increasingly sharp. In this, Germany moved firmly into second place, well behind Great Britain (which in 1913 supplied 31 percent of Argentina's imports and took 25 percent of its exports) but ahead of the United States, France, Italy, and Belgium. Indeed, from 1910 through 1913 German sales in the crucial area of iron and steel products exceeded those of the British.[16]

The great upsurge in German-Argentine trade predictably brought with it a host of new trading houses to the Buenos Aires marketplace; already in 1887 sixty-seven import, thirteen export, and twelve mixed houses were owned by Germans. Amidst many transitory foundings, a new generation of merchants took its place in German-Argentine society alongside the pre-1871 patriciate. It included the heads and partners of such concerns as Berger, Boeker, Brauss-Mahn, Bromberg, Bunge & Born (a new firm introduced by the Antwerp branch of the Bunge family), Dreyfus, Engelbert-Hardt, Fuhrmann, Hasenclever, Peters, Plate, Schlieper, Staudt, the Swiss-German Zuberbühler. As noted earlier, these firms dealt almost exclusively with German traders or served as direct agents of German manufacturers, and a number of older houses adopted similar practices. After 1900 a number of major German industrial concerns such as Mannesmann, Koppel, Deutz-Otto, Siemens-Schuckert, and AEG set up their own directly controlled outlets in Buenos Aires.[17]

A chief defect in the official Argentine statistics is their failure to indicate the point of origin of imports and the ultimate consignee of exports. The recorded volume of German-Argentine trade is thus reduced by an unknown factor. Certainly, a significant proportion of the trade between Buenos Aires and Antwerp—Alexander Jonin estimated it at between two-thirds and three-quarters in the 1880s—was consigned to or from central and southern Germany and should have been recorded as German rather than Belgian. (As some confirmation, it will be noted that an unusually high number of major German trading firms in Buenos Aires, including Arning, Bracht, Brauss-Mahn, Bunge & Born, de Bary, Fuhrmann, Notteböhm-Möring, and Tornquist, had branches or familial connections in Belgian commercial circles.)[18]

Thus the official Argentine statistics do not make fully clear the fact that at least from the 1890s onward Germany suffered a permanent imbalance of trade with Argentina. After struggling with the statistics for the decade 1894–1903, Heinrich (or Enrique) Kohn, the capable editor of the *Buenos Aires Handels-Zeitung*, concluded that over the ten-year span the ratio of the value of Argentine sales to German sales had been on the order of three and a half or four to one. Statistics of German trade compiled later in the United States showed a balance of trade in Argentina's favor in every year from 1909 through 1913: according to this source, aggregate German sales in those five years amounted in value to 280 million U.S. dollars, but German purchases were worth almost precisely half a billion dollars. German businessmen and financiers adopted the obvious course: to attempt to redress the balance of payments with the earnings of German shipping and insurance firms and, more important still, with those of direct German loans and capital investments within Argentina. But the world of capital investment is even more tenebrous than that of trade statistics, and tendencies are visible only in their grosser outlines.[19]

In the 1890s, the Banco Alemán Transatlántico joined with other lending institutions in London in the Council of Foreign Bondholders, which consolidated and refinanced the debt of the province of Buenos Aires to the amount of thirty-four million pesos; it later underwrote public loans of three and a half million apiece for construction of the Port of Santa Fe and for municipal improvements in Buenos Aires. The BAT also participated in the founding of a branch of the Frankfurt construction firm of Philipp Holzmann and helped to finance the latter's first major project, 6.4 million gold pesos worth of customs warehouses in the Port of Buenos Aires. By the outbreak of war, Holzmann and other major German construction firms such as Siemens Bau-Union, Otto Francke, Gödhart, and Wayss and Freytag had won lucrative contracts for the city's port works, grain mills and elevators, sewer systems, electrification, tramway network, and its first subway. They were also highly active outside the capital, in such projects as the meatpacking plant and the naval drydock in Bahía Blanca, the Mitre Canal, grain elevators in Rosario and smaller ports of the Litoral, and the public wine cellars in San Juan.[20]

Other capital was invested in land mortgages and companies, development of the timber resources of the Northeast, especially quebracho wood and its derivative, tannin (export of which to Germany doubled in value between 1909 and 1913), and speculative drilling in the newly discovered Comodoro Rivadavia oilfields. There, the first strike had been made in 1907 by a crew under the German engineer José Fuchs; the Erdöl Company of Rudolf Nöllenburg began commercial production before the war; the firm's holdings passed to the Swiss International Petroleum Union during the war and thence to Stinnes' Astra. There were a few minor investments in utilities (e.g., the Telefónica in 1887) and one major one: the Compañía Alemana Transatlántica de Electricidad, or CATE. It opened its first power plant in Calle Paraguay in 1900; in short order it absorbed smaller pre-existent facilities and acquired the Buenos Aires monopoly of power and light. At first CATE also operated tramways, but by 1909 it had struck a number of agreements with the Compagnie Générale de Tramways de Buenos Aires in Brussels and the Anglo-Argentina in London whereby all unseemly competition was obviated: CATE divested itself of tramways and in return received exclusive rights to the provision of electricity so long as the several concessions should last. By 1910, the city's rapidly increasing power requirements caused CATE to construct an entire new power plant complex at Dock Sud, formerly an uninhabited swamp beyond the Riachuelo at the southern edge of the city's frontage on the La Plata. Although CATE's Buenos Aires operation was its largest—indeed, it was one of the largest unified systems in the world at the time—the concern also held interest in similar utilities in Montevideo, Valparaíso, Santiago, and Mendoza and in the Compañía Argentina de Electricidad (CAE), which operated in Buenos Aires Province to the north of the capital. Several writers coincide in a round estimate of 250 million gold pesos for the aggregate worth of German capital investment in Argentina in 1913; of this, the largest components represented the holdings in CATE, public loans, and coastal shipping. In the international competition for an investment position in Argentina, Germany stood third on the eve of war, well behind Great Britain, not far behind France.[21]

The principal merchants, financiers, and utility managers formed a tightly knit economic oligarchy in Buenos Aires. They were the beneficiaries of Germany's headlong technological, industrial, and capital-exporting development and of the simultaneous growth of Argentina's capacity to supply foodstuffs and fibers to Germany and the industrialized world. They thus became incalculably wealthier than their predecessors of the *Handelsstand* of one or two generations before, as well as more prone to snobbery and ostentation. In important respects, however, their economic behavior had changed little. They were still given to purchasing landed estates for both profit making and prestige purposes: Bendinger, von Bernard, Boethlingk, Diehl, the Engelbert-Hardt Co., Funke, von Heinitz, Hirsch, Kemmerich, Klein, Krell, Nordenholz, Plate, Roth, Scheibler, Schroeder, Staudt, Tjarks, and Wendelstadt, among others. At the turn of the century, Karl Kärger, the embassy's agricultural attaché, noted that successful businessmen tended to invest their profits above all in sheep ranches, to produce wool for the export trade; he calculated that German-owned *estancias* of all types covered a total area of some 150 square leagues. Urban real estate speculation was another important use to which profits were put. And German businessmen—Altgelt, Arning, von Bernard, Duckwitz, von Freeden, Lahusen, Martin Meyer (of Hamburg: father of Carlos Meyer Pellegrini), Möring, Napp, Sattler, Schlieper, Tornquist, Vernet, Zimmermann, Zuberbühler—were prominent in the affairs of the Bolsa de Comercio, which came increasingly to be the center of currency and commodity speculation until 1899, when the ratio between the foreign trade gold peso and the domestic paper peso was definitively pegged and speculation was curtailed.[22]

On the other hand, aside from ventures designed to uncover commodities that could be commercialized (timber, petroleum, the continuing fitful search for other mineral resources) or to expand pastoral and agricultural production, the German merchant class made few gestures toward developing Argentina's industrial potential. The exceptions to this generalization are minor. The breweries and sugar refinery cited above produced for a domestic market, as did the early distilleries of Klappenbach and the Halbach brothers and the later Germania distilleries whose production was centered in Rosario and Mendoza; however, by 1900 capitalization was mainly from abroad. The textile mill founded by Carlos Zuberbühler in San Carlos in 1891, the shirtwaist factory of Sternberg, Mitau & Grether (f. 1892), and the mechanized shoe factory cum tannery spun off by the old line trading firm of Mantels in 1888 are among the rare examples of German participation in this elementary stage of factory development. The foundries and shops of the Schwarz brothers, a few smaller metalworking factories operated by German-speaking immigrants, and furniture factories such as those of Sackmann and Otto all date from well before 1900 and tended to disappear thereafter. In fact, before World War I, the most durable German contribution to Argentina's development above the level of primary production was the work of such firms as Kratzenstein, Peuser, Stiller & Laass, Kraft, Van Gelderen, and others in establishing the printing and publishing industries, in which Buenos Aires would hold for a time the leadership of the Spanish world. The majority of the economic elite, however, remained content to carve out a German enclave in Argentina's export economy and to strengthen its dependency on the German metropolis. But World War I would destroy this happy complacency and force adoption of a slightly different approach.[23]

The situation of the German-speaking artisanate of Buenos Aires moved in the opposite direction between the 1870s and the turn of the century. In a few specialized trades—the book trades, certainly, and high grade cabinet making, in which they were known for their copies of French Empire styles—German artisans retained a precarious eminence. Their comrades discovered, however, that their traditional policy in Buenos Aires of *theuer und gut*—"high cost and high quality"—
—could not withstand the low rate competition of Italian shoemakers and tailors, locksmiths and saddlers, all occupations in which Germans had once been preeminent. As early as 1886 the Austrian Leopold Schnabl observed that "the largest part of handicraft industry is in [Italian] hands" and that the Italians had come to monopolize such trades as masonry and stonecutting, architecture, housepainting, plastering, saddlemaking, food handling, and baking. He attributed this development to the Italians' great capacity for "hard work and self-denial." To the easy habits of the long-established German artisans he contrasted the "antlike policy of the Italians—neither bold nor conquering, in no way heroic, but rather laborious and modest, a step-by-step forward movement along the paths of working-class life."[24]

The distress of the *Handwerkerstand* was compounded by the growing preference of the upper reaches of Buenos Aires society for the cachet conferred by European-made wares and of less affluent *criollos* for the industrial shoddy of British and continental factories. During the export boom and population growth of the 1880s, moreover, the urban cost of living rose sharply. The most pernicious effects were felt in housing. Scarcity produced soaring rents, and even relatively well-paid skilled workers were faced with the alternatives of removal either to the spreading downtown tenements, or *conventillos*, or to the developing suburbs. The latter were preferable on many counts, but such a move would cause workers, as the *Buenos Aires Vorwärts* put it, to be "looted" by the tramway companies. This new socialist weekly (founded 1886) analyzed intelligently the deterioration in the living conditions of the artisanate, as well as its causes in the workings of the trade and investment boom. Its editors also spoke acidly of the growing class differences within the German community—hitherto unknown, but which "one now must of necessity feel." [25]

The declining independent artisanate was absorbed into a more occupationally diverse middle-class population. At higher levels of status, professionals, academics, and technical experts—all three categories mainly in Argentine public employ—increased markedly in numbers after the 1870s. Behind this development lay a tradition of respectable antiquity, for since the time of Rivadavia well-educated German immigrants had been carrying out public commissions on an ad hoc basis —for example, the merchant F. W. Schmaling, Rivadavia's political ally, who helped to reorganize the first national bank of the 1820s; or Louis Vernet of Hamburg, the first (and only) Argentine governor of the Falkland/Malvinas Islands. The public career of J. G. Frers as an educational administrator in the 1850s has been mentioned. Somewhat later still, the trained agronomist Ernst Oldendorff headed the new Department of Agriculture for Sarmiento; Oldendorff represented Argentina at the United States' Centennial Exposition in Philadelphia in 1876 (and abandoned Argentina for the U.S. in 1877). The comprehensive report on Argentina prepared for circulation at the same exposition was the work of the immigrant journalist Richard Napp and German colleagues.[26]

The movement of German academics to Argentina that set in in the 1870s depended, however, to a much lesser extent on such hit-or-miss arrangements. For one thing, in this period second and third generation German-Argentines, many of whom had received their university training in Germany, began to emerge to prominence in the overlapping circles of politics, public administration, the universities, and the intellectual salons. Carlos Maschwitz, whose banking career has been noted, also served as head of the national Railway Administration; he was succeeded in this position by Alberto Schneidewind, and Schneidewind was followed in turn by Emilio Schickendantz. Already in the 1880s more German experts than Englishmen were in the public employ as railway builders and administrators. The politicians Adolfo Bullrich and Franz Seeber, both of whom served as *intendente* of Buenos Aires in the 1880s, were fluent in German, belonged to German associations, and visited the Fatherland; as Theodor Alemann put it, however, "socially they stood within the charmed circle of their *criollo* social environment." Seeber reportedly was instrumental in the importation of the German pedagogues who founded the Instituto Nacional del Profesorado Secundario in 1904 and was a strong advocate of remodeling the army on Prussian lines. Around the turn of the century,

Argentines of Germanic background such as Alejandro Korn, Carlos Octavio and Alejandro Bunge, Cristóbal Hicken, Eduardo Holmberg, Santiago Roth, and Carlos Zuberbühler began to make their reputations as intellectuals and academics.[27]

Undoubtedly the cumulative influence of prominent German-Argentines, acting on individual initiative, in bringing German learning and expertise to Argentina was great, but the practice of importing German academics for specific assignments and on fixed contracts had also received great impetus from President Domingo Faustino Sarmiento. In 1870 Sarmiento named his friend, the naturalist Hermann Burmeister, formerly of Halle, to the post of director of the new National Academy of Exact, Physical, and Natural Sciences to be created within the somnolent University of Córdoba and charged Burmeister with recruiting German-trained scientists to staff it. Burmeister was able to engage a cadre of proven academics—Siewert, Stelzner, Vogeler, Lorenz, Schulz-Sellack, the Hollander Weyenburgh—but in short order fell into an obscure but violent dispute with them and returned to his former position as head of the Natural History Museum of the province of Buenos Aires, which he held until his death in 1892. Burmeister and the Córdoba group (which continued to renew itself from German sources) were the true progenitors of the modern tradition of German academic teaching and scientific research, both theoretical and applied, in Argentina. By World War I, several hundred German academics had spent portions of their careers in Argentina, and many, particularly among the early comers, had remained permanently. They formed the scientific commission that accompanied Roca's Conquest of the Desert in 1879–1882. They remained entrenched in the sciences at Córdoba and came to dominate the Institute of Physics, the Astronomical Laboratory, and the Natural History Museum of the new National University of La Plata. Others found positions at the National University of Buenos Aires and later in the provincial universities.[28]

University-trained professionals also found scope for their activities outside the academy. German technical personnel were dominant within the National Bureau of Mines and Geology and the Institute of Military Geography, and they found influential positions in the technical branches of public administration (hydrology, topography, meteorology, in particular) at both federal and provincial levels. At a comparable level of status were the senior engineers brought over after 1900 to plan and carry out the extensive and lucrative civil and electrical engineering projects for which German construction firms had won contracts. In 1904, the Ministry of Public Instruction engaged, through the Prussian Education Ministry, a group of pedagogues under

Dr. Wilhelm Keiper to found the Instituto Nacional del Profesorado Secundario in Buenos Aires. This cadre, with some turnover, remained at work until 1916, when the contracts of the German schoolmasters failed of renewal. By that time, however, they had made the Instituto, with its attached *colegio* as laboratory school, the republic's elite center for the training of secondary level teachers.[29]

The history of German academic work, or *Gelehrtenarbeit*, in Argentina is a topic (largely unexplored) in and of itself. It transcends that of the Buenos Aires community—if for no other reason than because, although almost all the academics passed through Buenos Aires at one time or another, a majority of them did not reside there. Looking ahead, however, one important point deserves to be made here. The German artisanate was already in decline by the turn of the century, largely through the impersonal workings of the international division of labor. The academics would be the next element of the German-speaking community to find themselves under ultimately irresistible pressure, though for different reasons. The German academics at first, and generally until World War I, achieved easy acceptance (and prosperity and status) because they helped fill a large lacuna in the urban *criollo* social order. However, slowly at first, then in increasing numbers after World War I, *criollos* began to move into precisely those bureaucratic, professional, and subprofessional occupations that the German and other high-status Europeans had formerly virtually monopolized. It was a competition that the latter could not withstand. As will be noted in detail in subsequent chapters, many thousand middle-class German immigrants would learn this, to their great cost, after 1918.

One small though conspicuous category of upper-status Germans would be mostly (though not entirely) exempt from this generalization: the military advisors. In the late 1890s, the deterioration of relations between Argentina and Chile over the boundary question, and the threat posed by Chile's formidable German-trained army, caused President Roca to put into effect a project he had contemplated for some time: the modernization, also on German lines, of the Argentine army. On the recommendation of Colmar *Freiherr* von der Goltz, trainer of the Turkish army, a retired colonel of cavalry (later brigadier general of the Argentine army), Alfred Arent, was contracted through the Prussian War Ministry to head the military mission. The cadre, which consisted of some ten to fifteen officers, each serving, normally, a three-year tour, remained on duty until 1914, when all were recalled to Europe. Arent proved a poor choice, however, and succeeded in ruffling some very ornate plumage. On discovering a military establishment which included 600 staff officers (almost all comfortably ensconced in Buenos Aires), 900 line officers, and 7,000 enlisted men, he briskly proposed a revised table of organization which would have reduced the number of staff officers to 305. An outburst of nationalistic indignation duly erupted in the Buenos Aires press: it forced the resignation of the war minister, Lieutenant General Luis María Campos, who had negotiated the Prussian contract, and very nearly caused the abrogation of the contract itself. He also feuded with Campos' successor, Ricchieri, and with his own second in command and had to be withdrawn in 1902. Arent's subordinates and successors were more successful, however, in implanting German military doctrine in the newly founded Supreme War College (f. 1900) and the Escuela de Tiro (f. 1906). They acquired numerous disciples among ambitious junior Argentine officers, 15 of whom were detached annually for two-year tours of regimental troop duty in Germany; a smaller number of staff officers were sent in 1912 and 1913 to observe the autumn maneuvers, and a select few attended the War Academy in Berlin. At least one of the German training officers served simultaneously as sales representative of Krupp Armaments, although this fact was not to be made general knowledge.[30]

The majority of the community's newer residents, however, were of more obscure station. The remnants of the artisanate melded with small shopkeepers, *Gewerbetreibende*, who included, among others, those stereotypes of the German small town: oculists, pharmacists, photographers, innkeepers, butchers, booksellers. This expanding petite bourgeoisie also came to include, after about 1900, large numbers of white-collar workers, or *Angestellte*: the accountants, clerks, salesmen, and office managers of the trading firms, banks, and utilities. CATE alone was reputed to employ "hundreds" of clerks and was notorious for its low salaries, oppressive working conditions, and mediocre personnel; in the community's folklore the initials C.A.T.E. stood for *Compagnie Aller Traurigen Existenzen*—"Company of All Sorry Existences." Like that of the academics, and for similar reasons, the situation of the white-collar workers would worsen drastically after the war.[31]

The community's working-class component also grew in the decades after 1870. The most notable of the newer working-class immigrants were printers, compositors, lithographers, and others in the book trades who found employment in the already established German publishing concerns of the city. Many of these people were political activists who had been driven from Germany by Bismarck's repressive Socialist Laws. They figured prominently in the founding in 1882 of the socialist association, Vorwärts, and later in the formation of the Argentine Socialist party. Working-class German neighborhoods developed also among the wool and felt workers and railwaymen in Barracas al Norte near Plaza Constitución, the manual operatives of CATE's power plants, and the brewery workers of Quilmes. Some 10 percent of the known prostitutes in Buenos Aires in 1887 were Germans.[32]

In this process of rapid social differentiation, the bonds of community loosened. "To external appearances a single entity, the body of the community [*Gemeinde*] has fallen apart internally, has lost its organic coherence," wrote the Austrian Leopold Schnabl in 1886; at best, "the pleasures of existence are cultivated in small intimate circles."

> Now with the growth of the colony's numbers, the differential distribution of wealth, and the growing competition, a number of well-known hereditary evils have reappeared. . . . [One is Envy]: one gossips maliciously [*tratscht und klatscht*] with such abandon that it would seem that the first of the Ten Commandments were to speak ill of one's neighbor. . . . This is paired with another social evil: the Spirit of the Cashbox, this old unholy illness of the German spirit. . . . The *Junker* class has unfortunately established itself in altered form—as Nobility of Finance, as Patriciate, as The Richest Fraction—in the midst of the German bourgeoisie of Buenos Aires. . . . The big traders strut through life with the pride of a sanctified caste. Their houses are closed to all those whose visiting cards do not bear a coat of arms in seven digits.[33]

Changing residential patterns reinforced the gathering social differentiations within the community. The original German-speaking neighborhoods had been scattered about the core of the old riverside city. With Buenos Aires' great population surge of the late nineteenth century, however, the more prosperous elements of the community were displaced northward to the residential districts of Palermo and, especially, Belgrano. Less affluent German-speaking neighborhoods also developed on the periphery of Belgrano; simultaneously the working-class German *barrio* in Barracas acquired its own identity. By 1914, a working-class community would also have emerged near CATE's installation at Dock Sud, and working-class and petit bourgeois elements would have begun their movement outward toward Villa Devoto and Villa Ballester. For the time being, most of the older German associations, with their predominantly male membership, retained their quarters in the downtown commercial district, but the newer residential *barrios* also developed their own associational life. It reflected accurately the dual processes of socioeconomic change and assimilation to Argentine culture.

New schools were obviously required. Those founded in Barracas al Norte (1893), Quilmes (1898), and Dock Sud (1912) were unmistakably working-class. They provided a minimum of three (Dock Sud) to a maximum of seven (Barracas) years of schooling. Fees were moderate but were set upon a graduated scale—the higher the school year, the higher the cost—which insured that, for many, schooling would be of short duration. Elsewhere the distinctions were slightly more subtle. The Belgrano School (1897) and the Germania School (the old Congregational School, which was renamed when it moved from downtown to Calle Ecuador, not far from Plaza Once, in 1903) came to include secondary levels and were known as the most prestigious (and costly) in the community. The school governing boards held to the principle that no child of German parentage should be denied a German education because of his parents' straitened financial circumstances, but scholarship students were not allowed to forget their station. Years later, some would recall with bitterness the wire fence that had separated them from the children of the well-to-do in the recess yard of the Belgrano School. In 1910 the Monroe School (later the Humboldt School) was founded in Belgrano to accommodate the children of tradesmen and white-collar workers; a six-class school, in time it would become the largest in the German language system of the city. But perhaps the most significant of the new schools was the Cangallo School, founded in 1898. Theodor Alemann and other dissenters from the community's orthodoxies played leading roles in the founding governing board. They accepted the fact of assimilation, and from the beginning the Cangallo School concentrated upon a Spanish language curriculum that would prepare the children of German-speaking parents for Argentine careers.[34]

The Evangelical church, too, was forced to decentralize religious services. Pastors were recruited from Germany for new urban congregations as well as a growing number of rural congregations; in 1897 the La-Plata Synod was created to administer the expanding ecclesiastical structure. In that year the membership of the Buenos Aires congregation included 737 "businessmen," 52 "artists and teachers," 56 "female persons," and 162 "artisans and laborers." Undoubtedly, the congregation was closely identified with the community's respectable upper-status elements; but the disproportionately low number of working-class communicants also underlines a fact of which the community's nationalists would ultimately have to take account: workers were in general more prone to migrate as unattached young persons to Argentina, to marry exogamously, and to drift away from both Protestantism and the German-speaking community altogether. Only in 1899 did the synod make its first efforts to provide Lutheran religious services in Spanish, to accommodate second and third generation communicants.

First generation German Catholics, for their part, had been in a minority in the nineteenth-century community, and it had been axiomatic that they were more easily swallowed up by the surrounding Catholic *Kreolentum* of the city. However, by the turn of the century, Catholic (or "mixed") families of diverse Germanic and Argentine antecedents certainly formed a large element of the community. Until that time, it had not seemed a pressing matter to attempt to organize them. Beginning in 1897, however, several associations of German Catholic laymen were founded, culminating finally, in 1911, in the St. Bonifacius congregation with its own chapel and German priests. Until World War I the number of communicants who sought it out in preference to the city's other abundant Catholic services was small. After the war, although the proportion of first generation Catholics increased, the congregation did not prosper, and its work was taken over by German regular orders.[35]

The opposing pulls at work within the community—toward further Argentinization, toward closer identification with the Wilhelmian Reich—could be felt in other aspects of associational life. Since the time of Rosas, it had been a shibboleth of community self-government that no German association should give even the appearance of partisanship toward internal Argentine politics. In the 1830s and 1840s, the community's leaders had, of course, been making a virtue of necessity. Vulnerable then in the absence of backing by a European great power, they had been complaisant in their dealings with the dictator, and in return they had received relatively benevolent treatment at his hands—certainly compared to that accorded the English and French communities. The tradition of noninvolvement had continued to serve well during the periodic upheavals of the decades following Rosas' fall in 1852; and, or so it was believed, it had contributed to the easy access to influential positions enjoyed by German experts and academics that has been noted above.

But this ban was decisively broken in 1882 with the founding of the socialist association Vorwärts. To the indignation of the respectable, Vorwärts became affiliated with the Second International, and in short order its leaders were instrumental in the founding of the Argentine Socialist party. The weekly *Buenos Aires Vorwärts*, which remained in existence from 1886 to 1897, consistently urged its readers to acquire Argentine citizenship and to work for the democratization of Argentine politics. A similar editorial policy was adopted by the *Argentinisches*

Tageblatt, whose readership and influence were considerably greater. The *Tageblatt* group also included political activists, a number of whom took part in the popular uprising of 1890 and the subsequent founding of the Unión Cívica Radical. In 1893 the newspaper's editors were vigorous partisans of the agrarian insurrectionists, many of them Swiss, of Santa Fe Province. The community's moneyed elite continued to view such political obstreperousness with displeasure, however, and responded with the threat of blacklisting laid upon German workers observed reading *Vorwärts*, or the advertising boycott of the *Tageblatt* organized in retaliation for the paper's support of the German parliamentary Socialists in 1907. These weapons would be used again.[36]

For their part, the community's upper class created associations which effectively excluded the commonality, and these elite associations all bore the imprint of the new German Reich. It is nowhere better seen than in the edifice of the new Deutscher Klub erected in 1908–1909 in the 700 block of Calle (now Avenida) Córdoba, where it still stands. The earlier building at Córdoba 197, which had housed what was then the Athletic Club (founded 1855), was a modest one-story structure built around a central patio in the *criollo* fashion. The renamed (and more exclusive) Klub, however, was housed in a multistory wedding cake palace, the architectural expression of Hohenzollern pomposity; in its precincts only German was customarily permitted to be spoken. The same rule held true in the lodge at Tigre of the upper-middle-class rowing club, Teutonia, founded in 1890. But the capstone of parvenu snobbery was the German Riding Club, begun in 1910: it was open only to persons of "impeccable" origins who spoke German.[37]

At a somewhat lower level of status were the professional associations: the German Teachers' Association (f. 1902), the German Scientific Society (f. 1904; it evolved out of an earlier literary society which had led a fitful existence for two decades), and the Argentine Associations of German Engineers and of German Chemists (both f. 1910). These were less concerned with sociability than with the material situation of their members. They played the role of intermediary between their members and German employers and also, especially in legal and contractual matters, Argentine bureaucracy; they provided the affiliations that often permitted German professionals to prolong their residence in Argentina through second and subsequent contracts.

Nevertheless, after the turn of the century, such upper-status transients—and also their compeers among the bank officials and managers of German branch firms—tended increasingly to view their Argentine experience as but a step up in careers that should, in the best case, culminate in high positions in Germany. Their concern for the future education of their children forced the revision, more in accord with German norms, of the curricula of the community's prestige schools, the Belgrano School and the Germania School; by 1906 both schools were offering certification for the one-year-volunteer option (which could lead to an officer's commission) under German conscription law. In their roles as opinion molders they brought a greatly increased pre-occupation with the affairs of Germany and Europe to the community's public life; by the same token, their patent lack of concern for its internal affairs began to draw muted grumbling. A rough index of the pace at which this international movement quickened between 1900 and 1914 is found in the membership lists of the upper-crust Deutsch-er Klub. As of 31 October 1901 the Klub had 257 dues-paying members; of them, 36 were temporarily absent on business in Europe. In 1911–1912, 123 of 615 were on extended European sojourns, and 92 returned during the reporting period. In 1914, 152 of 646 were "temporarily absent"; 51 of these left after August of that year, presumably to assume military duties.[38]

In the last decades before 1914, the community's leaders—its more articulate patricians, its newspaper publishers, churchmen, school directors, *Verein* presidents, the Reich's diplomatic and consular officials —grew acutely conscious of its collective prestige, its *Ansehen*, vis-à-vis their European colleagues and competitors. They thus worked purposefully to maintain the image of a unified, solidly prosperous, and irreproachably respectable bourgeois community infused by the German virtues of order and industry, a community scrupulously non-political in its dealings with Argentine officialdom and self-sufficient, through its communal institutions, in attending to its own social welfare and self-governance. This cultivation of appearances was directed in the first instance toward the Argentines and, secondarily, toward the other European colonies; but it undoubtedly affected also, in the end, the community's own perception of itself. For except within the small band of Socialists affiliated with Vorwärts—and even they were notoriously susceptible to bourgeoisification—the mores and values celebrated on ritual occasions, transmitted in its schools, churches and associations, internalized by the majority, were those of the European middle class.

By 1914, the community numbered about thirty thousand, of whom some eleven thousand were nationals of imperial Germany, or Reichs-deutsche. To appearances, it was remarkably immune to the ethnic crosscurrents and absorptive social processes of the expanding Argentine metropolis. To be sure, public men attributed the Germans' great material successes in part, at least, to the racial gift of *Anpassungs-fähigkeit*, or "adaptability." But adaptability, it seemed, was prevented from slipping quickly into assimilation by several potent factors. Like the city's other upper-status foreign communities, particularly the British (against whom the Germans ceaselessly measured themselves), the German-speaking colony occupied a distinct position in the urban social order, one apart from both the native landowning and bureaucratic *oligarquía* and the vast commonality of *criollo* and immigrant workers—and fulfilled economic and cultural functions beyond the capacity of either. Its apparently sturdy insularity was buttressed by a certain territorial cohesion (in Belgrano), an alien religion, and above all by an institutional structure capable of enveloping individuals in Germanic culture and of transmitting it intact from generation to generation. Psychologically, this insularity drew strength from a pervasive sense of cultural superiority to the Argentine *criollos*. Identification with the thrusting new Reich of Bismarck and the Hohenzollerns was an important element; yet even amidst the sharpening international rivalries of the prewar years the Germans were also wont to range themselves alongside the French and British as the foremost of Europe's cultural pioneers at work on the Río de la Plata.

But after the turn of the century the realities were diverging rapidly at several points from the comfortable self-perceptions sketched above. The process of socioeconomic differentiation and the emergence of a finely graduated social hierarchy weakened the bonds of community; the metaphor of a congeries of barely tangential social sets or circles used by Leopold Schnabl to describe the community of the 1880s was even more applicable a quarter century later. Further, the sketchy evidence available suggests that, although the German community strove for endogamy, nevertheless, because of the much greater numbers of male than female immigrants, many men quite understandably sought mates outside. They did so, in the main, among coreligionists (Protestant, Catholic, Jewish) of Northern and Western European antecedents and at equivalent levels of socioeconomic status. Religion and social class, in other words, were at least as strongly imperative as sheer ethnicity in determining behavior. Finally, the political prestige and lucrative economic presence of imperial Germany in Argentina gave the Reichsdeutsche disproportionate influence within the community. Among the majority who owed no political allegiance to the Reich, however, there was latent resistance to the assumption that they would follow wherever the Reich might lead. World War I and the postwar era would expose all these fault lines and would finish off a good many illusions.

In the last years before 1914, the community's enthusiasm for evidences of Germany's new military might grew perceptibly. Already in 1895 an Army League had been founded, although it seems to have consisted in the main of veterans of the Franco-Prussian War. The presence of the military missions after 1900 lent much luster to the community's social life, as did the periodic visits of the cruiser S.M.S. *Bremen*, then on South Atlantic station, which served as the occasion for expansive banquets and fetes. To be sure, in 1909 Ambassador Waldthausen felt called upon to complain to the admiralty of its thoughtlessness in scheduling *Bremen's* port calls during the month of December; for in December, approaching the height of the Argentine summer, the community's more important members, as well as all Argentines of any consequence, were accustomed to desert the capital for the cooler seaside or mountains.[39]

It chanced, further, that in 1907 one of the subalterns detached to the training mission in Argentina was the son of Field Marshal *Freiherr* von der Goltz. In consequence, in 1910 the elder von der Goltz was named imperial Germany's senior representative to the celebrations held on the centenary of Argentina's de facto independence from Spain. Von der Goltz was deeply impressed by the military parades, speechmaking, and lavish decorations of the festivities, the promise of Argentina's economic future, the ostentatious prosperity of the German colony, the aristocratic demeanor of Argentina's haut monde (something he had not expected to find in a republic), and "the alacrity with which the government defends itself against all attempts to disturb order" (as well he might be, for the centennial was held under a constitutional state of siege in which civil rights were suspended). His subsequent writing and lectures on Argentina aroused much interest in Germany before the war and undoubtedly turned the attention of many exofficers in that direction afterward.[40]

Until 1910, the duties of military attaché to the diplomatic mission were handled on an ad hoc basis by one or another of the training officers. Von der Goltz' recommendations, however, and the installation by the United States, Great Britain, and France of military attachés at about this time caused the matter to be rethought in Berlin. The extraordinary cost of living in Buenos Aires proved a major objection and delayed a decision. It was not until early 1914 that a naval attaché, in the person of *Korvettenkapitän* August Moller, was named to Buenos Aires; his area of responsibility included also Brazil, Uruguay, and Chile. He would have an eventful wartime career and a most interesting one in the postwar years as well.[41]

It is well to keep matters in perspective, however. According to an anecdote which still circulates, the military men learned that, for all the glamour and prestige of their station, German-Argentine society was ordered rather differently than at home. At an ornate ball given by the Deutscher Klub in one of these last prewar years—or so the story goes—a dashing young officer, impeccably turned out up to and including the requisite von to his name, requested the honor of a waltz with the daughter of one of the wealthiest big businessmen of the city. "Nein, danke," she is said to have replied frostily: "I dance only with *established* houses."

Confidence, optimism, and self-satisfaction reached a peak within the community early in 1914. The Argentine economy had reentered a boom phase of its business cycles in 1909, and trade with Germany and in general had been leaping ahead. The German-Argentine League for the Promotion of Economic Interests (Deutsch-Argentinischer Zentralverband zur Förderung wirtschaftlicher Interessen), set up in Berlin in 1910 with about fifty individuals and firms as members, claimed some three hundred four years later. The kaiser himself was reported to have complained of the small flow of German capital to Argentina and to have stated his intention of bringing his personal influence to bear to increase it.[42]

In March 1914, a powerful German naval squadron visited Argentina. Unfortunately, the battleships *König Albert* and *Kaiser* drew too much water to come to Buenos Aires and anchored instead off the fashionable resort of Mar del Plata (where bad weather ruined much of their effect). However, the cruiser *Strassburg*—one in the eye for the French colony!—made port in Buenos Aires and there followed the usual round of banquets, balls, speeches, and visits to breweries (for the crew). At the end of the same month, Prince Heinrich of Hohenzollern arrived for a formal visit on the maiden voyage of the crack Hamburg-Süd liner *Cap Trafalgar*, and the community's enthusiasm was screwed to an even higher pitch. By the time he departed, a Navy League had been founded, and Heinrich had consented to stand as its patron. At the Jockey Club banquet in honor of the officers of the naval squadron, Ambassador von dem Bussche-Haddenhausen expressed his brimming happiness at seeing more and bigger German warships in Argentine waters; he could now, he implied, lay his burden down. He left Argentina shortly afterward in the entourage of Prince Heinrich. He would return after the armistice as a private citizen whose self-appointed mission was to help keep alive on foreign soil a remnant of the old Germany.[43]

2. World War I:
Privation and Profiteering

Argentina remained neutral throughout World War I, but its fortunes were nevertheless bound up with those of the European powers, especially the Allies. Thousands of English, French, Belgians, Italians, and others returned to the colors in their homelands. The great Buenos Aires journals of upper-class opinion, *La Prensa* and *La Nación*, were partisans of the Allied cause; in this they were verbalizing the sentiments of most educated Argentines, who themselves had been profoundly molded, directly or indirectly, by British notions of political economy and the French high culture of the belle époque. Emotional commitment was reinforced by economic interest, for, after a period of retrenchment and confusion that lasted into 1915, Argentina's pastoral and (to a lesser extent) agricultural industries became prime suppliers of foodstuffs, wool, hides, and other material to the Allied armies. But the war also exposed Argentina's extreme dependence upon outside sources of every variety of capital and consumer goods, for the warring nations could no longer supply them. The result was a regime of scarcity, alleviated only slightly by the modest beginnings of import-substitution enterprises. Furthermore, scarcity combined with high export earnings to produce inflation: the cost of living, already high by European standards in 1914, nearly doubled by 1920. With high prices and scarcity came growing labor militancy, which culminated in the cycle of bitterly fought strikes from 1917 through 1921.

In the midst of the war, in 1916, Argentina took a long stride toward representative liberal democracy—or so it seemed at the time. By the use of chicanery, fraud, and ultimately force, the landowning *oligarquía* had ruled—with occasional brilliance and one dismal disaster (Juárez Celman)—since the 1860s. However, opposition had been building since 1890 among urban petit bourgeois and rural smallholder elements. The vehicle of their dissent was the Unión Cívica Radical, whose leader was Hipólito Yrigoyen. Under Yrigoyen, the Radicals threatened revolution and practiced abstention from the *oligarquía's* electoral charades. Immigrants, for their part, suffered no pressures to acquire citizenship and were offered no inducements. The response of the great majority was indifference; *criollo* politics were thus better kept en famille. Nevertheless, foreign Anarchists and Socialists figured large in the beginnings of authentically radical politics and trade unionism. With such pressures building from below, in 1912 President Roque Saenz Peña—over the horrified opposition of much of his own class—forced sweeping electoral reforms through Congress. They took effect in the subsequent presidential election of 1916, which Saenz Peña did not live to see. In Argentina's first free general elections, Yrigoyen and the Radicals won by a narrow margin. Elite rule, or so it seemed, had given way to populist democracy.

In Buenos Aires' German-speaking community, the first, predictable effect of the outbreak of war in Europe in August 1914 was an up-swelling of patriotic sentiment, a papering-over of internal dissensions, and a closing of ranks in the face of what were soon seen—with surprise, sorrow, indignation—as the predominantly pro-Allied sympathies of the *porteño* population. By mid-1919, however, it was clear that the war's more profound consequences had been disturbingly paradoxical. On one hand, isolation in the midst of a largely antipathetic urban society caused numbers of individuals—acting from social, economic, or ideological motives—to break with *Deutschtum*. In some cases, the break was transitory; in others, irrevocable. Unquestionably, however, for the majority the war years served to regenerate the sense of community that had been slipping away in the prewar years. The sense of apartness, moreover, the self-perception as a beleaguered minority unjustly persecuted and vilified by the victors of 1918, would remain a psychological sinew of community throughout the postwar decade. But, on the other hand, the war continued and indeed greatly hastened the distention of the community's social order, for its economic effects acted very differentially upon social elements within it.

The estrangement that developed during the war between the commonality and the business elite (*Geld-Aristokratie*, in local parlance) might well have found no expression but for the collapse of the Central Powers in late 1918 and the German Revolution that accompanied it. These events in Europe awakened political reverberations within the German-speaking community of Buenos Aires. In the popular assemblies of November and December 1918 and their *sequelae* through the following year, the elite's comfortably assumed dominion over community affairs was challenged by an inchoate but widely based populist reform movement. The uprising collapsed in time of its internal dissensions and the economic force majeure of the traditionalists, but the animosity of the commons toward the *Geld-Aristokratie* remained inflamed through the 1920s, kept alive both by political conflicts whose origins lay in Germany and by further aggravation of the community's social malaise, which was preeminently of local, Argentine, origin.

At the outbreak of war, the bourgeois Germans of necessity with-drew from the capital's larger and looser cosmopolitan European com-munity, which had hitherto comprised a mobile caste based on exten-sive personal friendships, business associations, international marriages, overlapping memberships in clubs and societies, and joint social in-stitutions.[1] For some, the sundering was undoubtedly painful: the dry notation, for example, that during the first fifteen months of the war eighteen persons had left the Deutscher Klub for "political reasons" must conceal many varieties of personal anguish.[2] Public solidarity behind the Fatherland was broken at only one point, however: the executive committee of the socialist association Vorwärts openly de-nounced the war as a capitalist crime against civilization and expressed its indifference to the identity of the nominal victors. But this orthodox pacifist stand brought down upon them not only the indignation of the community at large but also that of the rank and file Socialists. Vor-wärts was convulsed by recriminations against the executive commit-tee, fist fights on the premises between pacifists and patriots, and mass resignations. By October 1914, only nineteen active members remained on the rolls, and a motion to dissolve the association was defeated only by a narrow vote within the executive.[3] Policy was thereafter sharply reversed; by November Vorwärts was firmly committed to the cause of the Central Powers for the duration. During the war years, in fact, the socialist Verein—one of the few German associations in Buenos Aires possessing quarters spacious enough to accommodate large gatherings—became a major community meeting point for patriotic rallies, lectures, benefit concerts, theater performances, and similar events, which the Socialists were pleased to sponsor jointly with other German associations of widely differing social composition and political orientation, including even the patrician Deutscher Klub. A mora-torium on factional political debate and dissension settled upon the community.

On 6 August, a number of the community's eminences—Chargé d'Affaires Count von Dönhoff, Consul General Bobrick, Vice-Consul von Radowitz, Eduard Herrmann, director of the Banco Germánico de la América del Sur—summoned the executive committees of some thirty associations to a meeting at the Deutscher Klub. Its business was to organize a war fund, or Kriegsspende. The gesture of a war fund was patterned after the highly successful effort of 1870, which had demon-strated to the Argentines, and indeed to the Germans themselves, the patriotic solidarity which the community could muster in an emer-gency. In the far wealthier and more ostentatious community of 1914, patriotism, competition in flaunting material resources, and (it was later said) judicious pressures exerted upon dependent employees combined at first to produce an impressive series of contributors' lists, duly published in the German language press. By mid-1915 the round sum of one million pesos was reported forwarded to the Reich, and a second collection, now termed a *Kriegerdank*, for the relief of widows and orphans, was begun.[4] Contributions began to flag noticeably, however, and in time the fund would become a source of embarrassment to the community's leaders.

The patriotic enthusiasm of the early war years was channeled into war work, of a sort, through the German Scientific Society (Deutscher Wissenschaftlicher Verein).[5] The wartime orientation of this prestigious society was largely the work of Dr. Wilhelm Keiper, who had served since 1904 as the head of the cadre of German pedagogues who had founded and developed the Instituto Nacional del Profesorado Secundario and who had been, since 1912, president of the DWV. Late in 1914 he returned from a clandestine trip to Germany—itinerary not recorded—charged with responsibility for developing German propaganda work in Argentina. He believed, with some reason, that the cause of Germany and the Central Powers could best be laid before influential *criollo* intellectuals if it were associated with German science. Under his frenetic leadership, the DWV recruited far beyond the narrow circle of schoolmasters and academically trained professionals that had hitherto constituted its membership, and it succeeded in raising its numbers from about 150 (at the beginning of 1914) to over 500 (at the end of 1915). In the same period, the society's published budget more than tripled to over 18,000 pesos per year, a sum that reflected not only increased revenue from individual dues but also large contributions from local German business houses and from the German-Argentine League for the Promotion of Economic Interests and the Foreign Office in Berlin.[6]

These funds supported a varied program. It included courses of instruction in German language and literature directed both toward second and third generation Argentine-Germans and toward *criollos* believed susceptible to cultivation. The DWV also sponsored a lecture series on the war and periodic rallies. Its most important mission, however, was that of subsidizing and disseminating printed propaganda material. Until October 1914, a hastily prepared *Boletín Germánico* was distributed on the streets of Buenos Aires. It was then replaced by the much more professional *La Unión*, founded by Hermann Tjarks, editor of the well-subsidized *Deutsche La-Plata Zeitung*. Much financial support was also given to an organ of the Spanish community, *La Gaceta de España*, and its editor, Juan Cola. In addition, until 1916 a wealthy pro-German *criollo*, Eduardo Retienne, put out at his own expense the high quality illustrated *Germania*; he reportedly withdrew from German circles in disillusionment at the profiteering of the *Geld-Aristokratie*.

Relations between Keiper's operation and prominent *criollos* who lent, or leased, themselves to the German cause were, however, more cordial. The most important military Germanophile was Lieutenant General José Félix Uriburu, a protégé of the prewar training missions who had seen regimental troop duty in Germany. Uriburu discoursed on *la guerra actual* at the Deutscher Klub; the piece was reprinted and widely distributed in Argentine military circles. His eulogy on the death of Field Marshal von der Goltz in 1916 also received wide attention.[7] The German-educated historian, Eduardo Quesada, whose personal library would later form the nucleus of the Ibero-Amerikanisches Institut in Berlin, published two pro-German tracts: *La actual civilización germánica y la presente guerra* and *El peligro alemán en Sudamérica*. Other collaborators were Alfredo Colmo (*Mi neutralismo*), Manuel A. Baré (*Delenda est Germania*, in three volumes), Juan B. Ramos, dean of the Faculty of Law of the National University of Buenos Aires (*La significación de Alemania en la guerra europea*), Dr. F. Benavides Olazábal (*En el mundo de la filosofía y de la guerra*), and Josué A. Beruti (*Beligerancia científica*).[8] Uriburu, Ramos, and Beruti would remain closely involved with the German nationalist Right in the postwar era.

To facilitate these and other publications, Keiper early in 1917 established the Empresa Editorial Germana (also known as the Unión de Libreros Alemanes). There, he and his associates produced propaganda material of all sorts: posters, reprints, brochures, the war diary of one Juan B. Homet, a purported deserter from the French army, analyses of the war over the names of *criollo* intellectuals—more than a million pieces in all, in Keiper's estimate.[9] The operation remained in existence from April 1917 until early 1921, when it was closed down by Dr. Adolf Pauli, the newly arrived ambassador of the German Republic. Keiper soon landed on his feet again as special advisor to the embassy on educational matters, government inspector of the German language schools, and rector of the exclusive Germania School.

One venture which served as grist for Keiper's mill rested upon apparently solid accomplishment: the Patagonia expedition of 1915–1916. The expedition was the offspring of a long-term program of geographical and geological exploration begun before the war by the Argentine-German botanist Dr. Cristóbal Hicken and the German-born geochemist, mountain climber, and founding member of the

Agronomy Faculty of the National University of Buenos Aires, Dr. Fritz Reichert.[10] Reichert sounded out Keiper, who in turn persuaded the "complex, overly pedantic, cumbrously thinking brains" of the German Scientific Society to accept formal sponsorship of the expedition and to contribute 1,000 pesos toward its realization. Reichert, however, was thrown upon his own resources to collect the remaining 9,000 pesos that had been budgeted. Although beset periodically by fears of his own social inadequacy, he accomplished his mission in an epic "begging campaign" which took him through the forbidding country of the "offices and counting houses of the high and mighty upper reaches of German big business" in Buenos Aires. He was apparently amply persuasive in holding out before the *Grosskaufmannschaft* the possibility of uncovering hitherto unsuspected sources of petroleum, minerals, coal, and lignite. To his surprised gratification, the money was pledged in short order.

Curiously, although both Reichert and Hicken were seasoned campaigners, neither man, for reasons not entirely clear, was able to accompany the expedition. It was therefore placed in the charge of Dr. Lutz Witte, a geologist in the employ of the Topographical Service of the province of Buenos Aires. Accompanying Witte were the chemist Alfred Kölliker, the geographer Franz Kühn (soon to lose his position at the Instituto Nacional del Profesorado Secundario), the topographer Adolf Tomsen, and the Danish born photographer and painter of the La Plata Museum, Johannes Jörgensen. "A concern for social welfare," as Reichert put it, moved the expedition's organizers to engage as cooks and porters five of the unemployed German seamen lounging about the Buenos Aires docks.

The expedition began with a minor international incident. Twenty-four hours at sea aboard the Hamburg-Amerika coastal steamer *Bartolomé Mitre* (which carried a German crew but flew the Argentine flag), the scientists were taken prisoner by the British auxiliary cruiser *Orama* and carried to Montevideo. The affair was soon resolved, however. Francisco Moreno, director of the La Plata Museum, pointed out to the British ambassador, Sir Reginald Tower, that the expedition bore the personal imprimatur of Victorino de la Plaza, acting president of the republic; and Tower obtained the scientists' release. The group then proceeded by way of Santa Cruz to the glacier zone west of Lake Viedma; there, in February and March of 1916, they carried out the explorations plotted for them by Reichert and Hicken. Their report was speedily prepared for publication by Keiper and appeared, lavishly illustrated with maps, drawings, and photographs, in two volumes in Spanish early in the following year.[11] Witte and Reichert contributed short and singularly unrevealing passages assessing the exploitable potential of the region. It is possible, though undemonstrable, that they supplied more detailed reports to the expedition's sponsors. In any case, Keiper could claim another triumph for German science in the service of the republic.

The organized war effort of the community was carried out, however, by a minority in relatively comfortable circumstances. Elsewhere, the community was undergoing social dislocations that would have great long-term effects. They had begun to be felt in the first week of the war. In common with the missions of other European powers, the German and Austro-Hungarian consulates on 2 August 1914 published announcements in the German language newspapers calling their nationals under military obligation to the colors. The confusion at the consulates rapidly mounted to unmanageable proportions; in what was probably an excess of patriotic bombast, they were reported "besieged" by "hundreds" of men, not only those liable to military service but also volunteers.[12] One contingent of three hundred reservists and volunteers, including fifty officers, succeeded on 4 August in slipping out of Buenos Aires harbor aboard the Italian liner *Tommaso di Savoia*; their safe arrival in Genoa on 21 August was reported three days later.[13] Apparently, however, not all the fifteen German officers serving as trainers to the Argentine army were able to conclude their affairs in time; there was, in addition, a round of gala leavetaking dinners organized for them by their Argentine comrades-in-arms during the first week of August. It was later reported that *Rittmeister* von Pfistermeister and several others found themselves, presumably somewhat crestfallen, amidst their stranded countrymen on the Buenos Aires docks. All the training officers, however, eventually reached Europe.[14]

In view of the British Royal Navy's domination of the sea lanes to Europe, the rashness of the call to arms, not to mention the response, quickly became clear to Consul General Bobrick. On 11 August he made it known that for the time being there was no possibility of obtaining shipping to Europe and no point in reservists' coming from the interior in the expectation of finding it. He exaggerated slightly, for as late as October 1914 the Italian consulate continued to issue passes to reservists able to pay their own passage on Italian ships. On 29 October, however, the British Admiralty announced that it would no longer honor such immunities.[15] Thereafter, for the duration of the war, the sea route to Europe remained closed to identifiable male nationals of the Central Powers. Nevertheless, an unknown but sizable number—156 men from the Buenos Aires community alone were killed in battle during the war[16]—succeeded in evading the blockade as individuals. They, however, were the exceptional cases, for by far the larger number of Germans and Austrians of military age in southern South America got no farther than the waterfront of Buenos Aires. As most of them in the first flush of patriotic ardor had thrown up jobs, broken leases, or sold off businesses and property, there they remained, a burden and embarrassment to the Buenos Aires community, for the duration of the war.

Even before his deflating announcement of 11 August, Consul General Bobrick had acted to halt the migration of young men to Buenos Aires. On 6 August, a riverboat bearing four hundred reservists from Paraguay (including the eight officers on training duty with the Paraguayan army) was boarded at Rosario by the German consul of that city. He informed the men of the unlikelihood of their obtaining sea passage in Buenos Aires and advised them to return home to Paraguay; riverboat passage from Buenos Aires would be arranged for them, he promised. One of the Paraguayan reservists, Ernst *Freiherr* Gedult von Jungenfeld, later wrote a memoir of his experiences; with certain allowances for the hyperbole of wartime it remains invaluable for its description of the vibrant excitement among the Europeans of Buenos Aires during the first weeks of the war. Von Jungenfeld ignored the consul's advice: he had been several years in the savannas of Paraguay, and his stay in Buenos Aires had, at first, a distinct air of holiday release about it. He was duly awed by the ostentatious wealth of the Argentine capital, the elegance of its parks and public buildings, and the extravagance of the public mourning for the recently deceased president of the republic, Roque Saenz Peña. The city was seething with European reservists, he found, not only nationals of the countries already at war but also Italians, Swiss, Dutch, and others. All were beset by uncertainty, and all were credulous in digesting the plausible and implausible rumors that ran like brushfire through the cafes and roominghouses. For news of the European war, he soon concluded, the Buenos Aires press was little more reliable than the cafe gossip. The *viveza criolla* of the newsboys, however, was equal to the occasion: von Jungenfeld describes a street urchin who approached him and a companion, studied their faces intently for a moment, then waved his newspapers aloft and shouted "Gran victoria alemana!" Naturally, they bought a copy, then watched as the youngster ran off to the next knot of passersby, studied *them*, and yelled "Gran victoria inglesa!" The newspaper, it goes without saying, contained news of neither the one nor the other.[17]

Von Jungenfeld's high spirits soon gave way, however, to puzzled resentment at the anti-German feeling he sensed everywhere amongst

criollos and neutrals. He found the attitude of the Argentines particularly reprehensible, for they, he felt, owed much of their material and
intellectual progress to the work of German "cultural pioneers." But
his mood was further darkened by his reception at CATE and the
German commercial houses he visited in search of temporary work or
a loan with which to try his luck at a passage through the blockade to
Europe. The rich Germans, he wrote tartly, were more than willing to
see their names put down for "lovely sums" on the collection lists of
the war fund then being organized, but they wanted nothing to do
with "us poor suckers." Abandoning hope of assistance in Buenos Aires,
von Jungenfeld returned to Paraguay, put his affairs in order, and
raised money. From the Brazilian consulate in Asunción he obtained
papers which certified him as a Brazilian citizen in possession of the
promise of a job in an Italian factory. Armed with these, he eventually,
after further adventures, made his way to Europe. He survived the
war and returned afterward to Paraguay.[18]

The reservists who remained in Buenos Aires were augmented immediately by hundreds of merchant seamen whose ships had been interned by the Argentine authorities. The existing welfare agencies
were, of course, unprepared to cope with the sudden emergency, and
the first makeshift expedients were far from satisfactory. The men were
reported to be living in burrows and hastily constructed shanties on
vacant lots in the dockside area.[19] Appeals were made to private families to shelter destitute reservists temporarily, apparently with only
modest success. To be sure, by the end of September approximately
100 reservists and seamen had been crammed into the German Seamen's Home. About 30 of these were allowed to become more or less
permanent residents; the remainder of the limited space was reserved
for transients. Altogether through 1914–1915, the Seamen's Home took
in 1,339 different persons for varying lengths of time; thereafter, as
other charitable agencies assumed a larger proportion of the burden,
the number held at between 900 and 1,000 per year through 1919.[20]

A hastily formed aid committee of the urban community raised a
certain amount of money through collections and theater benefits in
the last months of 1914. By Christmas, more than 1,000 individuals as
well as numerous families had received assistance from the aid committee; 850 men had been lodged aboard the interned steamer *Gotha*
at one time or another.[21] Early in 1915 a more permanent solution was
found when another German merchant ship, *Granada*, was converted
into a floating hostel for 100 or more men. Aboard ship, a free medical
clinic was held regularly by personnel from the German Hospital.
Nevertheless, characterizations of *Granada*'s amenities vary greatly

according to the source: the term "unworthy of human beings" appears in one of the more embittered postwar recollections.[22] Unquestionably, maritime discipline aboard *Granada* was severe: in one year, 1916, 148 men were thrown out of the hostel for drunkenness, infractions of shipboard rules, or "unruliness."[23]

Granada's lodgers were, however, relatively comfortable compared to the party of German seamen interned on the Argentine island of Martín García in the Plata estuary. They were the survivors of the disastrous voyage of the commerce raider *Cap Trafalgar* in 1914. In August 1914, the 18,710-ton Hamburg-Süd liner had come under the orders of the newly arrived imperial naval attaché, *Korvettenkapitän* Moller. At his direction the ship was fitted out at sea with cannon and crew brought by torpedo boat from Southwest Africa. But on 14 September *Cap Trafalgar's* wartime career came to a sudden though not altogether ignominious end when it was surprised by the British auxiliary cruiser *Carmania* while coaling under the lee of the Brazilian island of Trinidade. After a spirited exchange of gunfire, in which both ships took substantial damage and casualties, *Cap Trafalgar* attempted to escape. In doing so, it ran aground and sank—or, according to the British version, exploded or was scuttled. Its surviving crew, 10 officers and 288 seamen, was taken to Buenos Aires. There they settled down to internment under Argentine supervision, an internment that would last four and a half years. The parallel with the World War II *Graf Spee* affair is striking. In the end, however, *Cap Trafalgar's* crew would be involved in events unlike anything that occurred a generation later.[24]

As early as October 1914, a number of German employees of the partly British-owned department store Gath y Chaves saw fit to take out newspaper advertisements in which they affirmed that they had not suffered discrimination at the hands of their employers (after the war it would be charged that they had been compelled to do so and that the condition of their continued employment had been reduced wages).[25] By the end of the year a full-scale purge of nationals of the Central Powers was under way by British, French, and Belgian firms, as well as some Argentine enterprises. The rolls of the unemployed began to swell with technical and administrative personnel as well as manual and clerical workers. In Buenos Aires and Rosario especial bitterness was felt at the Argentine government's complaisance toward the firings from the British- and French-owned railways—indeed, there was some evidence that German technical personnel were released from the Argentine national railways at British instigation.[26] In 1916 the contracts of the German pedagogues of the Instituto Nacional del

Profesorado Secundario failed to be renewed. As noted earlier, the head of the group, Dr. Wilhelm Keiper, had already established himself as an indispensable man-of-affairs within the community, and he busied himself throughout the war as director of the community's propaganda effort. A place was found for Franz Kühn with the Patagonia expedition; after war's end he obtained a permanent position with the University of the Litoral, as did Karl Jesinghaus, a third member of the institute staff. Of the fate of the remainder, no record has survived.

But during the course of the war still a fourth category of German-speaking workers drifted into unemployment: technicians and white-collar employees of German-controlled firms. Personnel managers of these firms insisted plausibly that such cuts were necessitated by war-time shortages and uncertainties. It was later claimed, however, that many of the concerns that had dismissed German-speaking personnel had done so merely to become less identifiably German in the generally pro-Allied business circles of the capital, for neutral or even Allied employees of the same firms appeared suspiciously less vulnerable to such reductions. This process began early in the war but became greatly aggravated following the imposition of the British and American commercial blacklists (March 1916 and April 1917 respectively). It was noted, similarly, that, when positions fell open, German businessmen appeared to prefer non-German employees. As early as 27 September 1914, one F. Grossler, a reservist who had come from Santiago de Chile, complained in an angry letter to the *Tageblatt* of the indifference of the local German business establishment toward the plight of their countrymen, who, he said, were suffering in the bitter competition for jobs with a "mob of Polacks, Slovaks, and other such riffraff [*einem Pack von Polacken, Slowacken, und sonstigen Gesindel*]." In 1915 the annual report of the Association for the Protection of Germanic Immigrants confirmed, in somewhat more dignified language, that German business houses were indeed reluctant to take on the German-speaking unemployed. Both the association and the job placement center of the German Welfare Society (see below) chose, moreover, to make their facilities available not only to German-speaking workers but also to nationals of all the Central Powers—including, after 1915, Turks and Bulgars—and to "friendly" neutrals: Dutch, Scandinavians, Spaniards, and certain Argentines.

On the question of nationalities, the wartime records of the Association for the Protection of Germanic Immigrants offer persuasive evidence. In 1914 it succeeded in placing 1,467 persons, 898 of whom were Reichsdeutsche; in 1915, 1,922, of whom 563 were Reichsdeutsche.

From 1916 onward it also published figures on the numbers of unemployed as well as those placed. It is obvious that only a limited number of new unemployed were allowed even to submit dossiers.[27] Its published data must therefore be regarded as gross underestimates of total unemployment. At that, they showed 2,988 jobless in 1916, 1,635 of them Reichsdeutsche; 2,305 were placed, including 1,215 Reichsdeutsche. In 1917—a year of great general unemployment in Argentina—unemployed were 3,998 (1,901); placed, 3,656 (1,865). For 1918 comparable figures were unemployed, 3,953 (2,364); placed, 3,830 (2,316).[28] Following the armistice the callousness of German employers toward their own compatriots would become one item, among many, in the populist bill of indictment against the wartime behavior of the local German business elite.

Early in 1916 most of the community's welfare agencies were amalgamated in the German Welfare Society (Deutsche Wohltätigkeits-Gesellschaft, or DWG), one of whose statutory objectives was the "suppression of house-to-house begging." Its records confirm that unemployment and social disorganization bit deeply into all levels of the commonality and touched not a few once well-off business owners and professionals. From March through December 1916, the society supported 145 destitute families and 45 unmarried businessmen and technicians. Of the occupations of heads of families that were recorded, 32 were businessmen, 19 were other white-collar or professional workers (technicians, teachers, administrators, architects), 25 were skilled workers, 9 were semiskilled, and 10 were unskilled. The number of family support cases (including all types of assistance) rose to approximately 500 during 1917 and to more than 600 in 1918. The society's budget was something under 50,000 pesos for the first ten months of 1916; in 1917 it rose to 139,000 pesos. In 1918, with the loss of more than 400 sustaining subscribers, it declined to 123,000 pesos.[29] The *Granada* records also indicate the range of occupational groups affected by unemployment. Of the 983 men who passed through the hostel in 1916, for example, only 295 were seamen, unskilled workers, or peasants; the majority comprised businessmen, white-collar employees, skilled workers, and "diverse."[30] As late as the business year 1918–1919 (October through September), 293 of the Seamen's Home's 927 lodgers were other than seafaring men.[31]

The records of the community's organized employment services provide an equally accurate picture of the extent of occupational and status dislocation. In the month of December 1915, for example, the Association for the Protection of Germanic Immigrants was besieged by 1,297 unemployed and filled 125 positions. Of these positions, only

26 required a modicum of manual or white-collar training or experience on the land.[32] In all of 1917, 3,656 persons found employment through the association, and in 1918, 3,830. Of those placed, 23 were businessmen in 1917, and 9 in 1918; all worked as traveling salesmen on a commission basis. In 1917 it placed a total of 48 technical and professional persons, 31 of whom took positions as "domestic tutors" to the German and *criollo* well-to-do; comparable figures for 1918 were 24 (12). Other varieties of domestic service—as cooks, gardeners, servants, "couples"—absorbed a sizable proportion of the unemployed: 598 in 1917, 589 in the last year of the war. But the largest single category in which the unemployed were placed was that of simple "worker": nearly 2,000 in 1917, nearly 2,300 in 1918.[33] Large numbers were sent to the interior to work at the harvest; many others found casual occupation as stevedores on the Buenos Aires docks.

Among the numerous other uses found for them was strikebreaking. In September 1917, in the train of the great strikes that had begun earlier that year, the 1,400 manual workers of CATE, Germans in the great majority, downed tools in affiliation with the militant and violent Federación Obrera Marítima. The managers of CATE assembled a force of 200 loyal foremen, clerks, and strikebreakers in a desperate makeshift attempt to keep the power plant's generators in operation. To be sure, the imbalance in numbers was more than offset by the presence of provincial gendarmerie, whom Emil Hayn, CATE's technical director, described with evident relish as "wild characters, Indians and half-breeds, with five bold officers. The captain of cavalry laughed: 'Que vengan, van a morir todos.' ["Let them come—they are all going to die."]" Hayn disdained to deal with the CATE delegates, whom he characterized as "idiots," but he admitted that he trod carefully with the representatives of the FOM. He pointed out, or so he later boasted, that it was beneath them to associate with such as the CATE strikers. After three and a half weeks the FOM, having won certain concessions, withdrew, and the strike collapsed. "We were not overly concerned about our [CATE] strikers; they fell apart, and we rehired those who pleased us. We were aware that the greater part of them had merely been terrorized."[34]

By war's end it was proving relatively easy for the Association for the Protection of Germanic Immigrants to find employment for skilled and semiskilled workers. In 1917, 850 skilled workers in 41 trades and 196 semiskilled workers in 12 trades were placed by the association; in 1918 the figures were 650 and 152. Similarly, the German Welfare Society's annual report for 1918 noted that, due to the greater availability of technical positions, expenses for the support of unmarried business and technical personnel had declined markedly from the previous year.[35]

Even taking these developments into account, however, it is clear that the overall effects of the war upon the commonality ranged from harmful to totally ruinous. To the independent petite bourgeoisie, wartime meant, at best, straitened circumstances: shopkeepers, restaurant and hotel keepers, tradespeople, all saw their clienteles shrink to a core of loyalists of the Central Powers. In somewhat feeble retaliation, address lists of German or pro-German establishments were published beginning in 1916. The expansion of the labor pool available to German employers meant that the wages of their dependents in no wise kept pace with the rising prices of wartime and kept vivid the fear of instant dismissal. In the tightly buttoned ultrarespectable world of the white-collar *Angestellter*, unemployment, when it came, brought with it a spirit-corroding loss of status that could scarcely be alleviated by bouts of casual and exhausting manual labor. For men already of middle age, anxiety that the loss might be irretrievable deepened as the war dragged on.

In May 1917 an anonymous correspondent of the *Tageblatt* estimated that 10 percent of the community were rich or well-off, 30 percent had some sort of income, and 60 percent were at the margin of existence or beyond it. The attitude of the comfortably situated in that year is suggested indirectly by the writer's observation that "we must once and for all break with the assumption that the larger part of these vagabonds are 'work shy,' and have become a plague upon the land." The poor have pity, he wrote, but little means; "but the rich and well-to-do, where are they?" He concluded with a plea to direct the principal effort of the German People's League for Argentina, then being organized, toward the alleviation of such grave economic distress—to which the *Tageblatt*'s editors added an emphatic amen.[36]

Toward the end of the war, then, the stolidity of the commons began to give way to a creeping resentment toward the local elite, to whom the war appeared to have brought little but financial windfalls. The German business establishment—cut off after August 1914 from German sources of manufactures and credit, thrown upon its own devices for survival in an ostensibly neutral nation, but one whose economic and (until 1916) public life was deeply influenced by the British and their allies—faced a series of most serious difficulties. They attacked them purposefully, however, and—since the German economic enclave not only survived the war but throve on it—with remarkable success. The export trade, particularly that of the great German grain handlers, cut more circuitous channels than before the war but did not suffer any abatement—quite the reverse. Due to the effectiveness of the Allied naval blockade, on the other hand, import and the retention of established Argentine markets were rather more difficult matters. The trickle of contraband imports, augmented by the substitution of non-German manufactures, was only a feeble partial solution, and importers were aware that many markets would have to be won again after the war. If, moreover, the Germans' European rivals labored under many of the same disabilities as they, the North Americans did not; the latter, active during the war in exploiting the disappearance of European-made commodities and the weakening of European investments in Argentina, were perceived as likely to pose the major threat to established spheres of economic influence after war's end.[37]

In the short term, however, wartime profits were very large in the aggregate. As these reserves could not be remitted to Germany, local banking and business leaders tapped them to good effect to diversify the areas of German interests within the country. Further investments were made in public utilities under the aegis of CATE, in land, and in extractive industry. The most interesting in the latter category was Hansa Sociedad de Minas, S.A., which produced wolfram at mines at Los Cóndores, San Román, and La Brillante. The wolfram was sold to Allied purchasers until the armistice, when the operation was closed.[38] German business leaders also sought to expand the domestic Argentine market for such homely commodities as charcoal, firewood, mineral oil, beer, toiletries, patent medicines, glass, electrical motors, and small appliances. By war's end, numerous projects for the establishment of manufacturing ventures, with the participation of German technology and capital, were in the discussion or planning stage. All these projects were, of course, directed toward the further alleviation of the long-standing problem of Germany's unfavorable trade balance with Argentina. After 1916 they could be much more effectively coordinated than before, for in that year the leadership of the German business community was centralized within the German Chamber of Commerce (Deutsche Handelskammer, or DHK), which would in the succeeding decades exert a commanding influence over the policies and directions of the entire German economic establishment in Argentina.[39]

After the armistice, once indignation over the British and American blacklists had died away, it began to be admitted, then boasted, that the German business community in Buenos Aires had suffered remarkably little harm. Indeed, as the German Chamber of Commerce announced smugly, not a single German commercial house had been driven into bankruptcy by the malevolent intrigues of Germany's enemies.[40] Self-congratulatory anecdotes circulated. They concerned, for example, the agility of German businessmen in founding dummy corporations (usually behind Argentine, Spanish, or Levantine front men) at a rate that exceeded the ability of Allied agents to identify them— or the operation (until 1917) of the Wagner steamship line to North America to import American made and other goods. CATE had kept its boilers fired and distribution of power at prewar levels in the absence of British coal by burning immense quantities (2,500 tons per day) of surplus corn and bran, as well as charcoal and quebracho wood shipped downriver by newly developed forestry enterprises in which German firms held interests. Indeed, in 1917, when the British-owned gas plant in Buenos Aires failed through shortage of coal, CATE promptly took over that portion of the city's lighting system formerly served by gas.[41] In October 1915 the pressing need for locally available insurance coverage had led to the founding of the Germano-Argentina insurance company; on its "mixed" board of directors sat fourteen German businessmen and two Argentines. Its paid-in capitalization of 600,000 pesos suggests the amount of disposable capital at hand even early in the war.[42]

A rough estimate of gross wartime earnings of all enterprises is provided by the fact that the total worth of German investments in Argentina rose from an estimated 250 million dollars in 1913 to 265 million dollars in 1920, even though by the latter year at least 15 million dollars in blocked wartime earnings had been repatriated to Germany.[43] (It should also be noted in contrast that, of Germany's aggregate overseas holdings of 1914, eleven-twelfths were liquidated during the war.)[44] Thus after 1918 the German Chamber of Commerce was in a superb position to attract further German investment to Argentina. It could point not only to the patently sound position of the German business interests there but also to the fact that, of all Germany's major prewar overseas trading partners, only Argentina had remained neutral.[45] Moreover, Argentina's president since 1916, Hipólito Yrigoyen, had shown himself by his staunch neutralism and in somewhat enigmatic interviews in the postwar years as "friendly to Germany."[46]

Activists of the populist movement of 1918 countered, however, that business well-being had been bought at the expense of the sufferings of the commonality and in gross dereliction of duty to the Fatherland. The varieties of exploitation to which the German-speaking work force had been subjected had of course not gone unnoticed, and they became major issues in the bitter postarmistice denunciations of the *Geld-Aristokratie*. The defections of numerous old-line German firms from the ranks of *Deutschtum* had been noted by the press even during the war: these included Tornquist, Lutz & Schultz, Breyer Brothers, Louis

Dreyfus & Co., Liebig Extract Co., Bunge & Born, and the well-known publishing house of Jakob Peuser, which on 1 May 1917 became the Casa Argentina Jacobo Peuser and in the process discharged senior German-born personnel of long tenure who were replaced by *criollos*. It was believed, however, that these firms had merely behaved less hypocritically than some of their countrymen. This belief was epitomized, perhaps, by a standing joke within the community: the case of one Karl Pfeffer, a director of CATE, who in 1918 Argentinized his name to the improbable "Carlos Pimiento." In the postwar years, it was alleged by dissidents claiming inside knowledge that the shipping firms of Oehrtmann (whose head was president of the Army League in 1919), Götthard, and Hermann Krabb had sold off portbound ships to British and French concerns during the war; that Weil Brothers, Bromberg & Co., Fuhrmann, Otto Wulff, and many others had done a brisk trade in cereals and wood products with the Allies; and that the firms of Staudt & Co., Böcker & Co., and Wilhelm had sold such commodities as nitrogen, wolfram ore, and mica to British and French agents.[47] The success story of CATE came to be seen in a more jaundiced light. CATE's heavy-handed treatment of its German-speaking employees was well-known; it was charged also with having taken great pains to install electrical cable (imported before August 1914) to supply electrical power to Allied firms and with having scoured Argentina for electrical equipment that could be rebuilt to the specifications of these customers. The British-owned subways and tramways were of course dependent upon CATE's provision of electricity, and the close interdependence was recognized, tacitly, by both sides. The bombastic archnationalist Emil Hayn later acknowledged that at the beginning of the war CATE had been assured "unter der Hand" that the operation of the utility would not be interfered with; later, at the time of the 1917 strike, the British had aided CATE's directors with timely information and other good offices. He does not mention quid pro quo's, if any.[48]

Decline in enthusiasm for the war and the changing mood of the community can be measured almost graphically by the fate of the second war fund or *Kriegerdank* collection. By May 1916 the announced total had reached 677,000 pesos, but by October of the following year it had risen to only 693,000 pesos; and little was heard of it thereafter in the official press. Its administrators claimed in the postwar period that portions of the fund had been sent through Barcelona for the relief of war prisoners. However, no public accounting was ever given, and its ultimate disposition remained a mystery. The matter became another item in the Left's postwar bill of indictment against the community's elite.[49]

In 1917 the imperial German campaign of unrestricted submarine warfare brought near-disaster upon the community, for in April and June of that year three Argentine-flag merchant ships were sunk by U-boats.[50] The sinking of *Monte Protegido* near the Scilly Islands on 4 April provoked a series of anti-German demonstrations in Buenos Aires, the leaders of which, according to the *Tageblatt*, were unemployed seamen recruited by the Allied missions. They culminated in attacks on the Deutscher Klub and a number of German businesses on the night of 14–15 April.[51] That further consequences might be in the offing was suggested by the occupation of idled German ships by Argentine troops (the apparent prelude to outright seizure) and the scarcely veiled threat contained in Foreign Minister Pueyrredón's note following the sinking of *Oriana* and *Toro* in June that, "so long as German persons and property continue to be protected," the German government would do well to protect Argentine interests also.

In view of the rising public and congressional clamor for a *ruptura* with Germany or an outright declaration of war, the Foreign Office in Berlin retreated hurriedly. Ambassador Luxburg promised President Yrigoyen that no further Argentine ships would be attacked (the commitment, however, was to be kept secret so as not to endanger the effectiveness of the submarine campaign); in return, Yrigoyen reportedly agreed to prohibit Argentine-flag shipping from entering the war zone. At this strategic moment, however, the United States government released the texts of three Luxburg telegrams sent through the Swedish legation in Buenos Aires (the so-called Swedish roundabout, the penetration of which by the British cryptanalysts of "Room 40" had already provided them one of the greatest intelligence coups of the war, the Zimmermann telegram affair of early 1917). In them, Luxburg characterized Pueyrredón as "a notorious ass and an anglophile" and twice forwarded the brutal recommendation that Argentine ships then clearing European ports either be left strictly alone by German submarines or else "sunk without a trace [*spurlos versenkt*]." Luxburg was declared non grata and received his passports on 12 September. A period of extreme tension followed; in the end, however, Yrigoyen succeeded in maintaining his neutralist stand in the face of a pro-*rupturista* congressional majority and a vehemently aroused public opinion.

The German business elite was deeply shaken by the threat to their property holdings. The mobs aroused by the Luxburg affair in September 1917 attacked the Deutscher Klub again; they plundered paintings and furniture and burnt out part of the first floor. Municipal firemen stood around aimlessly, for the rioters had slashed their fire hoses. Prominent businessmen trapped within the building beat a pell-mell

retreat over adjoining walls and rooftops and through nearby buildings; and the somewhat leaden joke passed around the community that
for perhaps the last time the club had lived up to its old name of German *Athletic* Club.[52] The municipal authorities drew the line short of
a diplomatic incident, however, and the mob's advance on the German
embassy was turned back by police. Elsewhere, the police were less
solicitous: great destruction was wrought upon the *Tageblatt*, the pro-
German *Gaceta de España*, and many small businesses. Jürgensen's
and Bar Finisterre were smashed up, and the liquor stocks of Zum
Fürsten Bismarck and Teutonia were drunk dry. The *Tageblatt* declared irately that the rioters had hauled their booty freely through the
streets as the municipal police looked on.[53]

Luxburg was unable to make any effective reply to the American
charges, and it had to be acknowledged that the Argentine government, if not the mobs, had been justified in their action. On 13 September Ernst Alemann wrote in the *Tageblatt*:

> Responsibility for these regrettable facts falls fully and entirely
> upon Count Luxburg. The ambassador has not known how to
> awake any sympathy. His rather remarkable conception of the na-
> ture of his duty has contributed greatly to this. While over there,
> men and women have given their all in service of the Fatherland,
> here, Count Luxburg was seldom at his post. All too often he was
> recuperating in the province of Córdoba. In this respect he might
> well have taken a leaf from the book of Sir Reginald Tower, the
> tireless British ambassador. [Luxburg is not an unintelligent man];
> thus his diplomatic *gaffe* is even less explicable. . . . [In future],
> the overseas representatives of the German Empire should be
> named by government functionaries responsible to Parliament;
> no longer social position and friends at court, but rather personal
> capabilities, should be the essential criteria for nomination.[54]

The oblique hints in the *Tageblatt's* account refer to a story current
at the time but published in detail only years later. According to this
version, when the crisis broke Luxburg was at a hotel in the distant Sierra de Córdoba enjoying a dalliance with a young lady said to be a spy
in the pay of the Americans. Instead of hastening to Buenos Aires to
deal with the deteriorating situation, he dispatched his valet to fetch
the codebook needed to decipher the frantic telegrams arriving momentarily from Berlin. The messenger, however, was waylaid and hood-
winked by other Allied agents, who relieved him of his identification
papers and with them succeeded in making off with the codebook as
well.[55] Luxburg's successor, Chargé d'Affaires Count von Dönhoff, was

held in no higher esteem. He was detested by the commons for his arrogance and indifference to their problems; to the upper strata of the community he was known familiarly as "sleepyhead [*Döskop*]." As Ernst Alemann said, Dönhoff survived the crisis of 1917 by doing absolutely nothing about it.[56]

For the remainder of the war, many of the Buenos Aires Germans sought to maintain a discreet invisibility. According to one story, the management of the Quilmes brewery forbade its employees to send their children to the local German language school, although it continued to subsidize the school itself and thus also the *criollo* children who formed most of the student body.[57] Peter Harold-Hatzold was proprietor of a *recreo*—a beer-garden cum dance-pavilion cum playground—on an island at Tigre in the Paraná Delta heavily patronized by the urban German community. To transport his customers to the island, Harold-Hatzold operated a fleet of motor launches, all of which flew a small German flag at the stern. Toward the end of the war, however, he was told by "important men" of the colony that this was injurious to the German position and was advised to cease the practice. Failing to see the point—a German *recreo* was a German *recreo*—he refused to do so.[58]

For the favored 10 percent, prosperity and its delights continued; and its manifestations could scarcely be concealed in the tightly knit wartime community. By mid-1918, the newspapers regularly carried accounts of elaborate and costly school bazaars in Belgrano, lavish dinners, and elegant parties—at some of which the entertainments, including the donning of the costume of a "winsome bride" by a member of the diplomatic corps, were liberated far beyond the bounds of the somber prewar morality.[59] Even the previous year it appeared that the war effort of some of the more affluent businessmen consisted in its entirety of a boycott of the first-class carriages on the British-owned commuter railway that bore them daily to and from their villas in Belgrano—a boycott they might or might not recall to observe following a visit to Bar Adam, strategically located near Retiro Station, the north shore commuter terminus, for a *Wegstärkung* (pick-me-up) on the way home.[60] Later, A. E. Gross, the most vitriolic of the postarmistice dissenters, perhaps best verbalized the resentment and indignation of the commonality when he coined the stinging epithet *Schieberia*—"profiteers' paradise," with a hint of Siberia—to describe this outpost of German culture overseas during wartime.[61]

3. The Political Awakening of the Community, 1918–1919

News of the momentous events of November 1918—the collapse of German arms, the flight and abdication of the kaiser, the proclamation of a German republic under socialist auspices—fell in Buenos Aires upon a community far from prepared to cope with them. Wilhelm Keiper, whose gift for the apt cliché seldom failed him during nearly thirty-five years as the community's chief chronicler and publicist, wrote early in 1919: ". . . and then came the catastrophe—surely long-awaited and feared by those over there, but for us here like a lightning bolt from a clear sky."[1] The *Tageblatt*'s reaction to the armistice can only be characterized as pettish: for the edification of the Argentine crowds surging through the streets in celebration of Allied victory, it published a Spanish transliteration of the French text of the "Marseillaise," so that their raucous singing should at least give the minimum offense to the ears of the city's "civilized people."

Through 1918, three new political journals had appeared: the archmonarchist *Unser Deutschland*;[2] the "Austrian" and virulently anti-Semitic *Die Wacht*;[3] and *Die Neue Zeit*, the single-handed effort of the idiosyncratic left maverick, A. E. Gross.[4] The strident radicalism of all three is indicative of the way in which the community's self-imposed moratorium on political debate was disintegrating before the pressures generated by four years of isolation and, for most, privation and social disorder. On the morrow of the armistice these tensions, exacerbated now by the tumultuous turn of events in Europe, erupted in a season of frenetic political activity. On 16 November a call went out from Vorwärts for a popular assembly to "take the pulse" of the community in its reaction to the fall of the monarchic old order and the beginnings of a new democratic Germany. The drafter of the call, Oskar F. K. Fischer, acknowledged the existence of "horribly differentiated circles within our colony," but he insisted nevertheless that the popular assembly must present to Berlin resolutions affirming the solidarity of the entire Buenos Aires community with the new German regime.[5] Behind this claim of plenary powers for the popular assembly lay the determination, as another socialist writer later put it, to end a state of affairs in which ". . . some twenty big businessmen and the representatives and functionaries of the defunct German government, together with a number of their paid handymen, make public opinion here" and in which the commonality, through fear for its jobs and livelihood, had no choice but to "pay up and shut up [*zahlen und Mund halten*]." [6]

In all, three popular assemblies were held during late November and early December of 1918 in the rooms of Vorwärts in Calle Rincón. At the time Vorwärts seemed the most logical and appropriate locale, in part because of its ample physical facilities, in part also because of the transformation it had undergone during the war. Although a minority of Socialists grumbled at the spuriousness of the wartime camaraderie and at the conversion of Vorwärts into what they termed a mere "amusement club," the nonpartisan reputation that Vorwärts had acquired by 1918 undoubtedly contributed to the high hopes and expectations with which the popular assemblies opened.

Braving the heat and humidity of the advancing Argentine summer and the dangers posed by the smoldering influenza epidemic, about six hundred persons, on the average, attended the sessions. Betweentimes, a nonstop debate pulsed through Vorwärts, Germania, and other German clubs and was continued in Aue's Keller, Zum Goldenen Adler, Bar Adam, and others of the two score and more German bars and restaurants of the city.[7] The debate engaged the community's lower-middle-class and working-class population, upon whom, of course, the burden of the war had fallen. This was the traditional readership of the *Argentinisches Tageblatt*, and the newspaper, through its publisher, Theodor Alemann, now provided an authoritative ideological lead. At the armistice, the *Tageblatt* had come out strongly in support of the German Republic, predicting it would be "the most orderly the world has ever seen";[8] shortly afterward, Alemann wrote enthusiastically of the "awakening of the German colony [of La Plata]," which, he claimed, demonstrated that the Germans were not, as their betters had taught them to believe, "political ignoramuses."[9]

A rift rapidly developed, however, between Alemann's group of moderate Republicans and the Socialists; the latter, moreover, were themselves soon locked in struggle over their reaction to the ambiguous behavior of the German Social Democrats in Berlin in the last tense months of 1918. Alemann's influence was decisive in persuading the organizers of the popular assemblies to prepare broad resolutions of support for the republic. These included the establishment of democratic and egalitarian orders in Germany and Austria, with the abolition of all vestiges of aristocratic privilege; German-Austrian union; the inviolability of German territory (an acknowledged derivation from the Wilsonian program); and a just peace without victory.[10]

From the beginning, however, the popular assemblies were boycotted by the traditionalist Monarchists, who now began to style themselves the Kaiser Loyalists (*Kaisertreuen*). Their leadership was co-extensive with the community's economic elite. In their own complacent view, they had served resourcefully as the leaders and defenders of the sore-beset wartime community; nothing in their recent experience had prepared them even to envision the disappearance of the late-Wilhelmian structure of authority and privilege, much less to accept it. Thus, demoralized initially by the armistice and the German Revolution, and taken aback by the passionate upsurge of populist sentiment within the Buenos Aires community, they immured themselves for a time within the bourgeois magnificence of the Deutscher Klub. Soon, however, they were emboldened by the murky rhetoric, factionalism, and seeming aimlessness of the popular assemblies to begin to direct a stream of derision upon the proceedings in Calle Rincón, particularly through the medium of the *Deutsche La-Plata Zeitung*.

Replies were returned in kind by the leaders of the popular assemblies, and thus was born the exuberant billingsgate that would serve the community as the language of debate for more than a decade. The populist factions, republican and socialist, were known variously as the "Maximalists," the "Reds," the "Jacobins," the "Thin Men," the "second-class" or "wooden-class" Germans (an epithet which derived from the two-class seating arrangements of the Argentine railways), or the "journeymen without Fatherland" (which referred to Vorwärts' longstanding encouragement to its members to acquire Argentine citizenship and participate in Argentine civic life). Conversely, the traditionalists were known as, among other things, the "Patricians," the "Bonzes," the "Fat Men," and the "first-class" or "cushion-class" Germans. By the first years of the 1920s, when much of the continuing strife within the community had centered upon the colors of the German flag, the traditionalists, who continued to display defiantly the old imperial banner, were commonly known as the black-white-red crowd. By this time, too, they had been reinforced by bands of disgruntled anti-Weimar émigrés and were sometimes described, simply, as the "followers of the swastika [*Hakenkreuzler*]."[11]

But the monarchist reaction was not confined to name calling. There ensued a faintly comic affair which made it clear that they would not easily relinquish authority within the community. At the second popular assembly, that of 26 November, an ad hoc Committee of Fifteen had been elected to draft the resolutions to be sent to Berlin. Its membership had been chosen specifically to represent the hitherto unrepresented: that sizable body of individuals who, purportedly through straitened economic circumstances or ideological nonconformity, had not found accommodation within the community's network of German language social clubs. Most of the fifteen would later return to the obscurity from which they had emerged; some would not. The committee comprised Doctors Sorkau, Schüler, and Max René Hesse (a physician at the German Hospital who would later, in the 1930s, embark upon a successful second career as a novelist), and Simon, Friedrich, Felix Bagel (a journalist then on the *Tageblatt* staff who would later become a special bête noir of the local Left), Bochet, Lauble, Gross (whose leftist *Die Neue Zeit*, begun in September, was already creating outrage among the respectable), Henning (a watchmaker), Hans Biller (a man of the theater), Kremser and Fischer (both identified as Socialists), Eckert, and a mysterious figure recorded only by his initials, K. H. None of these men, it was noted, was a member of the Deutscher Klub—a state of affairs that would, however, be remedied.[12]

Before the committee could bring in its recommendations, however, it was made known, by word-of-mouth and through the press, that the committee's existence was unnecessary, if not indeed usurpatory, inasmuch as the executive leadership of the community was already safely vested in a Committee of Five—and had been, in fact, for more than a year.

Following the organization of the war fund collection early in the war, it was explained, the obvious utility of maintaining the Council of Executive Committees (Vereinsvorstände, also known as Kolonie-Ausschuss or, simply, Colony Committee) in existence had been seen; and delegates of the major German language associations (excluding the Vorwärts Socialists) had continued to meet every month under the auspices of the Deutscher Klub to coordinate the community's commercial, propaganda, and other war-related activities. At the height of the Luxburg crisis of mid-1917, the Council of Executive Committees had created a special Committee of Five from among the community's wealthiest and best-connected citizens to "assist" or supplant Count von Dönhoff in assuming the burden of representation before Argentine officialdom in the event of a total rupture of diplomatic relations or, in the worst case, an Argentine declaration of war on Germany.

In the event, of course, the crisis passed without calamity, but the Committee of Five had remained in existence. "Certain trusted individuals" had been informed verbally of the arrangement, but the need for secrecy had prevented any general public announcement (in fact, only two men, the businessmen E. Möring and J. Hosmann, were ever identified unequivocally as members of the five).[13] Now, however, in late 1918, the Committee of Five was prepared to represent the community in its dealings with Berlin. The popular response to this bland announcement was one of outrage, for, as A. E. Gross put it, "ninety-nine percent" of the "German rabble" in Buenos Aires had been unaware of the committee's existence; the "leading classes" had thought it unnecessary to inform them.[14]

At the third (and final) popular assembly, on 12 December 1918, a majority of the Committee of Fifteen presented resolutions which restated the moderates' position: hopes for international collaboration for a just and lasting peace based on the self-determination of peoples; opposition to dismemberment of German territory; German-Austrian union; equality of rights and duties for all citizens; and free elections to constitutional assemblies. The assembly, however, was paralyzed on the left by mounting disorder, factionalism, and disillusionment, all aggravated by the news arriving momentarily from Berlin. Opposition on the right was also reemerging, and at least four members of the fifteen—Simon, Friedrich, Sorkau, and Bagel—played equivocal or disruptive roles. Many years later, in fact, Bagel, seeking admission to the Deutscher Klub, allegedly explained away his behavior in 1918 by claiming to have served as an agent provocateur at the behest of the imperial naval attaché, *Korvettenkapitän* Moller. The draft resolutions were voted down in tumult, and the popular assemblies adjourned sine die.[15]

The reversal had the important consequence of persuading Theodor Alemann and his associates to transfer their operations to the Buenos Aires local of the German People's League for Argentina (the Deutscher Volksbund für Argentinien: the DVA or, usually, the Volksbund). Well before this time, the Alemann group had felt the desirability of creating a third nucleus of community leadership distinct from both Socialists and Monarchists. Alemann's predilection, which came to exasperate many of his friends, was to reject partisan politics altogether: "Monarchy or republic, we remain nevertheless German brothers," he had written in the *Tageblatt* on 16 November. He sought to turn the Volksbund to pressing immediate concerns susceptible of pragmatic solutions. These included two projects long under discussion: the founding of a German language consumer cooperative and the reform and democratization of the community schools, as well as a third concern which assumed menacing proportions as the year 1919 wore on: means of coping systematically with the anticipated mass migration of Germans to Argentina. Although for a time the Alemann faction captured the executive committee of the Buenos Aires local, none of their projects could be even seriously undertaken, much less brought to fruition, for within the organization the Kaiser Loyalists made their stand. During the first half of 1919 it would be the cockpit of the community's increasingly bitter political strife.[16]

The Volksbund had been created, on Luxburg's initiative, early in 1916 on the pattern of similar organizations founded contemporaneously in Brazil and Chile. In January he broached the project to the Council of Executive Committees, and a founding commission was promptly formed from among the community's best-known public men: proprietors of the two German language dailies, Alemann and Tjarks (Tjarks, however, died in April of that year), the ubiquitous Keiper, Wilfert (chairman of the German Teachers' Association), and the businessmen Jeckeln, Springer, Hartmann, Ley, Gaitzch, Kraus, Leonhardt, and Plate.[17] Through the first half of 1916 the founding commission, under Keiper as chairman pro tem, prepared the Volksbund's constitution. The national executive was to be elected by the assembly (the commission plus delegates of locals then being organized); it was provided that in future this would occur at the annual meeting. On 2 July 1916 the assembly then in existence approved the articles and a national executive was named. The first president, who was reelected to office in 1917 and 1918, was Franz Dietrich, a wool-producing *estanciero* who owned more than 21,000 hectares throughout the province of Buenos Aires.[18] Keiper became editor of the Volksbund's official organ, *Der Bund*, and was the organization's most active organizer during the war.

As early as June 1916 it was noted that the leadership of the Volksbund was "strongly centralized" in Buenos Aires, in marked contrast to the rural orientation of the Brazilian and Chilean Bund organizations. Since the Argentine capital already possessed a powerful array of German associations, while the countryside was notably weak in this respect, the purposes that the Volksbund might serve if it continued in this direction were not entirely clear.[19] In response to such criticism, Keiper and his coworkers doubled their efforts to organize locals in the scattered Germanic settlements in the countryside. They regularly announced the creation of new locals (*Ortsgruppen*) in remote localities up and down the republic: eighteen by the end of 1916, forty by the end of 1917, forty-seven by the end of 1918.[20] The new foundings during these years were markedly fluid, however, and it is evident that many of them were very fragile plants. Some may have existed only in the dutiful reports of harried vice-consuls and honorary consuls who had been entrusted with the actual work of breathing life into rural locals. Membership totals in the countryside are suspect for the same reason. In any event, in September 1917 *Der Bund* claimed a national total of 3,027 members, 1,050 of whom were associated with the Buenos Aires local. The only other locals with more than 100 members each were those in the secondary cities of Bahía Blanca, Córdoba, Rosario, and Mendoza. A year later, 4,100 members were claimed.[21] Annual meetings were duly held in Buenos Aires in July 1917 and July 1918.

Despite the wartime moratorium on political discussion, however, the beginnings of the Volksbund were attended by substantial conflict. At the founding session of 2 July 1916 it was piously declared that the Volksbund was to be a "nonpolitical, purely cultural association," which would observe no class or confessional distinctions. It would embrace all the Germanic peoples of Argentina, by no means only Reichsdeutsche. And it would, of course, honor its obligations to Argentina— "this land under whose laws we live."[22] Nevertheless, muted animosity toward the authoritarianism and upper-class domination of the Volksbund began to emerge almost immediately. The annual dues of six pesos were beyond the reach of the majority in their straitened wartime circumstances, Alemann felt. The lack of publicity with which the first and subsequent national executives were elected drew sharp criticism. Similarly, the national executive retained absolute control over the founding and fiscal management of the locals—a provision that would be of crucial importance in the events of 1919.

The immediate wartime purposes of the Volksbund were a second area of strife. Although the organization had ostensibly been founded by dignitaries of the local Buenos Aires community, and its announced ends were cultural and pacific, it was evident enough that the actions of Luxburg and Keiper were dictated by their roles as imperial officials. Keiper's propaganda operation had been moderately successful in reaching well-placed *criollo* manipulators of public opinion and policy; but it would be well also to mobilize a mass following to impress upon the Argentine public mind the strength of an aroused Argentine *Deutschtum* solidly arrayed behind the banner of the Wilhelmian Reich. Thus, the annual meetings were to be held in a big city, where they could most appropriately "give the Argentine population an impressive picture of [*Deutschtum's*] solidarity."[23]

Within the membership at large, the Volksbund's potential services to the distant Reich took a poor second place to those it might render in alleviation of local distress caused by the war. Many saw in it a pressure group through which to protest against the discriminations inflicted upon German business firms, tradespeople, and employees by partisans of the Allies and, when possible, to retaliate. It was proposed many times that the Volksbund create work projects to relieve the rampant unemployment among the German-speaking. Although nothing came of these, the beginnings of a centralized employment agency began to emerge in 1917. Medical services were made more easily available: in June 1917 the Volksbund became a corporate member of the German Sickness Insurance Society, and all members of the former enjoyed the privileges of the latter. Still others saw in the Volksbund an agency for the regulation of standards and financing of the German schools throughout the republic. By the latter years of the war, when it had been agreed that the Volksbund's primary efforts should be among the rural German-speaking peoples, projects were afoot to create model *estancias* for the retraining of postwar agricultural immigrants and for petitions to the Ministry of Agriculture to alter the grid style land-surveying system in order to facilitate the founding of compact European style peasant villages rather than isolated farmsteads.

Ultimately more far-reaching in its consequences was the perplexing matter of defining the term "Germanic." By the end of the war it had driven deep rifts between the Reichsdeutsche and the Volksdeutsche, or "racial" Germans. The events of 1918–1919 made the schism complete. In the minds of the national executive committee and their upper-status supporters in the Buenos Aires community, Reichsdeutsch came to be equated with a traditionalist, monarchist, German nationalism. They thereby further estranged the majority of the Volksdeutsche as well as the German-born supporters of the Weimar Republic. Even before the Volksbund's statutes had been approved in July 1916, Alemann and other Volksdeutsch spokesmen had begun to insist that the organization be named the "Germanischer [Germanic] Volksbund für Argentinien," because to them the "German" (*deutscher*) was all too closely derived from "German Empire" (*Deutsches Reich*), and Alemann persisted in this position until he was driven out of the Volksbund, temporarily, in mid-1919. They pointed out, correctly,[24] that the Reichsdeutsche made up only a minority, albeit a highly influential one, among Argentina's German-speaking peoples. Although these people supported imperial Germany's wartime aims, as they understood them, they flatly rejected the argument that, should Germany be defeated, all of worldwide *Germanentum* would suffer cultural disaster and obloquy with it. As Alemann later wrote with some asperity, it was absurd for the Reichsdeutsch sponsors of the Volksbund to expect German Socialists and Republicans, Austrians, Swiss, above all Argentine-Germans, to remain enthusiastic about a narrow German nationalism based in the monarchic principle.[25]

In fact, the Volksdeutsch factions sought to create an even broader *Kulturbund* for all those who found sustenance in Germanic culture: Scandinavians, Netherlanders, Luxemburgers, and of course Argentines, whether of Germanic antecedents or not. These proposals were frustrated, however, by the provision that non-German-speaking groups might be admitted only by special permission (requiring a two-thirds vote) of the national executive. Shortly before the end of the war, Christoph Martin, president of the Chilean Bund, felt called upon to point out the dangerous imbalance in the Argentine organization: "the DVA consists almost exclusively of Reichsdeutsche."[26]

The contrasting viewpoints were best verbalized by Wilhelm Keiper, for the Reichsdeutsche, and Theodor Alemann, for the Volksdeutsche. Keiper, as events would show, was no diehard Monarchist but, rather, a man of great political flexibility. He retained, however, a profound, unquestioned conviction of the superiority of Germanic culture and a belief in the "missions" that history had imposed upon it; logically these missions could only be fulfilled among the world's peoples with the sustenance of a powerful German nation. This was as true in Argentina as elsewhere, although he recognized that the mobilization of Argentine *Deutschtum* presented special problems:

> As in other South American countries, each with its own nuances, [Argentine *Deutschtum*] is highly diverse according to national origins and popular customs, disunited in essence and view of life; nevertheless, in its core it is inspirited by national consciousness and a racial sense of belonging together. [It is] a variant of German humanity overseas; as such it clearly demarcates itself from other foreign ethnic collectivities. In Argentine life, as in the life of Greater Germany—"wherever the German tongue sounds"—it has a special mission to fulfill—has already fulfilled it.[27]

In Argentina, Keiper believed, an artificial distinction had arisen between Reichsdeutsche and Volksdeutsche. This had come about both because of the varied European origins of Argentina's German-speaking peoples and of the Argentine and general Latin American legal principle of *jus soli*, under which all children born in Argentina of foreign parents were held to be Argentine nationals. He insisted, however, that German feeling as well as German law (*jus sanguinus*) operated differently. The more significant distinction, he felt, was between the Argentine-Germans and the German-Argentines. The former, he wrote, were mostly of pure German ancestry. They retained their German customs, speech, culture—in fine, felt themselves to be Germans. Although they might be, in law, Argentine nationals, Germany was for them something "self-understood"; whereas toward Argentina they felt nothing. Together with those legally entitled to consider themselves Reichsdeutsche, they formed the "block" upon which the work of Argentine *Deutschtum* was based.

The German-Argentines, on the other hand, were usually third or fourth generation Argentines and not necessarily of undiluted German ancestry. They performed their Argentine civic duties, indeed were and wished to be Argentines; but they retained nevertheless a vestigial sense of German origin and heritage and hence had not become pure *criollos*. The German-Argentines were a volatile collectivity, but if handled correctly—and this of course was one of the Volksbund's major missions—the German-Argentines could be forged into an invaluable "connecting link" between *Deutschtum* and *Kreolentum*. Thus, for Keiper, an individual's legal nationality, or birthplace, or even his imperfect command of the German language, made little difference; it was ultimately a matter of will: "he remains a German in the broader, racial and cultural sense, so long as he is conscious of this connection, and holds himself [and his children] to *Deutschtum*."[28]

Theodor Alemann was an indefatigable journalist and polemicist, and his views on the situation of Argentina's German-speaking peoples are scattered through the writings of more than three decades. His most mature thinking, however, was summed up in his *Die Zukunft des Deutschtums in Amerika* [*The Future of the German Collectivity in America*], published in Buenos Aires in 1917 at the height of the controversy over the Volksbund's orientation. In important respects his thinking ran parallel to Keiper's. He too assumed the vast cultural superiority of the German-speaking peoples to the *criollos* and, implicitly, their duty to carry out a civilizing mission among the latter; he expressed regret toward the descendants of Germanic immigrants who had "sunk" to the cultural level of their Argentine fellows.[29] He was, however, optimistic in his belief that, unlike the German-speaking immigrants to the United States, *Deutschtum* in Argentina and other South American countries could retain for years or generations its cultural identity. To insure this, however, purposeful work was necessary. He laid special stress upon two areas to which he had devoted much effort throughout his career: the strengthening of the German language school systems available to all social levels and the creation of areas of compact and closed German language peasant settlements. To be sure, he was aware of the ambiguities involved and of the compromises that had to be made under both headings. As his work with the Cangallo School had shown, he accepted the principle that a German language education could be made compatible both with the requirements of Argentine citizenship and with the need to prepare the children of less well-off or less mobile parents for Argentine careers. With respect to agricultural colonies, he (as well as his father, Johann, and his brother, Moritz) had for decades battled against the "*estancia* evil," in which they saw the greatest obstacle to the creation of an independent smallholding peasantry on the Argentine land. By the end of

World War I, he had begun to admit that sponsors of Germanic agricultural colonization had missed the best opportunities for peasant settlement on a large scale and that the situation was probably irretrievable.[30] This accurate perception dampened his faith but did not extinguish it.

Alemann differed most markedly from Keiper in his view of the political obligations of Argentine *Deutschtum*, for his point of reference was the Argentine republic, rather than some murky vision of a Greater Germany. He recognized that the offspring of Germanic parents, even when endowed with the most painstaking German education, was not a German but a new person, an *Argentine*, whose natural inclination and duty were to work to perfect the institutions of Argentine republicanism—and whose political loyalties were hence unequivocal.[31] Although nowhere explicitly stated, Alemann's vision was clearly an Argentine variant upon the Swiss Confederation from which he and his family had sprung: a functioning cultural pluralism within the framework of a loose republican polity. Circa 1920 such an ideology for Argentina was perhaps already obsolescent, though not altogether fantastic.

Despite the evidences of traditionalist strength within the Volksbund, the moderate faction could well believe that much of the debate over the organization's purposes had become irrelevant with the armistice. Led by Alemann and Dr. Kurt Schüler, they gained control of the executive committee of the Buenos Aires local; to judge by the outcome, they commanded a large voting majority among the rank and file membership. As noted earlier, the Buenos Aires local was in turn by far the largest of the Volksbund's forty-odd locals within Argentina; if, in fact, membership returns from the interior were, as often claimed, grossly padded for propaganda purposes, it may have comprised half or more of the Volksbund's entire national following. The national executive committee continued, however, to be dominated by intransigent Monarchists. Early in 1919, the founding national president, Franz Dietrich, was replaced by Emil Hayn, the former technical director of CATE and until his departure for Germany in 1928 one of the most ubiquitous figures on the local Right. The subsequent struggle developed as a personal duel between Hayn and Theodor Alemann. It was won by the former when, as the culmination of sharp and complex parliamentary moves justified by the Volksbund constitution, the annual meeting of June 1919 dissolved the "red" Buenos Aires local, appropriated its treasury, and replaced it with a tiny but loyal rump unit. To obviate similar contretemps in the future, the national executive served thereafter simultaneously as executive committee of the Buenos

Aires local. The monarchist coup provoked the resignation of upward of one thousand Buenos Aires members of the Volksbund.[32] Hans Lindemann, who had replaced Keiper as editor of *Der Bund* (he himself would soon break with the Monarchists and later, in 1921, become first chairman of the Republican Association), admitted that the purge had increased the risk of alienating "the broader classes of our Germanic brothers and above all, the Argentine-Germans"; but, he explained carefully, had it not taken place, "influential members would have turned their backs upon the Bund."[33]

Theodor Alemann, whose good will remained unquenchable, rejoined the Buenos Aires local early in 1920 but found it impossible to realize any of his cherished projects. On 9 April 1920, he wrote wearily that the organization had fallen far short of the wishes of the founders:

> At first, there was a Reichsdeutsch majority, but many Austrian, Swiss, and Argentine-Germans as well. Now, however, the national executive consists solely of Reichsdeutsche. Not only that: within this one-sided composition the fact must be denounced that they are almost without exception supporters of the monarchy. There is a tendency to exclude all who have decided for the republic. . . . The Argentine-German population is far more assimilated [than the Chilean-German]. There is far more to be done here, and it cannot be done one-sidedly. The Argentine-Germans remained loyal to the German cause during the war, but they are born Republicans. Thus they are now driven out [of all the German associations] by monarchist executive committees.[34]

To this Hayn replied in an open letter two days later. In it, he nonchalantly tossed off a hint of the opportunism that would guide the political behavior of the local elite for the next two decades. "We are not Monarchists," he wrote, "but nationalists. We continue to stand by the monarchy because it has realized our national ideals. Should the republic ever do so well, perhaps one day we shall become Republicans." It is not recorded whether Hayn's patriotism ever required him to become a Republican. In the late 1930s, however, long after his return to Germany, he took to boasting of his role as one of the "precursors" (*Vorkämpfer*, in the then-fashionable nazi jargon) of national socialism in Buenos Aires.[35]

Under Hayn as president through most of the 1920s, the Volksbund's scope remained limited and its membership small. At the end of 1919, after the purge, *Der Bund* claimed a total national membership of 4,150, 1,330 of them in Buenos Aires.[36] These figures are highly improbable, even though the countercharge was frequently heard that employees of the German banks, CATE, Staudt, and a number of other kaiser-loyalist firms were compelled to take out membership.[37] In the latter years of Hayn's stewardship, the claimed national total did not rise above 5,000.[38] It regularly suffered the gibes of the irreverent as the "People's League without People." Wilhelm Keiper, whose relationship to the Volksbund grew looser after war's end, admitted that the charge was not without justice, although he ascribed the unfortunate state of affairs to the fact that, "as was only natural, the national executive was made up of the leading men of the community; with all good will, they did not and could not possess the close empathy with the common people that might have given the Bund the character of a true racial [völkischer] association."[39] Its major function was said to be that of providing well-paid sinecures for down-at-heel Monarchists. Indeed, the Volksbund budget had been one of the issues that agitated the affairs of the Buenos Aires local prior to the showdown of June 1919, for the Alemann faction had demanded—in vain—to know why the projected budget for 1920, 36,400 pesos, was triple that for 1918, even though the Volksbund's peacetime functions remained largely to be defined.[40]

Ostensibly dedicated to improving communications with, and social services for, the scattered Germanic communities of the interior, the Volksbund's executives rarely bestirred themselves outside Buenos Aires. As the volume of German immigration swelled in the postwar years, the Volksbund was bitterly criticized for its failure to provide the information and guidance that might have prevented the founding of many ill-conceived agricultural colonies, a failure usually put down to the Volksbund leadership's close business and social relationships with Buenos Aires-based promoters and land speculators. It is suggestive of the Volksbund's feebleness in carrying out its self-appointed responsibilities on the land that in 1927 a German Peasant League (Deutscher Bauernbund) was organized by a number of experienced German-speaking smallholders of the interior. The peasant league went bankrupt, however, and was dissolved in 1929–1930, largely in consequence of its efforts to resettle Russian-German peasant communities from the drought-stricken zone of La Pampa Territory to the subtropical Chaco.[41]

But, in Buenos Aires, the Volksbund placed itself squarely astride the immigrant stream. In creating its Counseling Center for Immigrants (Beratungsstelle für Einwanderer) and absorbing, finally, the much older and more experienced Association for the Protection of Germanic Immigrants, the Volksbund controlled the two largest and most effective employment placement agencies available to newly arrived German-speaking immigrants. In what was at almost all times during the postwar decade a grossly saturated labor market for manual and white-collar trades, these agencies operated selectively to supply cheap, undemanding, and politically orthodox labor to the major German employers in and around the capital city.

The Volksbund's right-wing political orientation remained quite undisguised, but, under Hayn's somewhat indolent leadership, the level of political activism was not high. It was restricted chiefly to financial support for right-radical political journals, sponsorship of lecture tours by popular war heroes such as the flying ace Ernst Udet and the naval officer Hans Berg of the commerce raider *Möwe*, gratis distribution of war memoirs and other nationalistic writings to the financially strapped German schools of the interior, and an uncompromising black-white-red stand in the continuing flag dispute. But in 1928 Hayn, having been duly feted by the "entire colony" at the Deutscher Klub and eulogized as the "father of the German community," [42] departed for Germany and was succeeded as *Vorsitzender* of the Volksbund by Dr. Martin Arndt. From Hayn's beginnings, Arndt expanded the network of communications between Buenos Aires and the interior German communities. Under him there began to emerge an efficient federation affecting much of the German associational life of the interior and subordinating it to the direction of the traditionalist elite of the Buenos Aires community. The Volksbund would have an important role to play in the nazi *Gleichschaltung* (coordination) of 1933 and would be the chief organizer of its rituals.

A second affair whose origins lay in the war years convulsed the community during 1919 and contributed to its growing political polarization. The party of German seamen, the survivors of *Cap Trafalgar*, who had been interned on Martín García since September 1914, was at first the beneficiary of frequent and openhanded visits from the Buenos Aires community. In time, however, interest waned, and the men were left to their own devices. At Christmastime 1916, they improvised a masked ball, at which two stokers, identified only as Schmidt and Gent, fell into a bibulous and apparently good-humored altercation with one of the ship's petty officers. The matter, however, was reported through channels to the imperial naval attaché, *Korvettenkapitän* Moller, who chose to regard it as mutiny. As there were no German disciplinary facilities available, Moller appealed to the Argentine authorities, who obligingly transported the two men in chains to the penal colony in Tierra del Fuego. There they remained until well after the armistice. In 1917, Moller, perhaps alarmed by news of the first German naval mutinies, aroused further detestation on Martín García by arranging work furloughs in Buenos Aires for officers and "reliable" seamen.

In the aftermath of the armistice, the cause of Schmidt and Gent was taken up by A. E. Gross in his journal *Die Neue Zeit* and by Augusto Bunge, descendant of one of the most illustrious Argentine-German families and at the time a socialist deputy in the Argentine Congress. Although Moller's counterrepresentations were vigorous, Bunge ultimately succeeded in obtaining the men's release. *Die Neue Zeit* also took up the case of the "unreliable" seamen who remained, in vociferous impatience, on Martín García as the early months of 1919 passed. In March 1919 the men prepared a manifesto in which they complained of inadequate food, clothing, and housing, arrears of back pay, officers' privileges, and above all of monotony. Officials of Vorwärts brought it to the attention of Count Donhöff at the embassy, from whom they received no satisfaction; Gross also published the manifesto and sought, unsuccessfully, to bring the matter before the Volksbund. Moller, persuaded that the men had fallen under the influence of bolshevik agitators (including Gross), procrastinated; he offered the excuse that *Cap Trafalgar*'s records had been lost when the ship was sunk and that he had as yet received no instructions concerning the men from the admiralty in Berlin. Matters were brought to a head, finally, by unnamed Argentine officials who, on 16 July, transported the men in a body to Buenos Aires. On 1 August, as Moller reported to Berlin in a tone which suggested a close brush with apoplexy, a crowd of "fifty or sixty," led by an "outspoken Bolshevik," invaded his office at the embassy to present their demands. After a ticklish interlude they were removed by Argentine police, whom Moller had called to his rescue. The only solution, in Moller's opinion, was to send the disaffected men back to Germany as soon as possible—"in small groups on separate ships."[43] This policy, however, could not easily be carried out in the maritime conditions of 1919, and there is no evidence that it was carried out. It is thus probable that many of *Cap Trafalgar*'s crew remained in Argentina to seek their fortunes.

Early in 1920 Moller was ordered to return to Berlin to report orally on his activities on station since 1914. He refused to do so, saying that the matters covered in his records were "discreet" and "very discreet" and that he therefore feared they would fall prey to the "fever of disclosure and passion for self-immolation" then raging in Germany. He informed the admiralty that he intended to burn his records and that "after 1 April 1920 I will not *in any way* serve the present German government."[44] It was a statement of deadly serious purpose.

Thus by the end of 1919 the Buenos Aires community had not only been awakened from its long apolitical slumber, it had also been cleft into two nearly irreconcilable factions. Paradoxically, in the view of the commonality the self-proclaimed bearers of authentic German nationalism—the Kaiser Loyalists—had shown themselves, through their opportunistic behavior during and after the war, as perhaps the *least* patriotic sector of the community; true Germanness lay rather among the hard-working little people, the *schaffende Volk*. The two currents —the traditionalist authoritarianism of the *Geld-Aristokratie* and the deep-flowing, mostly inchoate populism of the commonality—would come together again with the advent of Hitlerism in Argentina after 1931. But they would not mingle.

4. The Lure of Argentina in the 1920s: Big Business and the German-Speaking Immigrants

Argentina returned only slowly to peacetime normalcy. Strikes, shortages, and increases in the cost of living continued through 1920. Like other Western countries, Argentina was touched by the postwar wave of radical unrest—as in the student revolt at the University of Córdoba (the beginnings of the University Reform) in 1918 and the general strike in Buenos Aires in January 1919, which became, through bloody repression and an accompanying pogrom in the city's Jewish quarter, the Tragic Week. As elsewhere, the rightist reaction remained strong through much of the following decade.

Briefly a creditor nation at war's end, Argentina became a debtor again when the economy reassumed its familiar prewar character. By 1920 consumer commodities were available from the industrial nations of the Northern Hemisphere, and as before Argentina paid for them with vast quantities of its traditional exports: meat, grains, and wool. Aside from cyclical recessions of the economy, the 1920s were a time of general prosperity, expansion of the economic infrastructure, and advances in the material standard of living. With peace, the migratory movement from Europe resumed. However, the annual migration of harvesters (*golondrinas*) became a thing of the past; Italian immigration declined (though Spanish did not), and the slack was increasingly made good by the inflow from Eastern Europe. By the time mass immigration ceased with the economic collapse of 1929–1930, the postwar migratory movement had added a net total of over 900,000 persons to the country's population, which in 1930 was approaching 12 million.

The middle-class democracy of the Radical party rode the postwar boom and perished with it. Although rhetorically committed to nationalism, the Radicals did little to alter the basic structure of the Argentine economy. They quarreled among themselves; the authoritarianism of Hipólito Yrigoyen provoked the secession of the "antipersonalist" Radicals under Marcelo T. de Alvear during the latter's presidency from 1922 to 1928. But Yrigoyen's personal following remained broad; and in 1928, constitutionally eligible again for the presidency, he was reelected with ease. Aging, probably senile, he proved unable either to control the spoilsmen among the Radical faithful or, when they came, to cope with the shock waves radiating outward from the Wall Street crash of late 1929. He would not serve out his term.

Although alarmed, fleetingly, by the populist uproar of 1918–1919, the business elite of the German-speaking community, consolidated now in the German Chamber of Commerce, remained nevertheless confident of its position. Its reasons for doing so were summed up in 1919 by the German economist, Dr. Otto A. Krause: "At the moment, Argentina has become for Germany one of the most important, if not *the* most important, foreign countries in three respects: first, as our supplier of a series of the most necessary raw materials; second, as a natural marketing area for the products of our industry; and, third, as an appropriate goal for our emigration."[1] In the postwar period, the business community moved quickly to exploit the advantages that had accrued to them—advantages due partly to their own resourceful opportunism during wartime, partly (more fortuitously) to the obstacles that Germany would encounter in reestablishing commercial relationships elsewhere in the world. It was also of capital importance that the Yrigoyen administration continued to show itself well disposed toward German interests. Through early 1919, for example, the German Chamber of Commerce complained that the Allies were maintaining a "gray list" of firms with which it was inadvisable for non-Germans to deal (the Allied blockade, in fact, remained in place until July 1919). The chamber's representations were heeded, and by April Argentine diplomats had persuaded the British to cease their discriminatory practices against forty of the largest German firms.[2]

At about the same time the chamber made it known that it was now prepared to take action in the matter of the black list it had been maintaining since 1916. Once-German firms that had behaved in an unworthy manner during the war were to be ostracized from German business circles; firms considered loyal were to be assisted in acquiring franchises and connections that the disloyal had allowed to lapse. Little is known of this process of retaliation and redistribution, except that evidently the Chamber of Commerce's definition of unworthy did not correspond precisely to that of the community's dissenters. A number of firms, notably those of Bromberg and Boeker, accused on substantial evidence of wartime trading with the enemy, remained nevertheless influential within the postwar Chamber of Commerce[3]—indeed, Dr. Eduard Bromberg was president of the chamber from 1922 through 1926.

The chamber's first order of business, however, was to promote the rapid resumption of German-Argentine trade. In this it was highly successful. In June 1919 it was instrumental in assisting a German trade mission in negotiations with Argentine officials for a two-year credit of 100 million gold pesos for the purchase of wool, hides, and linseed.[4] The following year it could announce that trade had returned "almost to a normal level"; in 1922 it duly made known that Germany had regained its prewar share of Argentina's total trade.[5] By 1926 the prewar volume of trade had long since been surpassed; in 1927 the record for the interwar period was reached. In that year German sales in Argentina amounted to almost 300 million *Reichsmark*; German purchases of Argentine commodities were valued at 1,076 million *RM*. In the succeeding two years German sales rose even further to a maximum of 370.9 million *RM* in 1929. Simultaneously, however, German purchases began to fall off, and the total volume of trade slipped into decline. With the onset of the world depression, the decline became much more precipitous. By 1933 German sales in Argentina were approximately 100 million *RM*, and purchases were half again as much.[6] (One gold peso equaled slightly more than four *RM*).

The bilateral trade statistics cited here provide, of course, only a narrow perspective on the German economic position. For example, Germany increased its purchases of Argentine commodities to a maximum of 16.5 percent of Argentina's total export in 1927; nevertheless, such purchases could not be expanded indefinitely, for the objections of German landed interests as well as, probably, strategic considerations militated against making Germany unduly dependent upon overseas sources of foodstuffs.[7] Rather, as in the prewar era, the bilateral balance of payments was maintained by the earnings of German seaborne carriers, utilities, insurance and construction firms, and banking operations and loans. This situation was made much more complex, moreover, by the most significant economic phenomenon of the postwar decade: the mobilization of large sums of German capital which was directed toward the creation of a partly German-controlled, partly autonomous, industrial enclave within the Argentine economy.

In 1920 the economist Günther von Hirschfeld wrote of German economic prospects in Latin America: "there is only one solution: German export, for export's sake, must associate itself with the foreign capitalist, with the foreign overseas producer and seller of basic commodities—and/or set up its own establishments in collaboration with them, in order to earn not paper marks, but *gold!*"[8] In Argentina there were ample reasons for following such a course. There was, first, the recent experience of wartime, which had demonstrated to the German business community the desirability of freeing itself from total dependence upon German sources of manufactures. The brush with nationalization during the crisis of 1917, moreover, and the nationalism of the ruling Radical party suggested to the Chamber of Commerce the utility of inviting participation by as many well-placed and well-disposed Argentine citizens as possible. There were, finally, great tariff and exchange rate advantages to be gained by creating manufacturing establishments on Argentine soil—advantages, it should be noted, which were also well understood by North American businessmen during the 1920s.[9]

The process of diversifying and providing Argentine coloration for the German economic establishment was well under way at war's end. The Germano-Argentina insurance company, founded with a "mixed" board of directors in late 1915, had proven highly successful. The 1918 Annual Report of the Chamber of Commerce noted that many further projects for the investment of German capital in "local industrial enterprises" were then under consideration. Emil Hayn later recalled the euphoric business climate of the time and suggested that the new policies were not entirely the result of steely-eyed calculation:

> We were then the lords of the earth. As the terrible end to the war came, and with it the growing insight that this delightful state of affairs [*diese Herrlichkeit*—that is, the wartime boom] would end also, we began to develop substitute enterprises. Among friends in the Klub we founded small industrial enterprises, some of which in the meantime have come along very nicely. For example, we bought and built up electric utilities for small provincial towns, with good results . . . a limeworks, with quarry . . . a weaving mill for woolstuff and artificial silk . . . a gasworks, actually out of friendship for the German engineer who headed it.[10]

Among other foundings at the initiative of local businessmen and with Argentine participation were the wireless company Transradio (1920), which used the radio facilities built toward war's end at Monte Grande; La Protectora insurance company (1920); the Fábrica Argentina de Productos Químicos (1921); and Industrial y Mercantil Thyssen Limitada (1921).[11] Later events would confirm that these arrangements among friends took little account of the small entrepreneurs and artisans who had begun modest import-substitution enterprises during the war, but who were not privy to the councils of the Deutscher Klub or the interlocking directorates of the banks, utilities, and "established houses."

Although the outlines of the postwar German economic establishment in Argentina had thus been prepared by the German-Argentine business community, the magnitude of its fruition was due largely to the participation of German big business. For their part, German capitalists were uneasy under the shaky Weimar coalitions of the early postwar years, disturbed by the wartime-induced rise in labor and production costs, and threatened by the staggering reparations demands of the British and French. They thus proved receptive to the Chamber of Commerce's missionary work, which was carried on in Germany by the GELATEINO in Hamburg and the German-Argentine League for the Promotion of Economic Interests and the German Economic Association for South and Central America (of which von dem Bussche-Haddenhausen was president through much of the decade) in Berlin.[12] The movement began early: the 1922 Annual Report of the chamber noted contentedly that German capital had done well in both the Chaco cotton boom (due soon to collapse) and in the somewhat obscure operations of the petroleum firm Astra in Patagonia.[13] The latter is of special interest, as it belonged to the empire of the powerful German *Grosskapitalist* Hugo Stinnes. By 1925, after his death, the Stinnes interests were more broadly represented, particularly in shipping, which they shared with the revitalized Hamburg-Süd and Hamburg-Amerika lines. The decade saw the establishment of subsidiaries of other major German (and multinational) firms: Siemens-Schuckert (1921), Klöckner (1923), AEG Argentina (1925), Schering (1926), Merck (1929), Bayer (by 1929), Thyssen Lametal (by 1927), Krupp (1925), and several I. G. Farben affiliates such as S. A. Anilinas Alemanas and Agfa. Luis Sommi estimates ninety such foundings between 1919 and 1928. Particularly in chemicals and pharmaceuticals, these establishments served at first as the elaborators and distributors of semifinished products received from overseas. Profits were reinvested and manufacturing capacity increased until by the end of the 1930s they would be able to meet internal Argentine demand and to export to other Latin American countries as well.[14]

Many of the old-line concerns retained influential positions in the postwar era. These included the two banks, the BAT and the BGAS; the Germano-Argentina in insurance; the prewar manufacturing subsidiaries such as AEG Sudamericana and Mannesmann; the great construction firms (Wayss und Freytag, Dyckerhoff und Widmann, Grün und Bilfinger, Holzmann/GEOPE); a number of traditional import-export houses that diversified into both internal investments and distributorships of German manufactures (Brauss-Mahn, Lahusen, Hasenclever, Staudt, Boeker, Berger, Bromberg); and the largest of the German utilities, CATE.

The postwar history of CATE was uncommonly sinuous. In 1920 it was converted into an international consortium known as the Compañía Hispano Americana de Electricidad, or CHADE, with head offices in Madrid. A. E. Gross and other populist nationalists in Buenos Aires expressed disgust at the change—not only at what they took to be an attempt to disguise the German character of this prestigious concern but also at the requirement that the new company employ certain numbers of Spanish employees. This latter policy, however, does not seem to have been carried out seriously. In 1926 the socialist *Neue Deutsche Zeitung* noted that CHADE then employed three thousand German employees and claimed proudly that it was the largest single power plant in the world. CHADE's facilities were further expanded in 1929 with new ultramodern installations, mostly of German design and manufacture. Through a subsidiary, CHAD-OPYF, CHADE was also closely involved, along with Siemens-Bau-Union (engineering), Orenstein und Koppel (rolling stock), and Siemens-Halske (signals), in the completion of the Buenos Aires subway system, which was undertaken shortly thereafter.[15]

To older trading and investment firms were added such concerns as De Boer Hosmann (insurance and real estate; it was affiliated with the British-controlled Buenos Aires Building Society, Limited), the Ribereña del Plata (coal and wood, slipways and ship repairs), and the major investment houses, Kropp Comercial y Financiera and Koerting. As early as 1921 Dr. Hugo Eckener was promoting the Zeppelin to interested Argentine and German circles in Buenos Aires; however, when his project for regular transatlantic service was ultimately realized, connections were established only as far south as Brazil. But, as early as 1926, the German Aerolloyd was active in developing domestic Argentine aviation.[16] One writer estimates that, in sum, the total German investment in Argentina rose from 265 million dollars in 1920 to approximately 375 million dollars in 1926.[17] According to another estimate, this one based on Chamber of Commerce sources, between 1930 and 1933 an additional 213 million dollars in German capital was placed in Argentine holdings.[18] The great German capitalists Peter Klöckner and Fritz Thyssen—both already represented by substantial interests in the republic—paid personal visits to Buenos Aires in December 1929 and October 1930 respectively. It seems a fair supposition that their counsel or example caused other German capitalists to take appropriate evasive action amidst the onrushing collapse of the Weimar Republic.

The changes within the German economic establishment between World War I and the early 1930s are reflected in the composition of the Chamber of Commerce's executive committee. The founding committee of 1916 included representatives of the two banks and of the established houses (Brauss-Mahn, Lahusen, Boeker, and Hasenclever). Its *Syndicus* was Heinrich Kohn, who had been publisher of the bilingual business weekly, the *Buenos Aires Handels-Zeitung*, since 1889. However, Kohn died in 1921—the journal faltered on three years longer— and he was succeeded by A. Ramm-Doman, who was to play a minor though revealing part in the monarchist attempt to destroy the *Argentinisches Tageblatt* in 1924–1925. In 1932 the executive committee still included representatives of the banks and two of the old-line trading firms, Lahusen and Berger, but they were now complemented by men from the newer De Boer Hosmann and Ribereña del Plata concerns and from the German giants AEG and Thyssen.[19]

These changes worked primarily to the benefit of the uppermost strata of the business community. During the latter years of World War I numbers of artisans and tradespeople, seeking to turn the wartime scarcity of skilled workers and consumer commodities to advantage, had been active in setting up small independent enterprises. However, few of these enterprises survived the peacetime resumption of trade and immigration. Further, insofar as their proprietors sought to remain within the German-speaking cultural community and were dependent on German working capital, subcontracts, and clienteles, they were unable to withstand the postwar tendencies toward consolidation and oligopoly within the German economic enclave.

It is probably significant, for example, that the number of member firms of the Chamber of Commerce in fact declined from 130 in the year 1920 to 121 in 1927; however, as a consequence of the investment surge of the early 1930s the number rose to 161 in 1931.[20] The annual *German-Argentine Address Books* published by the German Scientific Society from 1916 through 1926 (omitting 1919) also provide data, though of an ambiguous sort. The *Address Books* are unsatisfactory in that the listings under occupational and commodity specialties were paid inserts and are thus obviously not exhaustive. Nevertheless, over a ten-year span they provide a controlled series of a sort, and with very few exceptions they all move in the same direction. The numbers of independent artisans and tradespeople drifted downward from the peak years 1917–1920 among bakers, picture framers, sculptors, printers, bookbinders, glaziers, jewelers, fine art dealers, mechanics, furriers, wallpaperers, taxidermists, watchmakers, couturiers, tailors, cabinetmakers, housepainters, pharmacists, music teachers and dealers, draftsmen, accountants, surveyors, and barbers. The six German bookbinders of 1916 had become three by 1926 and were now listed as booksellers. It was noted that the independent mechanics were now affiliated as subcontractors to Bromberg and other large diversified firms and that the cabinetmakers had become employees of concerns manufacturing office furnishings.

One type of enterprise within this socioeconomic sector that had traditionally attracted many Germans was that of *Gastwirtschaft*— bars, restaurants, hotels, pensions, *recreos*, and so on. At least fifty-one of these were in business in greater Buenos Aires in 1917. In a less complete listing for 1924–1925, three were apparently under the same management, four bore the old name but were under new management, and ten were new. Of the thirty-five that advertised in the *Deutsche Zeitung* in February 1927, twenty-five had come into existence since 1917. As these listings are not exhaustive there is no reason to conclude that the *Gastwirtschaft* sector (including owners, managers, and employees) was contracting; indeed, it may well have grown. But it was clearly subject to a very high rate of turnover.[21]

Thus by the mid-1920s the great majority of the community was being displaced, or had been displaced, to dependent positions in the tertiary sector of the economy. Economic independence, one of the most durable goals of the migrant to America, was being precluded. Indeed, the even more fundamental goals of material and social betterment were also drawing more remote. The economic insecurity that had beset middle-class existence during the war was prolonged and grew perhaps even more acute during the postwar decade, for this broad stratum would suffer the competition of renewed large-scale immigration—especially that of upward of one hundred thousand Germanic blood brothers.

The first projections for postwar Germanic immigration caused great unease in the Buenos Aires community, already deeply riven by the political tumult of 1918–1919. Certainly, as a special report from Buenos Aires noted in August 1919, "no one here believes in the figure of five million that has been estimated [by German newspapers], nor even the hundreds of thousands spoken of in less fantastic reports. Nevertheless, people are convinced that tens of thousands will come, and this is sufficient to create deep concern within the German colony on La Plata."[22] *Der Bund* put it more fatalistically at about the same time: the community, like it or not, must gird itself for a massive influx, "even though this were to be discouraged from all sides."[23] The community's fears were allayed temporarily as the first German immigrants did not begin to arrive until late 1919, then only in relatively small contingents. The Volksbund executive committee pronounced these first immigrants "excellent elements" and went on to intimate that it had the situation well in hand: "the problem is to be solved in the best interests of the immigrant, to the benefit of the German community, and to the advantage of all *Deutschtum* . . . so long as German immigration is directed purposefully and with proper planning along the right path, there need be no fear that the German immigrant will swell the international proletariat in Argentina."[24] As late as February 1920, however, the Argentine ambassador in Berlin, Dr. Luis R. Molina, told *La Prensa's* correspondent that "five million" Germans would emigrate to Argentina were it not for the unfavorable currency exchange rate. Molina went on to cite an interview with a German officer recently released from a British prisoner of war camp in Egypt who told him, or so he claimed, that "forty percent" of the inmates had been studying Spanish in their ample spare time "in order to emigrate."[25]

At the end of 1919 Theodor Alemann circulated a questionnaire on immigration among the most knowledgeable businessmen and promoters of agricultural colonies within the community, and at the New Year he published a summary of their replies.[26] Their analyses ranged from the mildly pessimistic to the brutally negative. Together with the observations of other informed persons during the course of the decade, these analyses form a generally accurate basis for an understanding of the hardships, disillusionments, and—often enough—disasters that the great majority of postwar immigrants suffered.

For example, many of the projects in the air on both sides of the Atlantic envisioned compact agricultural settlements—colonies, in the Argentine terminology. Little faith was placed in public (federal or provincial) undertakings; it was assumed, rather, that responsibility (and opportunity) lay primarily with private colonization companies. Such companies would seek to attract immigrants of rural origins who lacked sufficient capital to purchase farmsteads immediately. The immigrants were to be given long-term mortgages and furnished tools, livestock, and seed on credit. In the best circumstances they would liquidate their obligations and acquire clear title to their lands over a period of a decade or more. Ventures of this sort had a long, if troubled, history in Argentina. One of the more successful, the Jewish Colonization Association, was occasionally cited as a model whose statutes and procedures could be adapted to present circumstances (the fact that the JCA's purposes were philanthropic did not receive the same attention).

Alemann's informants, however, made several negative points. They observed that the consolidation of a system of extensively operated export-oriented *latifundia* and its "valorization" through the inflation of land prices were by now all but complete in the most accessible and productive areas of the interior. New colonies, therefore, were in the main condemned to remote and marginally productive regions where the chances of economic survival, much less prosperity, were drastically limited by high transport costs, by natural hazards such as the periodic flooding, insect life, and burgeoning subtropical vegetation of the Northeast or the precariousness of the annual rainfall along the outer rim of the Humid Pampa, and by the speculative and cyclical aspects of an export commodity economy. It was therefore unlikely that closed Reichsdeutsch colonies, on the pattern of the earlier Swiss and Russian-German zones of settlement, could be created at this stage of Argentine economic development. It was also pointed out that, although it was theoretically possible for German capitalists in Buenos Aires to initiate such ventures, most of them were unwilling to do so because of unfortunate earlier experiences. According to more jaundiced writers this was a euphemistic acknowledgment that profits were greater in short-term speculation.[27]

For the independent small agriculturalist, the outlook was somewhat brighter, provided he met several important qualifications. He must be of peasant origin; he must dispose of ample starting capital (estimates ranged from four thousand to twenty thousand paper pesos);[28] and he must be willing to spend a year learning the language, customs, laws, and techniques of the country before investing a single peso in a parcel of land (he was urgently warned against entering into any kind of rental agreement). If he sought to produce cereals or other export crops, he must be prepared to cope with the vagaries and highly capitalized nature of Argentine export agriculture. He must be prepared to suffer natural disasters and the isolation of many areas of the Argentine interior—indeed, isolation would corrode his spirit, he was warned, but would be even harsher on his womenfolk. He was warned, too, of the depredations of *criollo* landowners, local officials, soldiery, *langosteros*,[29] and the like. At first, most of the advice directed toward agriculturalists assumed that they would settle in the cereal zones or join in the development of newer lands, such as the orchards of the Río Negro, the cotton fields of the Chaco, or the *yerba mate* operations in Misiones; and many, perhaps the majority, did so. However, many other peasant immigrants founded market gardens, dairies, apiaries, pig and poultry farms, and the like, to supply local markets. These possibilities, and the apparent success they had brought, were recognized only belatedly. In 1927 the *Deutsche Zeitung* observed unhappily that Buenos Aires promoters had never sought the aid of German agrarian banks, cooperatives, and agricultural specialists and that consequently many opportunities in this area had been lost.[30] In any event, by the early 1930s the surviving residue of German agricultural settlement—in the Chaco, in Misiones, along the Río Negro, in the Sierra de Córdoba, in the environs of the big cities—undoubtedly consisted mostly of immigrants of peasant origin who had been able to bring capital from Europe, rather than ill-prepared *colonos.*

The failed peasant or *colono,* on the other hand, would find himself in a desperate situation if he remained on the land, for it was held that German immigrants were poorly suited to casual agricultural labor. It was noted that the 1917–1918 harvest, the greatest ever to date, had been brought in successfully with the use of locally available labor in the absence of *golondrinas* from overseas. During the war, moreover, the German unemployed who had been dispatched from Buenos Aires to work in the harvests had gained the reputation of "spoiled Middle Europeans" unable to match the physical endurance or accept the elemental living standards of the *criollo* and Southern European harvest hands. This opinion was not altered in the 1920s. In 1925 it was reported from Buenos Aires that, although "Argentina is flooded with destitute German unemployed," work on the land would afford little relief because "the German worker is not exactly cherished in agriculture, since he . . . cannot compete. He demands the customary types of human shelter and respectable food, and usually in the great heat performs significantly less than the races accustomed to warmer regions."[31]

The cities offered a greater range of possibilities, but again there were qualifications. Workers were warned that the social legislation and public assistance to which they had long been accustomed in Germany simply did not exist in Argentina and that the Argentine government would proceed ruthlessly against any foreigner imprudent enough to protest their absence, let alone to agitate for radical changes in the social order.[32] Further, Argentine industrialization was still in its infancy and there were few prospects for unskilled and semiskilled factory workers. As early as March 1920, a Dutch newspaper reported the return of numbers of destitute German workers of this category who had found no work in Argentina: "how they were to get to their home towns in Germany remained a puzzle."[33] It was also clear, however, that unskilled manual workers, depending upon their youth, endurance, and above all adaptability, could survive and perhaps even thrive in Argentina.

The prospects for skilled workers were varied. Railway workers, for example, were still barred from work on the British- and French-owned railways; and the postwar decade would reveal other anomalies, such as the inability of German bakers to compete with Southern Europeans and the great difficulty in placing skilled metalworkers and toolmakers. On the other hand, members of the building trades—masons, carpenters, painters, plasterers, cabinetmakers, plumbers—easily found employment during the construction boom that set in once the peacetime economy had been restored. This first boom was short-lived, to be sure; the socialist *Neue Deutsche Zeitung* wrote in February 1921 that in view of the deepening economic crisis it could no longer recommend to German comrades willing to work hard that they come to Argentina.[34] Except during such periods of depression, however, the situation of people in these and most other skilled trades remained relatively advantageous until the general collapse that began in late 1929.

The Socialists' reaction to the immigration question reflected, in fact, painful conflicts between interest and ideology. They feared—with reason, as events would show—the use of immigrants as strikebreakers, the formation of yellow unions, and the general cheapening of wage rates. They therefore incessantly urged workers to seek employment outside Buenos Aires, insisting that many of the best opportunities were to be found in the smaller cities and towns, in the Comodoro Rivadavia oilfields, and as smiths and mechanics on the great *estancias*. But they also believed that the most appropriate single solution to the inundation of countrymen without funds and marketable skills was large-scale settlement on the land. Thus they bitterly denounced the capitalists of the Buenos Aires community for their failure to lay out the investment necessary for agricultural colonies and training *estancias*, "the profits from which no one would begrudge them."[35]

Many skilled workers and tradespeople, of course, as well as many immigrants recorded as "businessmen," came to Argentina with the goal of owning small independent businesses. The evidence cited earlier in this chapter suggests that among the Germans the turnover rate for small businesses was high, and perhaps rising, and the number surviving to even a modest success was small. Observers in Buenos Aires did not see this at the time as a long-term trend; they stressed, rather, the heavy initial capital investment necessary—twenty thousand to thirty thousand paper pesos—for even a small retail business, workshop, or restaurant, and even more the savagery of competition: "one could well say that the most hardboiled wartime and postwar profiteer from Germany is, by local standards, a wide-eyed innocent; he will be swindled of everything he owns."[36] It is impossible even to guess at the number of times this prediction was borne out. All that is certain is that the petty entrepreneur, successful and struggling, prospective and failed, formed a large, fluid social stratum within the community of the 1920s.

But at war's end by far the most urgent warnings against migration to Argentina were directed toward *Kaufleute und Kopfarbeiter*—

white-collar workers, salespersons and dependent business employees, members of the free professions. On 10 July 1919 the *Frankfurter Zeitung* gave an accurate though understated account of the situation in Buenos Aires: the larger business houses "have learned to adjust to circumstances and have in part succeeded very well," but the "white-collar and manual workers have had to survive very difficult times."[37] By September of that year the Reich Bureau for Emigration (Reichstelle für das Auswanderungswesen) felt compelled to discourage business workers "most urgently" from considering a move to Argentina.[38] Pessimism did not reign everywhere, to be sure: the Socialists claimed at about the same time that the Chamber of Commerce had cabled the Foreign Ministry in Berlin the opinion that business employees with a working knowledge of Spanish had good possibilities of employment.[39] In Germany, the economist von Hirschfeld noted cheerily that the German businessmen stranded in South America by the war "have learned in those difficult years to adapt, to learn new trades [*umlernen*]; they have remained in closest contact with the economic changes there" and would of course prove highly useful in the future.[40] The bulk of the counsel reaching Germany was, however, couched in emphatically negative terms. An engineer active in Argentina since 1913 wrote, "it is impossible to make sufficient propaganda in Germany against migration here . . . [among other things] the proportion of professional idlers is extraordinarily large." The Buenos Aires local of the German-National Business Employees League reported, "the German firms are awash with job seekers; at the moment there are more than sufficient unemployed at hand." The Businessmen's Association of 1858 wired simply and despairingly, "be warned urgently and from all sides against migrating here!"[41]

With the economic crisis of 1921 the situation of the sales and business personnel and professionals collapsed altogether. It was reported that large numbers of Spanish-speaking employees—most of whom had only just recovered from wartime privations—were being released. The position of the newcomers was utterly hopeless.[42] The barrage of exhortations to stay out of Argentina and the white-collar unemployment of 1921 should have been, one feels, ample warning to middle-class persons unequipped with either the occupations or the temperament appropriate to Argentina in the 1920s. But the crisis of the *Kaufleute und Kopfarbeiter* would continue unabated, for they continued to flood into Argentina during the decade and—as the statistics below suggest—may have formed larger proportions of the yearly cohorts at the end of the period than at the beginning.

In round numbers, 72,000 German nationals and almost 15,000 Austrian nationals were recorded as immigrants by the Argentine authorities from 1919 through 1932. Of these, some 40,000 (or 55 percent) of the Germans and 4,500 (or 29 percent) of the Austrians are known to have reemigrated.[43] However, these statistics require further examination. They do not, for example, account for the excess of entrances over exits among steamship passengers traveling first class (second- and third-class passengers were regarded ipso facto as immigrants by the authorities, first-class were not). In the category of entries via river ports or overland they do not permit distinctions among tourists, commercial travelers, and true immigrants; and of course they allow no estimate of the number of illegal entrances.[44] Most important of all is the fact that the round numbers cited above refer, as was the Argentine custom from the beginning of immigration records in 1857, to the nationality of the immigrant. However, exceptionally, from 1923 through 1930 the Argentine authorities also noted his or her first language. In those eight years a total of almost 94,000 immigrants were classed as German-speaking, an excess of some 33,500 over the combined totals for German and Austrian nationals during the same eight-year period. In only two of those years was there a significant deviation from the rough proportion of three to two, and the two deviations virtually cancel each other out.[45] If this proportion were projected over the entire period from the end of the war to the imposition of stringent restrictions by the Argentine government in 1931–1932, and the anomalies noted above were taken into account, an estimate of perhaps 130,000 to 140,000 German-speaking immigrants would be in order.

Linguistic groups cannot be correlated to country of origin, but it is apparent from other evidence that the majority of non-German, non-Austrian immigrants consisted of peasants and small-town persons from old enclaves of German settlement in Eastern Europe and (in the later 1920s) the Ukraine and Lower Volga regions of Russia. There was an important movement (which had begun during the war) from the southern Brazilian states to the newly founded settlements in Misiones. Smaller contingents arrived from the lost German colonies in Africa and some few individuals and families from the United States and Canada.

Argentine statistics on the occupations declared by immigrants are incomplete. Those that are available, however, provide the basis for some interesting, though admittedly rough, comparisons, shown in Table 1. It will be noted that, if the *Kaufleute und Kopfarbeiter* categories (professional and technical, business and office) are added together, they make up 24.7 percent of the total in 1923, 21.9 percent in 1927, 28.1 percent in 1929, 30.5 percent in 1930, and 28.4 percent in

TABLE 1. *German Immigration by Occupation,*
1923–1932 (Selected Years)

	Semi-skilled and skilled workers	Agricul-tural workers	Serving persons	Profes-sional and technical	Business and office	With-out occu-pation
Unskilled workers						
1923 (N=5105, incl. 69 religious)						
179	1285	604	205	301	959	1682
1927 (N=5165, incl. 34 religious)						
254	1148	570	217	229	901	1812
1929 (N=4851, incl. 33 religious)						
101	942	381	164	319	969	1672
1930 (N=5139)						
114	1065	336	172	435	1131	1886
1932 (N=2089, incl. 52 religious)						
35	353	143	64	174	420	848

Sources: Argentine Republic, Dirección de Inmigración, *Memorias* and *Informes*, years cited. Argentine officials included both religious personnel and theatrical performers under the rubric professional. I have subtracted these. Theater people have been placed under skilled workers.

1932. In 1923 they nearly equal the contingent of workers (unskilled, semiskilled, and skilled), which amounts to 25.2 percent of the total. In the years 1929, 1930, and 1932, they exceed the proportion of workers (22.8 percent, 22.9 percent, and 18.6 percent respectively); in the latter year, 1932, the restrictions on immigration, which fell most heavily upon workers, are responsible in some measure for the difference.

In Chapter Seven, the records of the German language employment services will be examined. They do not correspond exactly to the years cited here, nor do they permit discriminations among nationalities (since, as during the war, they were available to all persons with a rudimentary knowledge of German). Nevertheless, they will show plainly that placement in a white-collar occupation was nearly impossible for the newcomer who came *auf gut Glück*—that is, without the ironclad promise of a job. In the same statistics the high levels of recruitment of unskilled labor and of serving people will indicate that an initial—and certainly, in many instances, permanent—descent into the proletariat was the common experience of the middle-class Germans who sought to "make America" in Argentina.

Many, of course, of all categories reemigrated—although reemigration was not an easy matter. Pride undoubtedly held people back, at least for a time; but finances were even more important. "Workaway" passages were scarce on the South Atlantic run; to be shipped home at the expense of the consulate or the German Welfare Society required that one be declared medically unfit. As the analysis of wages and living costs will show (Chapter Seven), there was little margin for savings in the average budget. A savings account was perhaps more feasible for an unmarried person, especially a worker not obliged to live up to bourgeois standards of gentility; on the other hand, job security was nonexistent and sudden layoffs followed by long spells of unemployment were the ruin of many plans.

Argentine statistics on reemigration are not particularly revealing, as they cannot be correlated to either the first language of the reemigrant or the occupational category—only the nationality. They tell nothing of the length of time spent in Argentina. In the matter of the large mass of German-speaking immigrants who were not of German or Austrian nationality, however, one may infer that, given the strength of the "push" factors that had driven most of them out of their former homelands, the rate of return must have been very low (they could, of course, seek their fortune elsewhere). In the reemigration of Austrians (29 percent) no pattern is visible over time. In the case of the Reichsdeutsche, however, several points are worth noting. Until 1923 the rate of reemigration among them remained relatively low (32.3 percent from 1919 through 1923). This reflects the capacity of the Argentine economy to absorb certain numbers of skilled workers, noted above, and more generally the advantageousness of being among the first comers. In those years, also, the precarious situation of German politics and the German economy offered small inducement to return. But, with the onset of runaway inflation in Germany in 1922–1923 and the simultaneous rapid filling of the United States quotas for German immigrants,[46] the years 1923 and 1924 represented the crest of the movement to Argentina—and the point at which the crisis of German immigration became acute. Already in 1925 reemigrants were 102 percent of immigrants (111 percent according to the Chamber of Commerce, which counted first-class passengers as immigrants also), and in no year thereafter until the early 1930s did the proportion drop below 75 percent. For the entire period 1925–1932 inclusive, the overall reemigration rate was just under 87 percent.[47] The movement and frustration suggested by these statistics are of especial significance for the Buenos Aires community, for of all the German-speaking groups the Reichsdeutsche were by far the most highly urban in origin and the most likely to end up haunting the employment agencies, welfare offices, flophouses, and back alleys of the German community. And the residue of the Reichsdeutsch immigration constituted an ever-larger proportion of the growing urban community: from roughly one-third of the 30,000 of 1914 to 45 percent of the approximately 45,000 of the late 1930s.[48]

This is not the place for an extended discussion of the causes of the German outmigration of the 1920s—the "push" factors. German birth rates just prior to World War I had been at an all-time high; infant survival rates had also been high; and this generation had not partici-pated in the war. For fifteen years after the armistice the cohort of those born between 1900 and 1914 flooded the German labor market and swelled the army of unemployed. Compounding the fundamental demographic problem were postwar economic dislocations and the ac-celerating inflation that culminated in currency collapse in 1922–1923 and revaluation in 1924. Hardest hit of all were exofficers (the Treaty of Versailles permitted Germany to retain only 3,796 on active duty), academics (in surplus even before 1914), and rentiers generally; these were the most likely to contemplate emigration. But the urge to emi-grate had an important psychological dimension also: the *Untergangs-stimmung* verbalized by Oswald Spengler, a brooding sense of Euro-pean civilization in decline. Among educated persons especially, this mood transformed mundane considerations in favor of emigration into what Karl Thalheim termed a "mass psychosis."[49]

The "pull" factors directing German emigration toward Argentina rather than elsewhere are of some interest. As Kurt Faber, himself an old Argentine hand, put it in August 1919: "Argentina is today in great vogue in the German Fatherland. The number of books on Argentina grows ever larger; a countless horde of agents crisscrosses Germany and portrays the new land of unlimited possibilities in the most glow-ing colors to the many—the all too many—for whom the table is no longer set in the Fatherland."[50] The average German emigrant—the ex–frontline soldier who had gone directly from school to the trenches, the small shopkeeper ruined by the inflation, the young person with a trade or degree or without it—was aware that many formerly hospitable areas—the United States, Canada, Brazil, Australia—were now closed, either legally or de facto through the persistence of wartime passions. And, despite the volume of sober and discouraging counsel available through such agencies as the Reich Bureau for Emigration and the

Overseas Institute in Stuttgart, he all too often listened instead to the "agents"—or to whatever it is that moves people to pick up and go.

We know some of the reasons. For example, early in the postwar days and into the period of runaway inflation in 1922–1923, many workers appear to have made (or been persuaded to make) to elementary "currency exchange error [*Valutafehler*]": they translated the wage levels paid in the solid Argentine peso into the purchasing power of the inflated German *Reichsmark* (in February 1922 the exchange stood at one gold peso to 1,200–1,800 *RM*). But they failed to reckon with the correspondingly high cost of living in Argentina and with long periods of unemployment that might liquidate savings.[51] At least one German-speaking municipality, Danzig, attempted to use Argentina as a dumping ground for its own unemployed. In 1926 a group of three thousand was assembled, reputedly on the initiative of the Argentine vice-consul in the city, one Dr. Jakob, and plans were laid to ship them in several contingents to Buenos Aires. However, the first Danzig contingent of two hundred, after lounging about the Hotel de Inmigrantes and the Salvation Army for some months, was finally shipped home again at the expense of the Danzig senate, accompanied by a barrage of indignant remarks.[52] When it had become apparent by the middle of the decade that the greatest problem of all was the horde of unemployable *Kaufleute und Kopfarbeiter*, German authorities recommended bluntly that these people would do better to take the unavoidable downward step from learned or white-collar occupations to manual labor in Germany (where social agencies could ease the transition to some degree) rather than in Argentina. A reply of sorts was given by a number of such men interviewed by Volksbund agents in Argentina: at least in Argentina, they said, they could accept declassed positions without incurring obloquy among family and associates.[53]

But one aspect of the "mass psychosis" was of especial relevance to Argentina. This was the "drive to own a little plot of land [*Drang zur eigenen Scholle*]" that had arisen, according to Thalheim, among industrial workers and other urban people sick at heart of a "ruined" civilization: "men no longer wish to be subordinates, workers for capitalist interests; they strive toward broader, freer possibilities of development; they wish to be their own masters on their own land."[54] It would be at the root of vast amounts of misery among the postwar emigrants to Argentina.

The vague yearning for "a little plot of land of one's own"—the *eigene Scholle Märchen*, or "fairytale," it came to be called—was first stimulated in Germany by news of the Argentine homestead law, which was circulated widely, evidently with the complicity of Argentine consuls in major cities, in 1919. The Reich Bureau for Emigration and other reputable agencies strove energetically to scotch this enthusiasm, pointing out that such a project had indeed been passed by the Argentine Congress in 1917 but that Yrigoyen had refused to implement it. Even had it been implemented there was little it could have accomplished, given the scant amount of usable public land available.[55] Nevertheless, the homestead law lingered on in promotional literature for several years.

Prospective emigrants fell victim to dozens of interested parties, white slavers, and swindlers; and the main area of activity of the latter was the land. Free lancers abounded, as did organizers of settlement cooperatives (*Siedlungsgenossenschaften*), who ran the gamut from venal to merely incompetent.[56] But much promotional work was also carried on by publicists from the Buenos Aires community. The most notorious of these was Felix Bagel, one-time member of the Committee of Fifteen. In 1919 Bagel published, under the pseudonym F. Alba, a tract entitled *Auswanderung nach Argentinien* (*Emigration to Argentina*) which presented Argentina in the most roseate terms to the prospective immigrant. Although slapdash and inaccurate, it is said to have earned its author and publisher seventy thousand *Reichsmark* in less than a year.[57] The Volksbund published handbooks and other literature for immigrants and is known to have prepared promotional films for showing in southwestern Germany. Much of the irresponsible —often termed "criminal"—propaganda put about in Germany was the work of the three steamship lines that regularly made the South Atlantic run: Hamburg-Amerika, Hamburg-Süd, and Stinnes. In 1923 they had no fewer than twenty-seven liners in operation to Buenos Aires.[58]

One settlement project which began reputably enough was that of a training *estancia* for the systematic introduction of European farmers to Argentine conditions and techniques. The basic concept of the training *estancia* had been worked out in the Volksbund during the last years of the war. Now in 1919 the august German-Argentine League for the Promotion of Economic Interests announced elaborate plans for such a venture. In this version, however, the training *estancia* was designed principally for exofficers of the German armed forces.[59] It received a great deal of publicity in both Germany and Argentina and undoubtedly raised many hopes, but it never came to fruition. And it had a tainted sequel. A German businessman, F. Wencke, donated 345 hectares of land near the Pampa town of Zárate to be used for the project and entrusted its administration to the executive committee of the Volksbund. Some years later it was revealed that the land had been sold, but the sale price and the identity of the purchaser were never clarified in the robust debate that erupted between the Volksbund and its critics. At all events the executive committee used the proceeds to construct a modest old people's home—named, naturally, after Wencke —in Buenos Aires.[60]

The list of agricultural settlement projects which ended in frustration was a long one. The most extensive failures were in the Chaco, where the postwar fall in cotton prices, four successive bad harvests (1924–1927), and overextension on the part of many planters combined to ruin the majority of German settlers,[61] and in the La Pampa Territory, where the drought of 1929–1930 destroyed newer settlements (principally Russian-German), which had pushed westward across the isothermic boundary between Humid and Dry Pampa from the older zone of Ströder colonies in southwestern Buenos Aires Province. In May of 1931, 450 colonist families and many thousand head of livestock were resettled to government lands in the Chaco; about 100 persons, mostly children, died along the way. A similar fate befell the band of peasants from Türkenfeld, near Munich, who followed the Benedictine Pater Sauter (the "mad monk Paulus") to a waterless region of the Chaco. For a time they were sustained by the charity of the Buenos Aires community, but in the end they were removed to Misiones, where they became day laborers in the El Dorado colonies. Other projects which either collapsed or required long-term charitable aid were La Patagonia (which resulted in protracted lawsuits in Germany), New Karlsruhe in Misiones, Jocolí and La Llave in Mendoza, and Dora in Santiago del Estero. With the exception of the promoters, the Buenos Aires community came to regard the agricultural colonies as several varieties of nuisance. Few of them became reliable suppliers of exportable commodities or consumers of German imports, calls for charity were chronic, and the community had somehow to make room for hapless ex- or would-be peasants.

The El Dorado colonies in Misiones had a particularly ambiguous reputation during the postwar decade. The first serious private colonization projects in Misiones had been started at the beginning of World War I by the Tornquist interests. Their most valuable nuclei were Brazilian-German peasants familiar with the subtropical environment. Following the war the pioneering population was augmented by varied German-speaking groups and many non-German immigrants as well. In the 1920s the best publicized and most controversial operations were those controlled by Anton Schwelm. Schwelm had been born in Stuttgart but had been taken to London as a child by his parents and had there acquired British citizenship. He had come to Buenos Aires during the war as an employee of the Bank of London and had first come to Misiones to buy quebracho logs to be made into crossties for the British owned railways. In 1919 he bought his first land in Misiones, and in 1924 his El Dorado Company absorbed the former Tornquist colonies of Monte Carlo and Puerto Rico.

From beginning to end, Schwelm's activities were surrounded by a welter of accusation and counteraccusation, and it is exceedingly difficult to make reasonable judgments at this late date.[62] It is indisputable that by the late 1930s the El Dorado colonies formed part of a zone of stable communities made relatively prosperous through cultivation of *yerba mate*, tobacco, tung, and citrus crops. On the other hand, El Dorado sent forth cadres of disgruntled failures vociferous in their grievances against Schwelm. The bulk of their complaints centered upon his alleged misleading advertising, particularly concerning the distances from prospective farmsteads to road and river transport facilities, and upon his evasiveness in granting clear land titles following the fulfillment of contractual obligations. El Dorado also attracted, in one fashion or another, considerable numbers of agriculturalists who arrived in Misiones destitute or nearly so. They include the survivors of the Sauter colony, mentioned above, and probably many from La Pampa as well. They also include 911 Germans placed as *internados* by the Hotel de Inmigrantes in Buenos Aires from 1926 through 1930 (from a total of 4,193 so placed) and another 240 (of 381) in 1932.[63] Some colonists worked five days a week on Schwelm's land at a monthly wage of 60 pesos in order to pay for their own *chacras*. The smallest parcel available was 25 hectares and cost 750 pesos.[64] Once begun on such a course, it was difficult for the *colono* to leave. Undoubtedly some, of great strength of will, joined the ranks of independent smallholders so glowingly depicted in El Dorado promotional literature.

Schwelm's own painstaking attention to advertising, overt and covert, clouds the issue. A number of travelers' accounts of the period are suspiciously uncritical in their admiration for El Dorado.[65] As the socialist press noted often, Schwelm's extensive advertising in the *Argentinisches Tageblatt* and the *Deutsche La-Plata Zeitung* made it unlikely that either of these influential dailies would be uncomplimentary in its references to Misiones. More serious still, it appeared that the German embassy itself had been enlisted in Schwelm's service. Criticism could hardly fail to be aroused when in September 1924 Bernhard Stichel left his position as the embassy's special counselor for immigrant affairs and was placed on Schwelm's payroll at a reputed two thousand pesos per month.[66] Passion outran facts, causing even the tough-minded officials of the Reich Bureau for Emigration to conclude their evaluation of El Dorado in 1929 by figuratively throwing their hands in the air and declaring, "El Dorado is . . . highly controversial."[67] Criticism of Schwelm mounted toward the end of the decade, and the volume of his counterpropaganda appears to have increased also. In Buenos Aires in 1932 considerable malicious pleasure —*Schadenfreude*—was expressed at the news that his operations faced bankruptcy. By this time also, anti–El Dorado sentiment was tinged by anti-Semitism. Several of the colony's financial backers in Europe were Jewish, and Schwelm himself, although a convert to Catholicism— who had once owned a yacht named *Svástica!*—had been born a Jew.[68]

The economic decline that began in late 1929 continued into 1930 and worsened into a general crisis with falling world prices and falling demand for Argentina's export commodities, as well as unparalleled levels of unemployment. Toward the end of that year the military regime of General Uriburu, which had seized power in September, initiated policies that would, in effect, end Argentina's historical encouragement of mass immigration. On 20 December the cost of an immigrant visa was raised from three to thirty-three gold pesos. During the course of 1931 the immigration of wage workers was halted almost entirely by provisions which limited entry to agricultural settlers, persons in possession of capital, returnees claiming Argentine residence or citizenship, or members of families of those otherwise admissible. After 1 January 1933 entry was restricted to immigrants who could show a work contract or other proof of a job awaiting them or attestation of support from relatives of the first degree already domiciled in Argentina.[69]

At the upper levels of the German-speaking community the deteriorating situation of the Weimar Republic after 1930 brought a new surge of economic activity. Among the commonality the depression, the sharp decline in immigration, the collapse of Argentine parliamentarism, all contributed to a poignant awareness that a distinct time and way of life had passed. In this mood of reflectiveness a number of the community's intellects tried to make sense of the postwar movement of their countrymen from Europe to the land of unlimited possibilities, and the conclusions they reached were mostly bitter. On the troubled history of Germanic agricultural settlement, the *Neue Deutsche Zeitung* had long since made the telling observation that "the stream of relatives following the original settlers from the homeland is extraordinarily small. No one wants the responsibility of encouraging relatives to undergo similar privations."[70] In 1932 Paul F. Heintze (himself earlier active in land promotions in the Sierra de Córdoba) wrote in *Der Bund*, "I hold every attempt to create settlements in the tropics and subtropics to be a regrettable total waste of German human and material resources." He went on to denounce bank directors and bureaucrats, land promoters and salesmen of agricultural equipment, and the writers of "frivolous" articles in *Der Bund* and elsewhere. But he admitted that, despite long experience in many parts of Argentina, he had no answers: "[I only know that] there can be no good reason for the Middle European to transplant forcibly his good northern race to the plague- and sickness-ridden tropics and subtropics, remote from the world." [71] In a similar vein Dr. A. Buckeley wrote of the urban experience of the immigrants: "The worker, the white-collar employee, the small businessman out here, all must work far, far more, and longer, and harder, to remain at the same standard as over there [in Germany]. Despite the problems of the German economy he runs a greater risk here than there of being without work and earnings. Here, businessmen and entrepreneurs can begin something only when heavily backed by capital—which they could do equally well over there. Out here, these are all commonplaces of folk wisdom [*Binsenwahrheiten*] that are unknown or not believed back home." [72]

Puzzlement, *Binsenwahrheiten*, above all, insecurity—for the community had undergone many unsettling changes since 1918.

5. Notes on the Immigrant Experience im Affenland

In 1953, F. R. Francke, publisher of the popular journal *Südamerika*, replied to complaints by post–World War II immigrants of the coldness and inhospitality of the "old settlers," the "well-upholstered moneybags" of the community. "Do you think," wrote Francke, "that [thirty years ago] they received *us* with open arms?" True enough, he agreed, he and numbers of his contemporaries had "made it [*haben es geschafft*]"; but—a touch of bathos here—the German Cemetery in Buenos Aires, meager graves in Misiones, the Chaco, Paraguay, bore testimony to the unknown thousands who had not, who had gone to ruin. (Successful immigrants did not die, apparently, or at least not in South America.) Sounding like the archetypal old soldier, he reminisced about the way he, as a jobless newcomer three decades before, had customarily slept in sections of storm drain waiting to be installed along Paseo Leandro Alem—when they were not already all occupied for the night by countrymen. But, he concluded, "those were other times and other contemporaries and—what I find the healthiest aspect of the matter—we thought nothing of it. In fine, we had come to America without illusions."[1]

Perhaps. One suspects, however, that Francke's verdict is evidence merely of the quicksilver quality of memory, of the existential need to preserve the authorized version of one's own history intact. Similarly, in interviews with survivors of the post–World War I immigration, one catches flashes of the naiveté, the "illusions," of the time; but too much has come between—unemployment, depression, Hitlerism, war, postwar closure of the community's institutions and sweeping demoralization—and the memory threads its tortuous way between truth and pain.

Nevertheless, the illusions have to be taken account of. The Germanic immigration to Argentina of the 1920s was characterized, after all, by what social planners might consider high incongruity between supply and demand and what others might call excessive pointless misery; and analysis in terms of mechanistic "push-pull" factors carries us only a short way toward understanding it. Memories assist, though they are an inconstant guide. Thus, to try to grasp more firmly at the attitudes, the psychology, the illusions, I propose to turn to the Argentina-literature of the time. The Germans, a most literate people, wrote voluminously of their adventures and misadventures in Argentina. It scarcely need be said that these writings are highly uneven in quality and reliability. They are suffused by personal vendettas, plagiarism, political tendentiousness, and paid promotional propaganda masquerading as straightforward journalism; the amiable spirit of Baron von Münchhausen hovers over many of them. But precisely because it is a popular literature, the attitudes and illusions of the authors, and of the publics for whom they were writing, stand out in high relief. And, taking it all together, certain coherent themes begin to emerge.

The excitement concerning Argentina that surged up in Germany after 1918 was matched by a corresponding outpouring of publications on the subject. The number of immigrant handbooks (*Wegweiser, Ratgeber, Berater*) increased, but otherwise they changed little: their thumbnail sketches of Argentine geography and history, notes on customs regulations, currency conversion tables, and lists of trades sought and not sought remained as flatfootedly factual (if often as ill-informed) after the war as before. Nor was there much change in the genre of scholarly-cum-promotional works by German-speaking geographers and other academics—except that, if anything, the quality declined: little published after 1918 compares favorably with the work of such prewar writers as Kärger, Schmidt and Grotewohl, or Schuster.

There is, however, an important qualitative change in the memoirs of German travelers and immigrants. Those written before the war generally fall into the familiar genre of good-humored, somewhat rueful *Wanderjahre* memoir. Kurt Faber, to cite only one example, worked his way across Argentina as a harvest hand (among other things) shortly before the war. Surely some truth lay then in his assertion that, in contrast to other nationalities, "the German is the only hobo [*Landstreicher*] out of passion; what others do out of need and consider a cross to be borne, the German does as a trade. This has not always contributed to the raising of German prestige overseas. But still!"[2] But in the post-1918 memoirs little of the exuberance, little of the *Wandervogel* impulse, remains. Rather, to a greater or lesser extent, they reflect "that historical pariah complex of self-pity and self-justification which the German people . . . developed after the defeat of 1918," as Alan Bullock has somewhat uncharitably put it.[3]

Like any popular literature, it is also highly ethnocentric and hence often insensitive toward Argentine sensibilities in ways which one might today find offensive. But however unflattering these perceptions of Argentina, they demand to be examined because they obviously affected the immigrant's response to the Argentine reality—the more so when that reality proved baffling or intractable.

In the great age of immigration, the Germanic newcomer to Argentina was confronted by a physical landscape—a squat, sweaty, dun-colored city smeared along a muddy riverbank and, beyond it, engulfing it, an illimitable empty plain and towering sky—unfamiliar, desolate, and ultimately menacing. Like the overwhelming majority of travelers down to the present day, he found the physical aspect of Buenos Aires uninspiring at best. The verdicts recur. In the 1880s, Leopold Schnabl concluded that, to the eye, Buenos Aires was depressingly monotonous. Like many Europeans, he was put off by the "chessboard" symmetry of the city's layout, block after block of "paltry, narrow-chested, poor" *criollo* houses "showing us only their undeveloped fronts." He made an exception of Tres de Febrero Park (Palermo) with its stately trees, but he revealed his lack of sympathy with its avenues of heroic statuary and the parades of the fashionable, publicly preening themselves in conscious imitation of their counterparts in the Prater or the Bois de Boulogne. "No," he wrote, "the city—either in its physical situation or its architectural elements—is not exactly what one would call beautiful." [4]

Two decades later—two decades of flamboyant economic growth and a flourishing of the haut monde to match—Hanns Heinz Ewers described the *paseo* in Palermo Park rather more emphatically as a display of tastelessness and harlotry. As to the city itself: "in one single cobblestone of the Boulevard Haussmann there is more culture than in all of Buenos Aires. It is the most desolate metropolis on this earth. It exists for only one wretched purpose: to make money." [5] In the 1920s, Alfons Goldschmidt described Palermo as "an asphalt Corso, where in the afternoon the pearl-laden, with drooping haughty mien, drive by in their autos, where the idle envy each other, where a revolting odor, compound of petrol, asphalt, and perfume, befogs the brain." Of the city itself he wrote: "it has a history but no tradition. It came from outside; it has no roots in the land. . . . It is European commercial and North American commercial . . . frenetic and humid, badly laid out and unhealthy, a chessboard of stone . . . tasteless parks and villas, all bedecked with kitsch." [6]

But, once past the first impact of the physical environment, the German immigrant found paradox. He was confronted by a frontier society in which everything was in the process of becoming; yet at the still center of this flux lay an indigenous culture—the Hispano-Argentine, *lo criollo, Kreolentum*—which seemed resistant to all change, immobile. It was vaguely "medieval" in its clericalism, illiteracy, and care-lessness of human life, yet without a serious history or tradition; hos-pitable, in its way, to the foreigner, yet curiously impermeable by him. Thus for enlightenment he turned to his more seasoned countrymen, and within a short time of his arrival he was almost certain to receive three laconic bits of advice from one or another of them. Much of his experience in Argentina can be organized in terms of the implications or coded meanings of these free handouts and his responses to them.

The first was the Argentine *dicho* that has been translated into every immigrant tongue: "El zonzo vive de su trabajo; el vivo[7] vive del zonzo"—"The fool lives from his labor; the hustler lives off the fool." Any immigrant who failed to internalize this folk wisdom was lost; but according to a long line of German writers it was of even greater sig-nificance to the Germanic immigrant than to most others. For he must remember that he was *Deutscher Michel*, "German Mike"—the average German who was good hearted, law-abiding, hardworking, reliable, scrupulously honest, credulous, perhaps even a bit thick in the wits. He was thus liable to endless varieties of exploitation by "the *Criollo*," all of whose salient personality traits were precisely the opposite of his own. A generation earlier, Leopold Schnabl had worked up the basic Germanic stereotype of the Argentine (more precisely, the *porteño*), one plagiarized by many of his successors but never improved upon:

> One would think that a half-century under arms, in revolutions, would have made the *porteño* hard, rough, and warlike. Nothing of the sort. . . . Not that there is any lack of personal courage . . . in Society the man who does not defend his honor with dagger or pistol is impossible. All the same, most duels end quite without bloodshed, which is just as well. Basically, there is no milder blood lust than that of the presentday Argentine. A bit of war-scare and heroic posturing, a bit of revolutionary rhetoric, suffices completely to satisfy his most cherished fantasy and keep him content.
>
> [He is, rather, a man of salons, a diplomat, for] reserve and mistrust are basic to the Argentine character. . . . Nothing can compare to the extreme hospitality with which he receives you: [he will invite you to his home to continue a business conversa-tion] and with this shrewd chess move his diplomatic talent has prepared him a double triumph. First, he is now able, with his high cosmopolitan polish, to corrupt you and take you in; and second, he has concealed the deep mistrust in which he holds you. He is not what he passes himself off to be; nor does he take you

to be what he *says* he takes you to be. His joviality is a mask; . . . he is a master of the art of appearances. . . . Unless you are fully on your toes, you will soon have fallen victim—lock, stock, and barrel—to his fascinating deftness and persuasiveness; and you will feel it in terms of *money*. . . . His philosophy is supple, expansible, and a mortal enemy to any limitations of a moral scruple nature. . . . In this world, which consists of deceivers and deceived, he prefers to be the hammer rather than the anvil. . . .

[The *porteño* is less ruthless than the North American, but this may merely be because] the *porteño* . . . is less enterprising than his North American brother, and also because, until now, better-off Argentine youth has learned fewer trades and professions in which to practice the art of scalping one's fellows. The native, to a remarkable extent, concentrates on a very few occupations, and ignores the rest. Trade itself he leaves to the foreign immigrant and is content to serve the latter as his lieutenant—as translator, broker, auctioneer, et cetera. He is often most handsomely overpaid for his assistance in these positions. . . .

[Every national character has its paradox]: for his part, the Argentine, who is anything but a man consumed by a sense of duty, nevertheless bows before one unbreakable holy law. This law is Social Custom.[8]

The newcomer seldom had to wait long for his first encounter with the legendary business cunning—the *viveza criolla*—of the *porteños*. It might occur even before he set foot on land. Until proper landing facilities were built at the turn of the century, the immigration officials bore, theoretically, the responsibility for ferrying immigrants from seagoing ships to the shore; often, however, immigrants were not informed of this and were left to the attentions of private, high-priced lightermen.[9] Inside the government-operated Hotel de Inmigrantes, where he was given five days' free board and lodging (a term often extended), the immigrant was relatively safe; the moment he stepped outside its doors, the predators closed in. There were outright thieves, of course, but he was more likely to fall victim to a nonviolent confidence trick—a *cuento del tío*, in the vernacular. There were false secret police, who could "fix" the "irregularities" in the immigrant's papers, for a fee. There were crooked gamblers and white slavers. There were practitioners of the ancient Spanish prisoner swindle and its many variations. A standard ruse was to entrust the immigrant with something of apparent value—a gold ring, a packet of money, a winning lottery slip, the unused half of a railroad ticket, which for complicated reasons the *criollo* was unable at the moment to deliver or use —against the money guarantee that the immigrant was asked to give as a token of good faith.[10] To the dyspeptic Goldschmidt, these were merely trivial instances of the overriding national passion. He described *criollos* who, he said, proudly showed him the imposing Congreso palace and attempted to estimate how many million gold pesos had been stolen during its construction. "They say, you see how rich this land is . . . ? Fraternal joy shines out of this report, as well as the business envy of men who were not on the inside."[11]

But it would dawn on the immigrant sooner or later that not all the predators were *criollos*, that, in fact, his own countrymen were at least equally dangerous. They would guide him to purported "employers" and promise to obtain the necessary "papers" for him, for a fee.[12] Entire workshops owned by Germans were said to have been staffed by the *medio-oficio* trick (described in Chapter Seven). At even higher levels, many of the post-1918 agricultural settlement schemes had no firmer basis than the active imaginations and hyperactive avarice of Buenos Aires–based German promoters (see Chapter Four). This stood to reason, according to Karl Huber, who had lived in the North for many years: "[Argentina is] to a very great extent the last refuge of broken down existences for whom things have gotten too hot to stay in Europe." Many immigrants who had been victimized by their countrymen probably agreed that Argentina, somehow, had received the dregs of Europe. Some would wonder, however, if there were not something in the very environment of America that debauched once-sound European stock.

But deep thoughts were for later. In the short term, Huber's advice, echoed by many others, was more to the point: "avoid any inclination to be trustful while under way; exercise the greatest care in every relationship; always be on your toes."[13] Confide your plans to no one. Trust no one. The price of these elementary lessons for survival in Argentina was often high. The immigrant who absorbed them was well on the way toward *acriollar*.

These admonitions touched not only personal and business relationships. The gravest and most fundamental criticisms that immigrant writers made of Argentina were, as they saw them, the frivolity of public administration, the corruptness of public men, and the absence of the rule of law. The depredations of officialdom fell, naturally, most heavily on the commonality; and German Socialists were among the most emphatic in drawing contrasts between the well-ordered German *Rechtsstaat* and the state of nature in Argentina, where such police power as the state possessed merely made the predators more dangerous still. The original *Vorwärts* weekly, for example, warned workers most urgently: "protect yourselves against lawyers, *procuradores*, and all such luminaries; they are here the worst of cutthroats. And in most cases the judges are no whit better."[14] In the 1920s, four decades later, the Socialists were still advising their working-class comrades to avoid any recourse to law, for in legal matters Argentine practice was precisely the opposite of what a European might expect: it was the "land of inverted concepts."[15] But not only the Socialists labored this theme. Cissy von Scheele-Willich and her exofficer husband had made a success of cotton planting in the Chaco. She wrote feelingly of the struggles of her countrymen on the land (where, if anything, the rule of law was more tenuous than in the city) and concluded that one of the several reasons for the Germans' indifferent success in Argentina was that the Fatherland's "widely developed public and social welfare institutions . . . our well-ordered police state" had not prepared them for America.[16]

Germanic disdain for Argentine civic and legal morality also drew authority from no less a personage than Otto von Bismarck. General Julio Roca, the story went, in the course of his extended trip to Europe following his first presidency (that is, in 1887 or 1888), paid a formal call on the Iron Chancellor. During the interview Roca dilated at great length on the economic and cultural progress of Argentina in recent years. Finally Bismarck, wearying of this, held up his hand and inquired coolly of Roca, "And tell me about the state of your justice? [*Und wie steht es bei Ihnen mit der Justiz?*]" This story circulated until the First World War and probably thereafter as well.[17]

These reactions to Argentina—to the unprepossessing face of the land; to the sadly derivative attempts at high culture; to the barbarism that began not far from the city's limits (not far from the door of the salon, for that matter); to its civic mores, underdeveloped and whimsical by European standards—coalesced into a reigning community attitude toward all things Argentine. This attitude was expressed in one crisp, singularly unpleasant epithet: *Affenland*—"monkeyland."[18]

A tiny privileged minority of Germans migrated to Argentina in the 1920s in possession of contracts for technical or professional positions that awaited them there. The immense majority, however, came with no such prospects. An immigrant in the latter category received a second piece of advice sooner or later—usually sooner, since emissaries of the Volksbund regularly boarded immigrant ships as they entered Buenos Aires harbor. This was: "no success without Spanish." It was often amplified by the suggestion that he spend a year or so knocking about the country learning its language and customs, after which he might begin to think of seeking a position with a German language firm. At all events, he would be wise to bank immediately a sufficient sum of money to cover his return passage to Europe. He need not, in other words, expect an enthusiastic welcome from the established Germans of La Plata.

From the mid-nineteenth century onward, in fact, the Buenos Aires community had never been particularly hospitable to newcomers. In the 1880s, for example, the promoter Carl Beck-Bernard had had to inform small businessmen bluntly that they should not count on the backing of capital from local German sources. He also noted that the trading houses recruited their employees exclusively through overseas business and familial contacts; they did not take on unknown newcomers.[19] Leopold Schnabl observed that, in the midcentury decades of political tumult and economic sluggishness, the German trading houses had sustained themselves through close management, rigid economies, and patience. In general, they had been in no position to absorb more than a few carefully selected business apprentices at irregular intervals, and, logically, they preferred newcomers who brought both experience and capital. At the same time, according to Schnabl, German employers, traders and artisans alike, had concluded that their countrymen were, in the main, far too demanding (of wages, creature comforts, rapid success) for Argentine conditions—particularly when one compared them to the patient, endlessly industrious, self-denying Italians, Basques, and Galicians.[20]

The new, purposeful German commercial development after 1871 and the swelling prosperity of the following decade had, if anything, deepened the coolness toward newcomers. The rough democracy of the early community gave way to what Schnabl termed the "spirit of the cashbox." The new plutocrats "have no time any more for the excellent young men bearing first-class credentials from German professional schools who seek introduction."

> One [businessman] gets rid of the unfortunate young man by giving him a few pesos as alms; at another firm, an underling, nose high in the air, says that the boss is not to be disturbed; a third observes drily that "too many educated proletarians" are coming out of Germany. Thus the newly arrived teacher, engineer, chemist, musician . . . discovers, often with confusion, that the distance that separates him from the soil of his homeland is not as monstrously great as the cleft that gapes between him and his money-proud countrymen in Buenos Aires. . . .
>
> Among all the German businessmen, artists, artisans, doctors,

engineers, military officers, literary men, and so on, who have made
their careers in Buenos Aires in the past twenty years, ninety-nine
percent have the friendship and good will of the foreigner, the
porteño, to thank for it, and only one percent the fraternal spirit
of their colonial countrymen.[21]

The only available statistical check on Schnabl's generalization is a
crude one; it suggests that he exaggerated, but not much. From 1872
(when such records were first kept) through 1923, inclusive, 27 percent
of all German immigrants (including dependents) were placed in their
first job in Argentina by the officials of the Hotel de Inmigrantes. These
placements as so-called *internados* were almost without exception in
the most physically demanding unskilled and semiskilled trades; Europeans with any pretensions to status could only view the Hotel de
Inmigrantes as the employer of last resort. In the 1920s the overall
internado rate among German immigrants was, in fact, slightly lower—
23 percent—than it had been over the preceding half century.[22]

The postwar immigrant, shaken perhaps by his initial reception,
might avail himself of the five days' free board and lodging at the
Hotel de Inmigrantes, or he might put up immediately in one of the
German-run hotels—Emmermann's, Hoffmann's, the Viena, the Kaiser-
hof (later the Jousten), the Royal, the Deutscher Bund (later the
Neuer Deutscher Bund), Zur Habsburg—in the city center; then he
would attempt to verify the advice he had been given. It would not
take long. If he was an office worker, he would learn that most of the
overseas branches of German firms recruited through their main offices
in Germany and that the remainder, and the independent houses, had
already at their disposal an immense pool of experienced Spanish-
speaking employees. The agronomist who fancied that his German
training would be heavily in demand was quickly disabused of the
notion: so long as land and transport facilities were available for extensive cultivation, and cheap labor for production, forwarding, and
processing, investment in technical innovation was an unnecessary
luxury.

Indeed, the holder of any professional or technical degree was already in difficulties. He was informed that first, in the public bureaucracy, Argentine nationals enjoyed preference for any openings
requiring such credentials and, second, in order to practice his profession legally in any case, he would first have to have his degree "revalidated" by Argentine examiners. This stricture would not apply if he
were a national of one of those countries with which Argentina had
signed treaties guaranteeing reciprocal treatment of professional de-

grees, but, as it happened, Germany (like most of the European nations) was not among those countries. Thus a pharmacist, for example, would learn that he was obliged to sit the equivalent Argentine examinations (in Spanish) and to pay an examination fee of some one thousand pesos.[23] The immense worth of a contract negotiated from Germany suddenly became apparent to him, for under Basic Law 4416 of the year 1904 exemptions from revalidation were made for persons contracted by public authorities or by firms holding public contracts. Under a decision of the assessor general in 1913, moreover, such individuals might continue to exercise their professions in Argentina after expiry of the original contract.[24] The varieties of chicanery open to both *criollo* officials and private employers can safely be left to the imagination. In any case, the immigrant's education was proceeding apace; he would have acquired an inkling of what was implied by the dictum of the Association of German Engineers in 1924 that, in the bitter competition for employment, "personal characteristics" were more important for success than "professional competence."[25]

As the days and weeks passed without employment, his resources would inevitably grow thin. His deteriorating situation was more likely to provoke merriment than sympathy among established oldtimers. In a less-than-endearing passage, A. E. Gross outlined the stages of the decline of the immigrant. During their first weeks in Buenos Aires, he wrote, the Germans were famous for appearing in incredible uniforms inspired by the writings of Karl Mai (an immensely popular author of the time, perpetrator of the American adventures of Old Shatterhand) —condor-hunting outfits, hung with tools for building jungle palisades—topped off by a pith helmet or, more likely, a small green felt hat, with feather. His initial inquiries having turned up nothing much, the newcomer might well place an advertisement in the German language newspapers:

> Intelligent young German, fine elegant appearance, tall slender
> stature, of fine family and rich experience of life, musical training;
> formerly active in the largest German concerns as leading director
> (department head, et cetera), seeks appropriate contacts.

No result. In the third stage, therefore, he would make his pilgrimage to the pawnshop district in order to liquidate his hotel bill. Some of his meager remaining capital might then be invested in another advertisement:

> Serious young German, willing to undertake any work, seeks mod-

est position (no expectations) as domestic tutor, kitchen helper, piano player, dishwasher, waiter, *mucamo*.

Still no result; so the fourth stage would find him giving his temporary Buenos Aires address as the "park hotel" on the Paseo de Julio or as "somewhere in the bank district" (*Bank* in German also translates as park bench) or staying with "Mother Green." Mercifully, Gross did not extend his fantasy beyond this point.[26]

At this point, in fact, the immigrant of bourgeois origin and pretensions found himself in a cruel dilemma. Common sense dictated that he avoid the brutalizing conditions of rural vagrancy and remain in the city, close to welfare agencies and possible employment. "At all costs [such persons] must remain in the city and consider themselves lucky when they find sustenance as dishwashers or commissionaires—at that, it can come to bitter starvation and begging," wrote one informed commentator.[27] On the other hand, however, such desperate recourses generated further difficulties:

> With heavy, often dirty, physical labor the clothing and the entire external appearance soon begin to suffer. This is a disadvantage which in this country cannot be overestimated. In Germany one has no idea of the importance that attaches to clothing and general appearance everywhere in South America. Someone who applies for a modestly elevated position—if only the lowest clerkship in an office—has no prospect whatsoever, despite the best credentials, if his appearance causes him to give the impression of someone come down in the world. It sounds absurd, but here, truly, a sharp trouser crease which sits well is worth more than a good reference. Nor should anyone in Germany believe . . . that the position in which one works makes no difference for career and getting on in the world. Here in Argentina it is *not* a matter of indifference that someone has worked as a common laborer, or dishwasher, or *peón*. In the local German colony and business world, everyone knows everyone else, and someone who has worked in a menial job finds his way toward a better position barred at most of the local firms.[28]

Such men, it was frequently observed, were as likely to continue downward as to rise. Many ended as derelicts—*atorrantes*—by no means an uncommon phenomenon in Buenos Aires.[29] Others returned to the Hotel de Inmigrantes, signed on as *internados*, and made use of the free trip to the interior.

Their wanderings took them over much of the republic. There was work in the Comodoro Rivadavia oilfields, unrelenting physical labor in a raw outpost on the desolate South Atlantic coast. For those who survived the first six months, there was a free trip to Buenos Aires. All too often this ended in an uproarious binge at the end of which the worker, groggy and lighter in the pocket than he had planned, found no alternative but to head south again for another six months. A few went north, to the sugar plantations and lumber camps of Tucumán and Salta, but the North had an unsavory reputation for its lethal climate and brutal police. Merely to have survived a season in the North was something of a triumph; the *Neue Deutsche Zeitung* carried news in 1923 of a band of comrades who had walked almost a thousand kilometers back to Buenos Aires along the railroad line.[30] There was work in the stone quarries of the Sierra de Córdoba, on the riverboats, in the railway shops of the interior junction towns, on railway section gangs, in the lumbercamps of Misiones. A *Landstreicher* could usually find temporary work or a handout in the Germanic farming settlements of Misiones or Entre Ríos or the Río Negro Valley or around the rough mountain town of San Carlos de Bariloche; some of the vagabonds became skilled small-time confidence men who migrated through most of the rural German-speaking communities of the republic.[31]

A more stable sort of rural employment was available to the middle-class immigrant who had gone luckless in Buenos Aires, that of village schoolteacher—or, as it was called in the German adaptation of the corrupt Anglo-Argentine version of Spanish, *Kamplehrer*. To be sure, the pay and emoluments were not princely. Like the pastor, the schoolmaster was put up in the homes of the farmers, a couple of weeks in each in turn. He was obliged, of course, to release the schoolchildren for the harvest; he had frequently to help with the harvest himself. In lieu of pay he might receive the use of a plot of land, which he worked himself. Sensitive to what he took to be the condescending mockery of the peasants, embittered by the outrageous fate that had abandoned him in the back of beyond, the *Kamplehrer* was also given to such periodic sprees in Buenos Aires as he could afford. According to Wilhelm Keiper—who like most of the German educators in Buenos Aires was scandalized and dismayed by the *Kamp* schools—about 140 of the 200 German language schools in existence in the republic in 1933 employed only "pick-up" teachers.[32]

Some of the hardier *Landstreicher* followed the harvest. One C. Lewin, who had lost a farmstead near Esperanza (Santa Fe Province) after six years of labor, joined the harvesters for several seasons toward the end of the war; he left a powerful brief memoir. He could no more than suggest the heat, fatigue, and mindlessness of harvest labor; he described in greater detail the food, the laborer's staples of *puchero*, *galletas*, and *mate*, to be wolfed down as quickly as possible; the confrontations with corrupt domineering foremen; knifefights, petty thievery, the occasional rape, and other major and minor brutalities. When the harvest came to an end in one district, the harvesters were paid off quickly and harried out of town, on occasion by police and armed citizens. In their hundreds they swarmed aboard freight trains, where a common pastime was to raid winecasks in shipment from San Juan and Mendoza to the coastal cities. The authorities had attempted to combat this by sheathing in metal the carriages in which the wine was shipped, but it did little good; the *linyeros* simply took augers to the bottom of the cars. (Their trail was easy to follow; the wagons they broached left a red streak between the rails for miles.) As a further corrective the railways had taken to arming the train crews, and shootings had become common. Lewin was particularly harsh on his German countrymen whom he encountered in his wanderings. He found them an embarrassment to Argentine *Deutschtum* and felt that, should they ever make their way back to Europe, they would there only strengthen "the criminal classes and the *Lumpenproletariat*." He portrays himself as a brand plucked providentially from the burning, but how this happened and what became of him are unknown.[33]

In 1926 Karl von Zitzgewitz, who, as an official of the Volksbund's counseling center had observed from close up the postwar flux and reflux of immigrants and had involved himself in passing with thousands of them, gave way to a cry of agonized compassion uncommon for the times and circumstances: "how many Germans who have found no work disappear yearly in the undertow of the metropolis, or, filthy and ragged, come to an ignoble end as poor miserable tramps wandering over the Argentine provinces—there are no statistics for this."[34] As a matter of fact there were statistics, of a sort: the lists of immigrants for whom mail was being held at the Volksbund or the Argentine Poste Restante, the Association for the Protection of Germanic Immigrants' annual tabulations of the thousands of letters forwarded (or not forwarded), the occasional advertisements in the German language newspapers in which the consulate, at the behest of relatives at home, requested information "concerning the whereabouts of . . ."[35]

The more general reaction to the postwar immigration was hostility, which took many forms. In the aftermath of the German Revolution a great fear swept through the community, fear that German Argentina would now be exposed to the bearers of the plague-bacilli of spartakism, socialism, bolshevism, and the "new times." Churchmen especially were vociferous in reaction: "Bolsheviks, Communists, Spartakists, all political people, are unwanted. The Germans here are racially good Germans; they do not bother themselves with politics, they want to know nothing of politics" (Pastor Bühler of Colonia Monte Carlos); "the Argentine Germans are willing to help, but only those who perform [*etwas taugen*]. The rest they let fall by the wayside. Unfortunately the latter form the majority" (Pastor Babick of the Buenos Aires congregation); "by far the majority are remarkably demanding, arrogant, godless, and deeply infected by socialism and bolshevism" (the Jesuit Max von Lassberg).[36] In other writers there was less concern for the moral health of the community than for German prestige in the eyes of the Argentines: "I have regretted that, through the medium of some Germans who now come to South America and express their discontent here, numerous entirely false and much too unfavorable impressions of Germany are circulated. This is in no way useful" (a prominent business source in Buenos Aires, August 1920).[37]

Many of the complaints about the newcomers, however, were merely restatements of well-worn themes. The immigrants thought they "knew better" than the Argentines or German-Argentines. They felt themselves too good for many jobs; their expectations in terms of standard of living were too high (the German worker demanded "a bed, a decent cold supper, and a bottle of beer"; but, if he wishes "to compete with the Latin or Yugoslavian worker, he must temporarily retreat to a culture level that lies far behind us").[38] It had to be admitted that German employers preferred Italian or other non-German workers and colonists. Concerning colonization projects it was reported early in 1920: "the members of the German colony have little interest in this, since most of them have had bad experiences with countrymen. Many who come here have not yet had it hard enough; many are thoroughly unreliable and bring the worst characteristics of the new times over with them." Later the same year, however, the Chamber of Commerce let it be known that local "moneyed circles" were prepared to support colonization—but Italian colonization, not German.[39]

It is difficult to know the extent to which the commonality shared these fearful or contemptuous views. Obviously, the newcomers represented economic competition and thus a threat to an already weakened position; nevertheless, resentment was almost never verbalized in plain economic terms. Some of it, surely, took the form of the heavy malicious humor of an A. E. Gross. In more reflective moments, however, old settlers could not help feeling that the community had undergone a violent reversal of fortune in 1914 and little but change and uncertainty since then—of this, the newcomers were the outward signs if not the cause. But it was also evident that the newcomers themselves were victims of a world knocked askew—that is, of the postwar impotence of the Fatherland. It was, in fact, all very confusing.

The newcomers, it scarcely needs be said, reciprocated the hostility. The Argentine-Germans, in their view, had managed to combine the social conservatism, propensity for cliquishness and backbiting, and smallness of vision of the old German pre-1871 extreme provinciality—*Kleinstaaterei*—with what they took to be the worst features of the *criollo* character. Goldschmidt on the Monarchists: "the Kaiser Loyalists say that they are loyal to the monarchy because the Argentine bourgeoisie fears the Revolution. In other words, they are not at all loyal to the kaiser; they want only to render service unhindered [to the Argentines]—in other words, a small life." On the Argentine-Germans generally: "they are not overseas-Germans, but 'inland-Germans.' . . . They are not part of the world when they are overseas, they are in their 'circle.' . . . They remain by themselves, but not because they want a closed racial community, but rather because they are unable to participate [in the larger society]. And they are unable to participate because they cannot conceive of others—criticize them, yes, but not conceive of them."[40]

Others of the newcomers, however, found it easier to believe that the Argentine-Germans had acquired their less attractive characteristics from overlong exposure to *lo criollo*, rather than (as Goldschmidt suggests) from too little. How else to explain their proclivity for speculation (rather than iron energy), for personal intrigue and ingratiation (rather than technical competence), for corrupt business practices (rather than honesty)? How else to account for the hypocrisy that lay in the contrast between the community leaders' bombastic adherence to the old Germanic virtues and national feeling and their aloofness toward, and exploitation of, their newly arrived countrymen?

For fundamentally the resentment of the newcomers derived from the varieties of rebuff they had suffered at the hands of the old settlers. Further, if the business community's elite had on occasion expressed heavy-handedly its preference for Italian and other Southern European workingmen, newcomers for their part were often open in their admiration for the British community, or what they took to be the more positive qualities of the British community. The point was not too well disguised in Walter Stölting's claim that, "when someone knocks on the door and says, 'Civis britannicus sum,' the simple fact that he is a British subject suffices to get him a position right away."[41] Theodor Alemann, though realistic in his appraisal of the chances for newcomers, was nevertheless sympathetic and used his personal influence to aid many. He was aware that the British imperial system (of which Argentina was informally a part) gave them certain advantages in this respect, but he too believed that the British were far more efficient and humane in their treatment of their immigrants.[42] Once again, this admiration (tinged with envy) of the British was nothing new in the German community. In the 1880s Schnabl reported the general belief that an Englishman seldom came to La Plata *auf gut Glück* and that there seemed always to be a position open when a compatriot needed it. Only Englishmen were employed in English trading houses, and at every rank they were better paid than their German counterparts. In the British community, "even the least significant person is somebody."[43]

The third piece of advice that the immigrant received gratis was *Umlernen*—"retrain yourself." In one sense, this urged nothing more than the acquisition of new skills and occupations. It should be unnecessary by now to belabor the point: most workers, even the most highly skilled, and virtually all middle-class immigrants except those on contract were compelled to work for varying lengths of time in trades other than those in which they had been trained; many professionally trained persons never exercised their profession. This was especially psychologically devastating to immigrants of middle-class background, for the value of schooling that at middle- and lower-bourgeois levels might well have demanded considerable material sacrifice was now set at nought. Work itself was reduced to its lowest common denominator, and the advantage lay with the most adaptable. Middle-class Germans could not but envy, and resent, the German worker, whose relative success in the Argentina of the 1920s has been noted. But by the same token there was envy as well as contempt among German artisans toward the simple Mediterranean or Slavic worker, whose needs as well as whose muscles were infinitely conformable to the demands of this new land. The effects of the *Umlernen* requirement were, one may suggest, of far-reaching significance, for in Wilhelmian Germany occupation was the cornerstone of self-identification in the order of things and of one's social status among one's fellows. The Germans, confronted in Argentina with the overriding need of *Umlernen*, with the destruction of all the supports and signposts that occupation should supply, fell into even greater personal and social disorientation than their already unpromising material circumstances might have occasioned.

But there was a broader psychological dimension to *Umlernen*—nothing less than the requirement to make oneself a new person. Few

immigrants anywhere can have a clear idea of the personality transformations they will have to make (or that will take place unrecog-
nized). However, seduced by the lingering image of the prewar colony,
among other illusions, the majority of the middle-class German immigrants to Argentina of the 1920s did not conceive that their move
would involve any personality transformations whatever. Rather, they
expected merely to transfer themselves physically to another area of
Germanic culture—a socially secure, prosperous enclave from which
to view an exotic, probably bizarre physical environment and subordinate native culture. (Clearly, the dictum that "every emigrant is in a
sense a dissident" cannot apply when the emigrant conceives his experience in quasi-colonial terms such as these.) But they found that
German Argentina was perhaps more demanding of adaptation to
alien patterns of behavior than they had anticipated. They also found
that the German component of German Argentina—which had not
experienced the war—was in general more socially reactionary than
was tolerable even to those who thought themselves out of sympathy
with the new times of post-1918 Germany; and it was, finally, highly
impermeable by outsiders anyway. At this point the psychological
processes of *Umlernen*—which here means, in fact, Americanization—
began to work more rapidly and often to produce varieties of personal
crisis.

Cissy von Scheele-Willich saw clearly how this operated. For her,
the key to success was *Disponierenkönnen*—"to be able to organize
and coordinate oneself." Her countrymen found this far from easy for,
as noted earlier, she felt they had great difficulty in taking charge of
themselves in an environment of lawlessness, without the support of
institutions of social welfare. People accustomed to a fixed occupation,
wage workers generally, were ill-equipped for the sort of self-reliance
that the Argentine frontier demanded. But the greater question was
"whether one is capable of altering oneself inwardly to meet the new
circumstances." Too many could not forget what they had once had,
never ceased to complain, would not break with "what had been."
Manual labor was "not appropriate to one's social standing." They
propped up status by boasting incessantly of what they had been before and remained obstinately blind to what "this life can give them
as replacement."[44]

In 1938, shortly before retiring to Germany at the age of seventy,
Wilhelm Keiper summed up half a lifetime's experience in La Plata.
The preconditions to survival in Argentina, according to Keiper, were
good health, a clear head, a powerful strength of will. No one should
ever forget for a moment that there was no insurance—against acci-

dent, illness, invalidism—no succor from the state, least of all for foreigners, nor that in Argentina men were free with their elbows and that the only law was the law of the strong. One who fell by the wayside remained at the wayside, and there was no pity to spare for him. This included many Germans "who have been left lying at the fringe of the battle for existence and who have not gotten up again . . . sunken and forgotten." It was, in fact, difficult to remain German in Argentina. A number of Germanic characteristics simply had to be shed: *Gemütlichkeit*, any comfortable geniality, as well as credulity and, indeed, any inclination to easy-naturedness—in short, the entire character of German Mike. One learned to trust himself and his intimates, but no one else ("for they all want something of you"). Being German thus became a private "Sunday feeling" which one might indulge only in the closest circle of family and friends. This is, of course, a close approximation of the *criollo* posture of *desconfianza*.

But there is more than an old man's bitterness to Keiper's summation, for he also concluded, with a chill strength, that in America the Germans lost their pettiness and narrowness of heart. They learned— some of them—to stand on their own feet and to look around them with a broader freer vision.[45] A few had "made America" in the conventional sense, with wealth, a triumphal return to Europe, a comfortable retirement. But in many more cases, and in many more ways, America had made them.

6. Political Conflict, 1919–1929

The political turmoil of 1918–1919 continued with little abatement through the first half of the postwar decade. In rhetoric and party alignments it replicated closely the polarization between the left and right radicalisms of Weimar Germany. Its peculiar intensity, however—even as a number of observers recognized at the time[1]—was due to the manifold stresses within the local community, to which of course it in turn contributed.

On the left, socialist veterans of the popular assembly and their newly arrived comrades from Germany formed a publishing cooperative in September 1919 through which to publish the weekly *Neue Deutsche Zeitung*. Until its demise in 1928 the newspaper served as a working-class counterpart to the older *Deutsche La-Plata Zeitung* and *Argentinisches Tageblatt*, with both of which it remained at daggers drawn. In its early years its administrative board included several Communists; however, the latter were purged in April 1924. It was loosely allied to the Cooperative of the Book Trade and Related Occupations (a broader based organization of the Germans who had been for many years influential in Buenos Aires' publishing industry), to more ephemeral craft unions of German-speaking housepainters and metalworkers, to the German section of the Argentine Communist party, and to the Group of German-speaking Socialists.[2] Later in the decade, the Reichsbanner and the Red Frontline Soldiers' League were added to the list of socialist organizations in Buenos Aires. Although Vorwärts served as the matrix and meetingplace for most of these groups, the association itself was politically inert through most of the decade. The decline in socialist ardor—never notably high since before the turn of the century—was ascribed variously to the bourgeoisification of its leadership and to the emergence of a second and even third generation of Argentine-Germans whose natural organ of political expression was the Argentine Socialist party. Somewhat defensively, Vorwärts' leaders justified its many nonpolitical entertainments as necessary to keep young male immigrants from the "insipid, spirit-killing so-called amusements of the cosmopolitan city of Buenos Aires."[3] Distinctly not within the socialist family was the cantankerous A. E. Gross, who reopened *Die Neue Zeit* in August 1922 and resumed his position as a party-of-one on the left.

Before this time, however, the assassination of Mathias Erzberger in Germany (26 August 1921)—an act described by the *Deutsche La-Plata Zeitung* as "not undeserved"—caused the local supporters of Weimar to close ranks to form a Republican Association against the "Monarchist intrigues." The first meetings, held at Vorwärts, did not afford the Republicans much encouragement, for attendance was low. In December 1921, the association's president, Hans Lindemann, noted with a touch of sarcasm that, "naturally, for the time being a reactionary mood has got to be dominant here, [inasmuch as] all intellectual movements from Europe, and artistic and scientific as well, only slowly find their way here." He added—shrewdly, in retrospect—that the German-Argentines would accept the democratic Weimar Republic only to the degree that *Argentine* democracy developed and grew strong. The immediate problems of the association, however, Lindemann ascribed to the pressure that monarchist employers had been bringing to bear on their employees to prevent them from joining: "unfortunately, the evil habit of attempting to injure one's countrymen economically because of their political opinions is all too common among the Germans here."[4]

Not long afterward, however, Theodor Alemann was persuaded to lend his name and prestige to the republican executive committee; soon the Republican Association came to include most of the *Tageblatt*'s editorial staff and the moderate faction of 1918–1919. Alemann later wrote that the Republican Association would have been unnecessary except for the "regrettable *Fronde*" among the Buenos Aires Germans, "the hangers-on of the Old Regime."[5] Thus one of the major projects of the Republican Association was the publication and distribution of pro-Weimar pamphlets among the German-Argentines.

Another objective was to demonstrate to Germany's diplomatic emissaries that not all the overseas Germans were bitter-end Monarchists. This touched a sore spot, as the attitudes of the diplomats themselves were highly ambiguous. As a socialist writer put it, "the best supporters of the German Monarchists are . . . a large number of propertied men among the overseas Germans. But these men are understandable, while the complaisant officials of the German Republic who associate with them are not."[6] It was noted that, as late as 25 May 1920, the Argentine national holiday, the German embassy, under the newly arrived chargé d'affaires, Dr. Olshausen, had been decked out in the imperial black-white-red bunting and that Ambassador Adolf Pauli, who arrived in Buenos Aires in December 1920, had been present at the Monarchists' German Day observation the following month but had been unwilling to attend or endorse the founding meetings of the

Republican Association. In time, however, the association was successful to the extent that Dr. Pauli was persuaded to show public support for the government he represented. By November 1922, celebrations of the anniversary of the republic—held in the Swiss House in Buenos Aires—were attended by 500 persons, including the German ambassador and his staff.[7]

On the right, there were few distinctions between the local Kaiser Loyalists and those who began to arrive with the postarmistice resumption of communications. As A. E. Gross put it, the latter were "not orphaned" by the former, to whom, perforce, the anti-Weimar émigrés looked for jobs and incomes.[8] The new arrivals were of all degrees of eminence: they ranged from a prewar ambassador to Argentina, von dem Bussche-Haddenhausen, who was well connected in the country (he had married Eleonora Martínez de Hoz some twenty years before), to *Freikorps* veterans and political gunmen on the run from the German police.[9] Two of the Germans' most influential *criollo* collaborators of wartime were now in strategic positions to aid the local Right. One was Juan P. Ramos, sometime dean of the Law Faculty of the University of Buenos Aires and a pro-German pamphleteer during the war years; later, in the 1930's, he would become prominent in Argentine right-radical circles.[10] As director of immigration in the early 1920s he was able to facilitate the entry of German rightists and, as will be seen, on a number of occasions to hinder or bar the entry of known German leftists.

The second was General José F. Uriburu, a protégé of the pre-1914 German training mission and outspoken supporter in military circles of the cause of the Central Powers; in September 1930 he would command the military coup that ended fourteen years of civilian Radical administration. As inspector general of the army, Uriburu found advisory positions and other employment for former *Reichswehr* officers, some of whom—Faupel, von Luecken, Kretzschmar, von Colditz, Perrinet von Thauvenay—had served in the pre-1914 training cadres.[11] Faupel was Uriburu's special advisor until his departure and replacement by the more equable Kretzschmar in 1926.[12] He was also the most politically active of the exofficers in the right-wing circles of the German-speaking community. In Buenos Aires he left no trace of the anticlericalism and other "left-wing nazi" tendencies he would reveal a dozen years later as Hitler's envoy to Francisco Franco's nationalist regime during the Spanish Civil War.[13] A large number of other exofficers were placed by the ubiquitous former naval attaché, Moller, who from mid-1920 to late 1922 operated the Officers' Counseling Center as the agent of CATE/CHADE, the banks, and a number of monarchist commercial houses. To be considered by Moller, exofficers were required to possess a command of Spanish, low financial expectations, a clearance from the Reich Job Placement for Officers (RANO), and "political conformity [*eine politische einwandfreie Gesinnung*]." This last was especially important, for Moller admitted darkly that "mistakes" had been made.[14] Wilhelm Herzog's communist informants told him in 1923 that exofficers had also been well received in Argentine police formations; this is not inherently improbable. In 1921, in fact, the Association for the Protection of Germanic Immigrants placed the remarkable total of seventy-five immigrants as policemen.[15]

Right-wing political organizations proliferated: to the old-line Army League (1895) and Navy League (1914), of which Emil Hayn was president after 1922, were added the Stahlhelm and Tannenbergbund (ca. 1924), the Black-White-Red Association (ca. 1922–1923), and the Buenos Aires local of the German National Racialist party (Deutsch-Nationale Volkspartei) (1923). Although national socialist sentiments were common among the postwar immigrants, there was no local organization of the NSDAP at this time. As the affair of Colin Ross would show (see below), the anticapitalist rhetoric, populist social policy, and unpredictable radicalism of the early nazis were unsettling to the local traditionalists and the movement would be held at arm's length until 1931.

However, of greater long-term significance than the purely political sects was the pervasive influence of the Monarchists in the executive committees of the community's manifold nonpolitical associations. These included the German Hospital, the Evangelical congregation— even the Church and its parish weekly are "Hitlerized [*verhitlert*]," wrote the pseudonymous "Hermit" in the *Neue Deutsche Zeitung* in 1924[16]—and most of the school governing associations. In 1926 the author of the "People's League without People" series in the same journal charged the *Geld-Aristokratie* with having dominated virtually all the community's institutions. He wrote elegiacally that, aside from Vorwärts and its affiliates, of the prewar associations only the Eintracht musical society, the Masonic lodge Teutonia, and the two sickness insurance funds had retained their pre-1914 independence and social purposes.[17]

One of the two principal agencies through which the monarchist elite extended its hold on the community's voluntary associations was the Volksbund. The latter's building at Calle Moreno 1059 housed the offices of the two German language employment agencies that it controlled and, by 1930, no fewer than fifteen other associations, including the German Welfare Society and the German Scientific Society; and it could make space available for the meetings of many more.[18] The other, and more important, was the Council of Executive Committees, which remained the community's executive organ after war's end. To some irreverent spirits, this was merely the capstone of the joinerism to which the community was notoriously addicted; as events would show, however, its capacity to make and enforce policy was formidable. Its power was above all economic. Diverse factors—the proliferation of German language neighborhoods and of the voluntary associations necessary to service them, inflation, and increased demand for social services—drove the community's budget above one million pesos per year by 1929.[19] In the same years, however, the ability of the commonality to support these private institutions at prewar levels declined sharply. Thus their principal financial support came from the great trading houses, investment consortia, utilities, and manufacturing concerns. Not surprisingly, then, the traditionalist, monarchist views of the *Geld-Aristokratie* prevailed in all but a few of the executive committees, the culmination of the trend that Theodor Alemann had seen as early as 1920.

In the early postwar era the council propagandized heavy-handedly: denunciations of the Versailles peace and of Allied attempts to try alleged German war criminals, birthday greetings to the kaiser and Hindenburg, propagation of the stab-in-the-back thesis which sought to shift responsibility for Germany's defeat in 1918 from the army to civilian politicians and disloyal left-wing and pacifist agitators. It assumed responsibility, too, for organization of the elaborate annual German Day or Imperial Founding Day festivities on January 18. In 1922, Ernst Alemann, representing the *Argentinisches Tageblatt*, was hauled to judgment and censured for the newspaper's criticism of the blatantly monarchist tenor of that year's observances. At about the same time, Vorwärts and the Republican Association were denied representation altogether on the grounds that they were, after all, "political" associations.[20]

Beginning in 1921, the council decreed that only the black-white-red colors of the empire would be displayed at the German Day observances. Both the *Tageblatt* and the *Neue Deutsche Zeitung* protested, demanding that the black-red-gold of the republic also be shown. The protests were ignored and the celebration went off as scheduled. It was attended, as the pro-Weimar press noted indignantly, by the German ambassador, Dr. Pauli. The flag question thereafter became a major irritant within the community, finding expression in many ways but reaching its annual peak every January with the recurrence of German Day. The Monarchists did everything within their power to make the event a mass outpouring of loyalty. The community's bands played the traditional marches of the Old Germany and ex-officers wore their uniforms again; athletic competitions were held; the children of the community's schools were drawn up in massed uniformed ranks; distinguished visitors from Germany or eminences from within the Buenos Aires community orated at length. Nothing, however, could alter the fact that German Day fell at the height of the Argentine summer, when most persons in a position to do so abandoned Buenos Aires for the seaside or *sierra*. The Monarchists were therefore obliged to inflate attendance figures, and these were then gleefully derided by the pro-Weimar press.[21]

A less innocuous imbroglio grew out of the flag question in September 1922: the war memorial affair. The Army League had verified the names of 156 men of the community killed in battle from 1914 to 1918 and proceeded with plans to erect a monument within the grounds of the German Cemetery. The Monarchists warned Ambassador Pauli (through Moller) that the colors of the republic would not be tolerated. Pauli chose therefore not to attend but felt duty-bound to show the black-red-gold of Weimar in some form. The ceremonies, on Sunday, 3 September, were attended by some 1,500 persons, including a judge of the German high court and former foreign minister, Dr. Simon; a former ambassador to Argentina, von dem Bussche-Haddenhausen; a former consul general, Bobrick; the incumbent consul general, von Sanden; and *Freiherr* von der Goltz of the prewar training mission. Herr Oehrtmann of the Army League unveiled the monument, and it was "received in the name of the community" by ex–Naval Attaché Moller. At some point during the ceremonies, a messenger arrived bearing the ambassador's memorial wreath, trimmed with black-red-gold ribbons. The messenger was seized roughly by several men; a path opened through the crowd; the messenger was thrown bodily out of the cemetery; and the corridor closed again. One Gustav Krause, a bookseller and member of the Army League executive committee, tore the ribbons from the wreath and trampled upon them, to loud approval. This violent outburst became public knowledge and provoked editorial handwringing over the state of German "prestige" in Buenos Aires. The Army League later apologized, grumpily and after a fashion, to Dr. Pauli but made it known that "the ambassador, as a republican functionary, has a false conception of the iron determination of the nationalistic German population of Buenos Aires to remain true to its old colors."[22]

Another source of the continuing strife was the arrival at irregular intervals of prominent Germans identifiable with one or another of the local factions. The first such visitor to arouse the ire of the Right was Colin Ross, member, in November 1918, of the Berlin Soldiers' Soviet and now a political journalist. Ross would later align himself with the nazis and become an advisor on Western Hemisphere affairs to Hitler. In the early months of 1920, however, he was patronized by both the *Tageblatt* group and the Vorwärts Socialists as a spokesman for the New Germany. He was given a wide hearing through public lectures and numerous articles in the Spanish and German language press. The following year, on a second visit to Buenos Aires, about which little information has survived, he was one of the few foreign journalists ever granted a personal interview with the reclusive Argentine president, Hipólito Yrigoyen.[23]

In 1920, Ross described himself as a Socialist and a supporter of the Ebert regime. He had opposed the Spartakists in 1918–1919—but now wondered aloud whether he had been correct to do so. His political concepts in 1920 were an amalgam of socialism, populism, and authoritarianism, and they clearly prefigure his subsequent drift to national socialism. In Buenos Aires he insisted that the monarchist old regime was extinct in Germany, but he acknowledged that monarchist sentiment nevertheless had, somehow, to be conciliated. The Socialists, too, had cause to be disenchanted with the Weimar regime, for so far it had failed to realize major socialist objectives, particularly division of the great Junker estates, expropriation of large personal fortunes, and justice for veterans and victims of the war. Ross insisted, however, that these shortcomings were attributable to the vindictiveness of the Allies, to the harshness of the Versailles peace, and above all to the divisiveness among the Germans themselves. By implication, the Weimar system was incapable of overcoming these handicaps; the solution lay, rather, in a reunification of the German people by means of a nationalist and socialist dictatorship, headed by an indomitable *Führer* and supported and guided by a strong and socially progressive army.[24] This ideology—amazingly—won the approval of the pro-Weimar factions in Buenos Aires; the *Tageblatt* took exception only to the militarist strain in Ross' thinking; the *Neue Deutsche Zeitung* characterized him as "pure humane social-thinking."[25]

The local Right, too, adopted a cool civility toward Ross, and he was engaged to speak before the German Scientific Society and other traditionalist associations. He did not get an opportunity to do so, however, for in March 1920 he denounced the Kapp Putsch in Berlin and insisted that any agreement between Ebert and Kapp would betray the German working class. The Monarchists thereupon boycotted his final appearance in Buenos Aires. Ross traveled shortly afterward to

Santiago, where he was arrested and later deported by the Chilean authorities as a "Bolchevik" agitator. He was denounced to the police in Chile by German right-wing groups there, but few doubted that the latter had been alerted by their coreligionists in Buenos Aires.[26]

Soon afterward, during the winter musical season of 1920, the eminent conductor Felix von Weingärtner arrived in Buenos Aires to direct the first performance ever of Wagner's *Parsifal* at the Teatro Colón. Weingärtner in 1917 had subscribed publicly to the peace movement within Germany; in retaliation for this breach of loyalty he was denounced by the local German Right, and his performances at the Colón were boycotted.[27] It was, however, the last incident of this sort, for the Council of Executive Committees was brought to realize that the great achievements of German music could win among the musically sophisticated Argentine elite a more generalized admiration for things German. The sensibleness of this view was borne out by the enthusiasm that greeted the prestigious figures of German music—Richard Strauss, Artur Nikisch, Lotte Lehmann, Fritz Reiner, Erich Kleiber, Otto Klemperer, Fritz Busch, among others—who spent one or more seasons in Buenos Aires during the decade.[28] By 1922, even Weingärtner, on a second visit, met with the "correct" cordiality of the elite circles of the German community. The warm reception by influential *criollos* of the German musical programs and performers led to an expansion of the cultural propaganda. In 1922 the Institución Cultural Argentino-Germana was founded to further this work by means of exhibitions, student exchanges, and lecture tours by prominent German artists and scientists. Its first president was Raúl Beruti who, like Uriburu and Ramos, had published pro-German pamphlets during the war.[29]

Lesser mortals obnoxious to the German Right were dealt with more harshly, for Juan B. Ramos, in his capacity as director of immigration, had wide discretionary powers in interpreting the already draconian antiradical legislation of the Argentine government as it applied to nonnationals. Among those who suffered Ramos' harassment were Professors Georg Friedrich Nicolai and Alfons Goldschmidt, who arrived in Buenos Aires aboard the steamer *Köln* in April 1922 to begin series of lectures for which they had been contracted by the University of Córdoba. Nicolai was an eminent philologist of the University of Berlin who had created a stir in 1914 by refusing to sign the scientists' manifesto in support of German war aims; later he had acted upon his views by going into exile in Denmark. Goldschmidt was a less well known Marxist economist. There had in fact been warnings of trouble well before they left Germany. When they attempted to disembark at Buenos Aires, they were detained by the immigration authorities and would have been deported forthwith but for the personal intervention of the rector of the University in Córdoba. On their release they were feted by the Republicans at Vorwärts and Aue's Keller and then left for Córdoba to take up their academic duties. Goldschmidt, in particular, aroused the continuing animosity of the German Right and of Argentine conservatives, an animosity shot through with anti-Semitism. He cut short his stay in 1923 and returned to Germany to write an ill-tempered memoir of his Argentine experience.[30]

The German communist writer Wilhelm Herzog was even less fortunate in his dealings with Ramos. Herzog, accompanied by his mistress, Sascha Witkowski, arrived in Buenos Aires aboard the Norddeutscher Lloyd steamer *Sierra Nevada* in September 1923. Herzog and Miss Witkowski were arrested aboard ship at dockside in Buenos Aires, together with a German businessman named Happe, a fellow passenger whose only delinquency, so far as was ever determined, was to have played chess with Herzog during the four-week voyage. The three were taken ashore and jailed for nine days at Ramos' disposition, part of the time incommunicado. The matter became a short-lived cause célèbre within the German-speaking community, and in the left-wing Argentine press as well. Both the Socialists and the *Tageblatt* group intervened on the prisoners' behalf, and Ernst Alemann succeeded in obtaining a writ of habeas corpus from a liberal-minded judge. Before the writ could be served on Ramos, however, the latter ended the matter summarily by organizing a police task force, removing the three prisoners from detention, and depositing them aboard *Teutonia* of the Hamburg-Amerika Line, which was in the process of weighing anchor for European ports. Herzog claimed that Ramos' agents, in order to substantiate an ex post facto charge of illegal entry, had crudely forged his visa while it was in their possession to alter the destination to Chile rather than Argentina.[31]

Of all such incidents, however, one which provoked little uproar at the time had perhaps the longest reverberations among the thoughtful members of the community. This was the snubbing, aggravated by a whispered anti-Semitic campaign, of the physicist Albert Einstein by the "pace-setting circles" of the community during his stay in Buenos Aires early in 1925. Einstein had been invited to Argentina by the University of Buenos Aires and was received by Argentine academics with great acclaim. As one socialist writer noted caustically, however, neither the German Scientific Society nor any other "respectable" organization accorded welcome to the man often termed the greatest of living German scientists, for the "hurrah-patriots" were simultaneously occupied with the visit of Admiral Paul Behnke, one of the commanders at Jutland, chief of the German naval staff from 1920 to 1924, and one of the architects, with Gustav Krupp and General Hans von Seekt, of Germany's secret rearmament.[32]

In January 1922 it was announced that General Erich Ludendorff would come to Argentina in the near future on the invitation of the Argentine politician Horacio Oyhanarte. Ludendorff's travel plans included a swing through Patagonia, a region that had long been of interest to German promoters of agricultural colonies and, more recently, to German oilmen. The French language *Courrier de La Plata* immediately announced the opposition of the French community to Ludendorff's visit. Somewhat chagrined at this, the Republican Association and other pro-Weimar organizations nevertheless made it known that they, too, would express their disapproval publicly. News of cancellation of the visit was made public in May 1922. Although Ludendorff's reasons for dropping the project remain unknown, it was assumed that the Monarchists were unwilling to risk exposure before Argentine opinion of the deep detestation in which Ludendorff was held by German Republicans—not to mention French, British, Italian, and other ethnic groups with ties to the former Allied Powers.[33]

With this exception, however, the parade of right-wing eminences through the elite circles of the German community during the course of the decade was long and impressive. It included the Zeppelin expert, Dr. Hugo Eckener, ex–Crown Princess Cecilie of Hohenzollern, with her sons Friedrich Georg and Louis Ferdinand (the latter of whom resided for several years in Argentina), such industrialists as Peter Klöckner and Fritz Thyssen, Generals Litzmann, Kress von Kressenstein, and Heye (in his capacity as chief of the *Reichswehr* in 1928), and conservative politicians such as Simon and ex-Chancellor Hans Luther. Luther's visit in late 1926 is worthy of some note because of the light it sheds on the political predilections of the local Right in the latter half of the decade. Luther's German National Racialist party had already won a sizable following in Buenos Aires since the founding of a local in 1923, and Luther's personal popularity had also grown great among the Monarchists through his role in the promulgation of the decree permitting the old black-white-red flag of the empire to be flown aboard German ships and elsewhere outside Germany. During his stay in Buenos Aires, Luther was the guest of honor at a special mass rally at the exposition grounds of the Sociedad Rural (31 October 1926). Later, at a banquet honoring Luther at the Deutscher Klub shortly before his departure from Argentina, Eduard Bromberg, sometime president of the Chamber of Commerce, declaimed, "the most heartfelt wish of us overseas Germans is . . . that in the foreseeable future the will of the German people will again elevate you, Excellency, to be their leader."[34] There is no reason to doubt that, at the time, Bromberg expressed a strong, possibly majority sentiment within the local Right.

The climax of postwar political strife within the community had already been reached and passed in 1924–1925 with the bald attempt of the Kaiser Loyalists to destroy the *Argentinisches Tageblatt* by means of an economic boycott. As Hans Lindemann had noted, the application of economic sanctions to enforce political conformity was by no means uncommon within the community. Dissident journals, such as the *Vorwärts* weekly of the 1880s and 1890s, the *Tageblatt* in 1907 (in retribution for its support of Germany's parliamentary Socialists), and Gross' *Neue Zeit* in the postwar days, had earlier suffered similar harassment. Nevertheless, the immediate motives behind the rightist campaign of 1924 remain unclear. Theodor Alemann recognized that it grew out of confrontations dating back to the popular assembly of 1918 but felt that an especial irritant to the Right had been his editorial "Non-Party Overseas Germans" of 20 April 1923, almost a year before. In the editorial, Alemann had declared adherence to the German Republic to be the *duty* of overseas Germans. He referred, not too obliquely, to "undisciplined" local Germans and reiterated an earlier assertion: "he who refuses to obey the laws of the Fatherland is the partisan."[35] By the standards of local political discourse, it was mild enough reproof.

He was certainly correct, however, in tracing another root of the trouble to the dispatches that the *Tageblatt* had been publishing from its special correspondent in Germany, the Spanish Socialist Julio Alvarez del Vayo.[36] Alvarez del Vayo's attitude toward Weimar was clearly one of approval. In a reflective essay, "After Five Years," printed in the *Tageblatt* on 9 November 1923, he characterized the republic as "the will of the German people" and indeed, in the circumstances, as its "last hope." He put the matter in this emphatic form because he was simultaneously filing reports from Munich on the Bavarian separatist movement and the attempted Putsch of 8–9 November (the "Bavarian tragicomedy"). His scarcely veiled denunciations of Kahr, Ludendorff, and their "errand-boy" Hitler were repeated in equally forceful language in *Tageblatt* editorials. In February 1924 Alvarez del Vayo began reporting, in the same vein, the trial of the conspirators in Munich.[37]

A year earlier, in 1923, however, the socialist press had claimed that the Right was seeking to silence all voices of dissent, or "radicalism," in order to present to the outside world, and in particular to potential

German investors in Argentina, the appearance of a German-speaking community thoroughly orthodox and committed to the old order. This assertion was apparently not taken seriously by the Alemanns at the time. Once the boycott began, however, Theodor Alemann expanded upon these charges in his own indictment of the local Right.[38] The active organizers of the plot were ex–Naval Attaché August Moller and Volksbund President Emil Hayn.[39] Moller had industriously made the rounds of monarchist firms to urge them to withdraw their advertising from the *Tageblatt* on the lapse of their current contracts on the first of April. He was accompanied by one Alfred Pass, an official of the local branch of the German National Racialist party, and by the *Syndicus* of the German Chamber of Commerce, A. Ramm-Doman. The presence of the latter lent weight to Moller's threat that a firm's noncompliance with the boycott could lead to "certain consequences."[40] The cancellations were to have taken the *Tageblatt* by surprise, but the plot was exposed prematurely through the indiscretions of one ex-*Korvettenkapitän* von Koschnitzsky, an associate of Moller; and on 28 February Theodor Alemann published the first of a series of front page editorials in what was for him highly charged language.

Alemann's sense of having been betrayed caused him to drop the magnanimous restraint of his political behavior since 1918. Drawing upon his own knowledge and his great range of friendships and contacts within the community, he laid bare the principal intrigues and maneuvers of the local Right since the end of the war. These included the capture and (as he saw it) the subversion of the Volksbund in 1919; the Ross, Nicolai/Goldschmidt, and Herzog affairs; Moller's role in the transmission of funds—including money ostensibly collected for charitable purposes—to secret anti-Weimar organizations, including the groups behind the Rathenau and Erzberger murders; the links between the Buenos Aires Monarchists and their equally reactionary, if less powerful, associates in Chile; and the activities of Faupel in organizing the network of right-wing associations in the city.[41]

The boycott began as scheduled on 1 April when the advertisements of nine large German firms disappeared from the *Tageblatt*'s pages. It continued for well over a year but in the end was simply abandoned. The financial pressure on the newspaper was great but was overcome by drastic economies, the founding of an information and travel bureau ancillary to the publishing operation, and the assistance of its supporters, many of whom reportedly paid subscriptions years in advance. The socialist Left lent its moral support to the *Tageblatt*, although editorialists could not refrain from reminding Alemann that the boycott was the coin in which his years of conciliatory political behavior were being repaid by the Monarchists.[42] Alemann directed a strong appeal for the help to the *Tageblatt*'s rural readers, who were beyond what he termed sarcastically the "good will" of the urban chieftains of business. The response, according to the *Tageblatt*'s editors, was thousands of letters of support from individuals all over the republic as well as votes of confidence from a number of interior locals of the Volksbund which had acted in defiance of their national executive committee.[43]

Theodor Alemann died suddenly on 22 September 1925 at the age of sixty-two. At his death the extent of his private charities, through Masonic and other connections, was made known. This added to the community's sense of its loss of a tie binding it to a more equable and humane past. It is notable that neither during his lifetime nor afterward did any rightist spokesman feel free to attack Alemann personally.[44] Nevertheless, the belief that the "Bonzes" had broken his health and spirit persisted among the commonality.

Coincident with the abandonment of the campaign against the *Tageblatt*, the stridency of political conflict within the community declined markedly; and it would remain low for the next five years. This reflected the restoration of tranquility to Germany in the latter part of the decade. The election of Field Marshal von Hindenburg as Reichspresident following the death of Friedrich Ebert in 1925 and the restoration of the imperial colors to the overseas Germans mollified much of the local Right; the Weimar Republic's survival and its apparent achievement of political stability made it ever more acceptable. In Argentina, this was related, of course, to the prosperity of Weimar at this time and the burgeoning of German-Argentine trade and capital investment; as noted earlier, 1927 was the record year of the interwar period for bilateral commerce. The fetes and rituals of the Right continued but with declining participation. By 1929 enthusiasm for the annual midsummer German Day festivities had ebbed so low that the Council of Executive Committees was forced to reject, with suitable indignation, a proposal that the event include "dancing"—"which would certainly fit well with the taste of the times"—to stimulate the interest of the younger generation.[45]

The internecine feuding on the left also diminished during these years. For unknown reasons the abrasive *Neue Deutsche Zeitung* (simply *Deutsche Zeitung* in its last year) ceased publication in 1928; relations between Vorwärts and the Republican Association were described as "excellent." The scope of the entertainments offered by Vorwärts increased—serious theater and *Schwänke*, New Year's Eve fetes, masked balls, choral groups, steamer trips to Tigre. A branch of Vorwärts was set up in the raw new working-class settlement of Villa

Ballester on the city's remote western rim. It was with a distinct air of smugness that the socialist association announced plans to acquire a recreation area in the countryside (as it would do—*Quinta* La Perlita —in 1932).[46] Numerous eminences—particularly men such as Haas and Keiper associated with the embassy—were invited to speak and attend sessions at Vorwärts. A sizable number of Monarchists also attended the celebrations held there on 11 August 1929 on the tenth anniversary of the Weimar Constitution. On that occasion the socialist executive committee gave as its considered opinion that, "in right-wing circles, the deliberately cultivated rejection of the republic is dying away."[47] But then, 1929 is a vintage year for quotes of this sort.

7. The Social Crisis of the Middle Class, 1918–1933

Many of the community's tormenting multiple transformations since 1914 were beyond the pale of politics. Economic displacement was at the heart of the community's malaise, for the insecurity and lowered income levels to which the commonality had been subjected during the war were perpetuated in the postwar decade. Following the armistice, in fact, its economic situation was worsened by a number of developments. One which affected the large stratum of dependent wage workers and white-collar employees especially sharply was the postwar inflation, which reached its peak in 1920 and subsided only slowly over the following decade.[1] These same groups were the most hard beset by the competition—and subsequent job insecurity and wage cutting—created by the postwar German immigration.

The social concomitant of economic decline was a steady erosion of status in terms of the German language reference group. This, one must assume, was devastating enough to the spirits of those who still observed the prewar commandments to maintain the external signs of a tightly buttoned genteel respectability and to assume personal responsibility or guilt for success or failure.

But economic and social sources of unease were compounded by the growing threat to cultural identity. Heavily in the background lay distant, but deeply felt, historical phenomena: Germany's defeat in the world war, the Treaty of Versailles (particularly its war guilt clauses), Weimar Germany's situation as an enfeebled pariah among the nations; but, more immediately, apprehensiveness concerning the possibility of absorption into *Kreolentum* remained constant among the urban Germans during the postwar decade. For, simultaneously with the economic and social reverses undergone by the commonality, significant numbers of urban *criollos* were rising to income and occupational levels formerly monopolized by European bearers of culture. The extent to which the Germans (and Buenos Aires' other foreign communities) perceived this transformation cannot be determined with any exactitude. As will be noted below, however, it is certain that many individual Germans perceived it most keenly when they found themselves in direct competition for jobs with their *criollo* compeers.

Still another dimension of cultural unease was concern for the future of the community's younger generation. Such concern found expression in the protracted and impassioned debates over the content and purposes of German language education—debates which, in the end, could have no clear resolution; only time would resolve them.

But the general reaction to the growing pressures of assimilation, including those on the schools, was further confused by political considerations. For after 1918 the community's traditionalist elite appropriated unto itself the rhetoric of German nationalism and undertook to hold the community to *Deutschtum*; and, through their command of employment, clientage, welfare, credit, and financial support for the community's institutional structure, by the early 1930s they had achieved at least the appearance of success. However, their nationalistic narrowness left the greater portion of the Volksdeutsch population indifferent, just as their monarchism and authoritarianism alienated Republicans and Socialists. Moreover, their claim to be the bearers of the old Germanic virtues could not fail to ring faintly bogus in view of their ruthless and corrupt business practices, their parvenu social snobbery, and their subordination of the concerns of the hard-pressed Buenos Aires community to the grander interests of German and international capitalism. Thus it is hardly surprising that by the late 1920s the mood of the community was a compound of cynicism, nostalgia, and despair. Nor is it surprising that, when it came, a movement which combined a resurgent German nationalism, a call to re-dedication, a promise of moral renewal—in a word, national socialism —should at first awake a highly positive response.

In this chapter I intend to present the evidence for the social tumult of the decade and attempt to describe the community's social hierarchy as it congealed toward the year 1930. The next chapter will treat of the several issues, particularly the school question, comprised within the overriding phenomenon of assimilation. In the concluding chapter I propose to consider the psychological as well as the organizational aspects of the reception of nazism within the community between 1931 and 1933.

The German language labor market in Buenos Aires was the crucible of the social transformations of the city's German community during the 1920s. The available data shed light not only on the extreme difficulties confronting most immigrants in finding any means of support whatsoever—and hence upon the high reemigration rates of the latter part of the decade—but also on the expedients to which they were forced in order to survive. These expedients demanded of most of them changes in occupation and of a great many—those of middle-class origins above all—a precipitous descent in the socioeconomic order. The odds against escape from such a declassed position were long, moreover, because of the long-term unfavorable market for white-collar skills and because also of deep social prejudices against persons known to have worked with their hands.

A variety of German language placement offices was available in Buenos Aires. Several were occupationally specialized, such as Moller's Officers' Counseling Center, the Seamen's Home, and the several associations of gardeners, waiters, innkeepers, chauffeurs, musicians, schoolteachers, commission-salesmen, and engineers (although the latter announced loftily in 1921 that "job placement scarcely comes into question"). An important agency for office workers was the Deutschnationaler Handlungsgehilfen Verband (German National Business Employees' League), a dependency of the conservative German National Racialist party. Vorwärts did not operate an employment bureau but could offer information and advice to workers. The German and Austro-Hungarian Women's Associations were active in acquiring German-speaking domestic help for their well-to-do members. In the desperate year 1923, even the YMCA, whose head was a German-speaking Netherlander, was recommended to job-seeking immigrants. But the three most important agencies were the German Welfare Society (DWG), the Association for the Protection of Germanic Immigrants (VzSgE), and the counseling center (Beratungsstelle) of the Volksbund. The DWG turned over its employment bureau to the VzSgE in mid-1921, and the latter was in turn absorbed by the Volksbund in 1926–1927. Of these, the VzSgE handled the largest volume of applicants and, through 1925, published the most complete statistics.

Unfortunately it is impossible to distinguish between old settlers and the newly arrived among the ranks of job seekers. Newcomers were undoubtedly the majority; nevertheless, wartime unemployment was only slowly liquidated, and the periodic slumps of the Argentine economy, such as those of 1921, 1926, and late 1929 to early 1933, also threw veteran hands out of work. The statistics are unsatisfactory in other respects also. The VzSgE and the Volksbund were available to non-Germans. Sporadically the VzSgE published breakdowns of the nationalities of its clients, but these data cannot be correlated to occupational categories or income levels. Not all job seekers were permitted even to submit applications, particularly at critical periods. There are no indications of the length of tenure of these jobs; undoubtedly, unskilled workers and *peones*, as well as many other laborers, manual as well as white-collar, held their positions for only short periods.

Table 2 is largely self-explanatory. A number of observations are, however, in order. Although a rough balance existed between supply

TABLE 2. *The German-Speaking Labor Market, 1919–1928*

	1919			)‍
	VzSgE	DWG	VzSgE	D
Occupational categories				
	Applied: 2444		Applied: 269:	
	Placed	Placed	Placed	Pl
Unskilled workers	1693	767	1751	
Semiskilled workers	486	266	736	78:
Skilled workers	372		580	
Seamen	40	—	27	
Agricultural	56	—	65	
Professional and technical	37	25	36	1
Business and office	44	59	57	2
Serving people	723	133	700	
Totals	3451	1250	3952	82
Repeatedly unsuccessful inquiries	—		—	

of and demand for semiskilled and skilled workers, within these large groupings there were serious anomalies. Masons, housepainters, carpenters, and other construction workers found work easily at most times, whereas it proved almost impossible to place bakers and locksmiths. By 1923 the Association for the Protection of Germanic Immigrants and the Volksbund were deeply involved in the business of providing rural properties to farm operators (*Landwirte*). Unfortunately, little evidence has come to light to indicate the destinations of the majority of these people. The clearest evidence of proletarianization appears in the data for placement of serving people. In this category, the Association for the Protection of Germanic Immigrants' figures for the years 1919 through 1921—723, 700, and 844—were already remarkably high; but in 1922, when the association began to supply data also on the declared occupations of the applicants, the point became even more obvious. In that year, no "couples" offered themselves, yet 242 were placed (this total fell short of demand, in fact). Many more persons found themselves working as serving girls and gardeners than had

	1921			1922	
bund ungsstelle une– cember) d	VzSgE	DWG	V'bund B'stelle (excl. August and September)	VzSgE	
	Applied: 2143 Placed		Placed	Applied	Placed
	1572			176	0
	567		43	603	742
	732			956	888
	18			31	41
	97		90	431	1460
	42		207	129	55
	41		27	415	77
	844		130	246	911
	3913	391	497	2987	4174
	—			18,589 (June– December)	

described themselves as such on their applications. Concerning couples, the grim warning was forwarded to Germany that even this desperate expedient was closed to those burdened with minor children.[2] In the following year, 1923, 56 male servants (*Diener*) applied, 132 were placed; 7 couples applied, 214 were placed; 148 serving girls applied, 222 were placed. To this, one correspondent added the curious note that, should all else fail, there was work available "under the heading of servants and couples (*Ehepaare*) so long as it is a question of unmarried people."[3] In 1925, finally, 169 serving girls were identified on applications; during the year, however, there were 447 openings, and ultimately 250 were placed. Comparable figures for male servants were 169 / 273 / 226; and for couples: 24 / 219 / 219.

Still another employment bureau was available to immigrants, that of the Hotel de Inmigrantes. As noted in Chapter Five, the jobs in which immigrants were placed by the Argentine officials were almost without exception of the most menial sort: harvest hands, sheep herders, general farm handymen, stevedores, quarry workers, road gangs,

TABLE 2. *The German-Speaking Labor Market, 1919–1928 (cont'd*

Occupational categories	1922 (cont'd)		July 192 June 19
	V'bund B'stelle (February, April, May only) Applied	Placed	V'bund B'stelle Applied: Placed
Unskilled workers Semiskilled workers Skilled workers	18	6	54
Seamen	—	—	—
Agricultural	28	14	77
Professional and technical	55	17	125
Business and office	14	4	14
Serving people	42	20	113
Totals	157	61	383
Repeatedly unsuccessful inquiries			

et cetera. High status immigrant groups, such as the British, rarely if ever made use of this service. Placement as a so-called *internado* did, however, carry with it one perquisite: a free trip to the interior if a job awaited one there. During the late 1920s many Reichsdeutsche found themselves without alternatives and became *internados*. From 1923 through 1926 a quarter or more of each year's cohort of Reichsdeutsch immigrants was placed by the officials of the Hotel de Inmigrantes; the peak was reached in 1924 at 31.6 percent. The proportion declined steadily over the following years to a low of 12 percent in 1930 but rose again to 18.2 percent in 1932. In the latter year it was, exceptionally, well in excess of the ratio of total *internados* to total immigrants (6.7 percent).[4]

The brimming labor pool contributed to oppressive working conditions and meager incomes (to be noted later) and kept the threat of layoff or dismissal hanging over the heads of the community's working-class and white-collar elements at all times. Few people fortunate

1923		1924		1925	
SgE		VzSgE		VzSgE	
plied	Placed	Applied	Placed	Applied	Placed
564	1488	384	2029	223	918
1089	1363	800	1482	507	1357
2085	1506	1209	1664	817	1588
46	15	37	21	21	23
555	323	576	790	298	286
246	50	137	48	68	37
731	42	453	63	221	25
545	1109	656	1292	352	852
851	5896	4252	7389	2507	5086
604		26,147		24,586	

enough to hold down steady positions did not know personally of others—the inept, the quarrelsome, the nonconforming, the unlucky—who were not. German-speaking employers did not hesitate, of course, to take advantage of the situation. Speaking of the immediate postwar period, Emil Hayn expressed the viewpoint of the community's *Bonzen* in his customary pungent manner: "in Buenos Aires, we had four thousand white-collar employees and laborers . . . in general we exercised extremely finicky selections (*scharfe Auslesen*)."[5] Manual workers were normally hired and paid by the day; the length of the work day was at the discretion of the employer. One of the most common abuses to which they were subjected, especially by their countrymen, was the *medio-oficio* arrangement. On the pretext that the immigrant was not yet familiar with the language and working conditions of the new country, a semiskilled or skilled worker was offered half the going daily wage for his craft. Many, desperate to work in their proper occupations and often lured by the promise that with time and experience

TABLE 2. *The German-Speaking Labor Market, 1919–1928 (cont'd.)*

	January–June 1926	1927–first quarter 1928
	VzSgE	VzSgE/V'bund
		B'stelle
		Applied: 2823
Occupational categories		(January–June 1927)
	Applied: 1266	Placed (combined
	Placed	totals)
Unskilled workers	850	1791
Semiskilled workers		
Skilled workers	1234	3090
Seamen	—	16
Agricultural	136	328
Professional and		
technical	29	21
Business and office	30	47
Serving people	447	1162
Totals:	2726	6455
Repeatedly unsuccessful	12,169	23,502 (1927)
inquiries		5,660 (first
		quarter 1928)

they would be advanced to *pleno-oficio* status, accepted—only to be discharged when they had gained experience and began to press for the wage levels due them.[6]

Vorwärts provided many practical services to workers. It was the only German language association to provide free Spanish lessons—a fact usually ignored by conservative writers who regularly denounced immigrants for their unwillingness to learn the language of the land—and it made available medical insurance through the affiliated General German Sickness Fund (Allgemeine Deutsche Krankenkasse). Its officials were active in setting up and supporting at least three German language craft unions: those of the publishing industry, housepainters, and metalworkers.[7] They also persuaded the Association for the Protection of Germanic Immigrants to refrain from recruiting strikebreakers and maintained vigilance to see that the agreement was kept. Immigrants were alerted to various *criollo* organizations, some of them backed by the right-wing Liga Patriótica, which sought strikebreakers and to a serious effort on the part of German employers to create a yellow Artisans' Craft Union (Handwerkervereinigung) in 1923–1924.[8]

Individual German firms were occasionally denounced for abusive labor policies. In 1920, for example, the construction firm GEOPE (Compañía General de Obras Públicas), formerly Philipp Holzmann et Cie., was reported to be plagued by labor disputes and to be actively seeking new, presumably naive, German-speaking immigrants to replace its dissidents.[9] The affairs of CATE/CHADE remained troubled in the early postwar years and received much attention. The *Neue Deutsche Zeitung* reported in September 1919 with a touch of contempt that CATE's white-collar workers, who had opposed earlier strikes by the manual workers, were now themselves attempting to form a union and were seeking the support of the utility's blue-collar personnel. The paper predicted that the attempt would fail, as it apparently did. Early the following year there occurred another round of labor strife at CATE, and its directors were accused of recruiting recent immigrants as strikebreakers. At this point, however, the CATE executives gave ground to the extent of sponsoring a company union, the Unión de Empleados y Obreros, which they placed under the direction of one Neigenfind.[10]

Thereupon, the utility's labor practices, at least with regard to manual workers, underwent a remarkable reversal. In 1920 the living conditions at Dock Sud were, in the common opinion, deplorable. Six wooden dormitories were then available for four hundred workers and their families; those who could not be accommodated were left to shift for themselves in an area remote from the built-up quarters of the city. The prices of food and basic necessities at the company store and in the immediate neighborhood were inordinately high. By 1929, however, at the time of the inauguration of the new and greatly expanded facilities of the power plant, a model company town had been established and a full-blown paternalism was in effect. The social services included two subsidized company stores (the larger one in the city center, the smaller in Dock Sud), social workers, subsidies for childbirth, child care centers, a mutual aid fund, cafeterias, a clubhouse and a sport field, communal baths, manual training courses, and subsidies to the two elementary schools in Dock Sud, the German School and State School Number 35. These fringe benefits greatly supplemented the wages paid by CHADE, which were themselves well within the far-from-princely norms for manual workers in 1930.[11]

With the abundance of down-at-heel *Kaufleute und Kopfarbeiter* competing for each job that fell open, their situation was, as might be expected, rather bleaker than that of the manual workers. Although

Vorwärts sought actively to attract white-collar workers, it is doubtful whether many could overcome their prejudices or were willing to brave bourgeois disapproval to use its facilities. Thus the unionization available to them was tinged a deep yellow: the Sindicato Unico Mercantil, to the founding of which at least a dozen German firms had contributed,[12] or the German National Business Employees' League, mentioned above. Certainly the protections they enjoyed were minimal. One of the unwritten conditions of employment in the more patriotic firms was a willingness to be squeezed for contributions to the numerous postwar relief funds, which continued at least through the massive collection at the time of the French occupation of the Ruhr in 1923. As during the war, the administration of these funds was cloaked in mystery; undoubtedly some of the money was embezzled, and very likely, as Theodor Alemann later claimed, large sums were diverted to anti-Weimar groups in Germany. The local Left also claimed that employees of the same firms were obliged to take out membership in the Volksbund, whose rolls otherwise, after the purge of 1919, would have been even smaller than they were.[13]

It was, however, the lack of job security, together with the absence of attendant welfare provisions such as had long been common in Germany—maximum hours, sick pay, vacations, employers' contributions toward sickness fund dues, pensions—that was at the heart of their grievances. Salaried employees were rarely if ever under contract. They could be, and were, set upon the street from one day to the next. To be sure, as *empleados* they were entitled under Argentine law to one month's pay in lieu of notice. If the money was withheld, however, even this modest legal protection was virtually meaningless, for the employee had then to apply to a *Juez de Paz* for redress—and it was assumed as a matter of course that the latter were paid a sort of retainer by the employers.[14] Given the extreme precariousness of middle-class status in the Buenos Aires community of the 1920s, the shock of sudden dismissal was severe enough for anyone, but for men of middle age it was traumatizing. Younger men were preferred: "the age limit [beyond which a man becomes unemployable] is drawn here far lower than in Germany."[15]

The pressures on the white-collar stratum were tightened by the growth of a *criollo* middle class and its thrust for respectable employment in bureaucracy and business. As the experience of wartime had shown, few German firms felt constrained to employ Germans exclusively; in the postwar era they increased the numbers of young *criollo* employees. (On the other hand, lack of Spanish and/or influential contacts barred most Germans from *criollo* firms; and, although many had studied English or French, persistent wartime animosities barred them from the important British, French, and Belgian commercial establishments in the city. It was reported, however, that the North Americans were generally willing to let bygones be bygones.)[16] German-speaking employees were undoubtedly exploited in terms of hours of work and productivity; they claimed also that they were harassed by *criollo* employees who performed less than they and that their employers all too often resolved conflicts between them and *criollos* in favor of the latter. One white-collar worker who left a short memoir of his experiences told a familiar tale of thirty applicants for one job, of letters of application that went unacknowledged, of being taken on finally (by an unnamed firm) at a daily wage of seven pesos, of *criollo* subordinates who made his life miserable, and of nearly being shot by *criollo* employees who had been discharged.[17]

Other than the engineers and technicians brought out to Argentina under contract, professional people also found themselves caught between exploitive German employers and ambitious *criollos*. As the employment statistics indicate, only a relative few were able to establish a foothold at all. The way they customarily did so was described in 1933 by the Reich emigration office: "For German engineers and chemists, the rule has been for years now that at first they could find employment only in extremely subordinate positions which often had nothing to do with their professional occupations; [they remained in them] until such time as they had the opportunity to demonstrate unusual ability or adaptability." The writer went on to observe that now, in 1933, even this rigorously selective system had ceased to exist, because of the economic crisis and also because of the increasing supply of *criollo* university graduates.[18] Indeed, the growing pressure of *criollo* professionals on their German-speaking compeers seems to have made itself felt somewhat earlier. The German Scientific Society *Address-Book* listings show that from 1916 to 1926 the number of German physicians declined from fourteen to ten, the number of dentists from eight to three. In the same period, independent consulting architects, engineers, and chemists disappeared altogether.

The data on wages in Table 3 have been compiled, except where otherwise noted, from German language sources. They show little alteration over the course of the fifteen years following the war. The material on the cost of living in Table 4 is also taken from German sources. It should be emphasized that the estimates are for German-style living levels. Commentators were ambivalent on this point, for, if they occasionally berated their countrymen for addiction to small luxuries, they also held, implicitly, that *criollo* living levels were simply

TABLE 3. *Wages in Buenos Aires (Except Where Noted)*
(in Paper Pesos per Month Except Where Noted)

	1919	1920
Unskilled workers		5–8.50 per day at Comodoro Rivadavia
Skilled workers		4–10 per day; 80–90, rm/bd, for smiths etc. on *estancias*; 200–300 printers
Agricultural workers	45–60, rm/bd for resident labor; 6–7 per day minus food for harvesters	Couples (kitchen help plus handyman) 100–120, rm/bd
Technical and professional workers		
Business and office workers		300 very good; 150–175 average
Serving persons		Couple (cook plus gardener) 90–110, rm/bd

unacceptable for Europeans of a certain culture.[19] It will be noted that, although wage levels remained virtually constant, the cost of living in various categories crept slowly upward during the postwar decade and a half. This is especially visible in the minima required.

As can readily be imagined, the community's welfare efforts, amalgamated since 1916 in the German Welfare Society (DWG), were hard-pressed during the postwar years. To judge from the tone of the

E 3. *Wages in Buenos Aires (Except Where Noted) (cont'd.)*
aper Pesos per Month Except Where Noted)

	1922	1925
	4.50–5 per day	2.50–5 per day; 5.50 at Comodoro Rivadavia
	6.75 per day (Dirección Nacional de Trabajo)	6–10 per day; 6–9 at Comodoro Rivadavia
250 newsmen, in-ng piecework	150–500	120–500, av 200; 0.80–1 per hr (tech); 200–500 (prof)
200 business person-200, rm/bd, hosp in; 80–200 salesman; plus 2% max in dept ; 120–180 plus 2–5% lesman; 175–225 keeper; 500–1000 led accountant		

Annual Reports, the charity was dispensed grudgingly and was probably accompanied by a great deal of hectoring of the recipients. The
DWG grumbled about:

> . . . the emigration from the German homeland, which all too often
> occurs in utterly senseless fashion . . . [1923]

> . . . the snap decisions to emigrate . . . the lack of preparation,

TABLE 3. *Wages in Buenos Aires (Except Where Noted) (cont'd.)*
(in Paper Pesos per Month Except Where Noted)

	1927	1928	1929
Unskilled workers			
Skilled workers	6–7 per day (low 4.5 for weavers, high 9.33 for upholsterers)		170.30 (Dirección Nacional de Trabajo)
Agri-cultural workers	4.46–4.47 per day minus food (harvesters)		
Technical and pro-fessional workers			
Business and office workers		7 per day (one instance)	
Serving persons			

lack of competence, small appetite for work, inability to adapt [of the immigrants]. [1924]

The unconsidered emigration which continues to this moment—of people who are totally inappropriate for the struggle for existence in this country, and for whom it is necessary to find funds to send home lest they swell the army of those who must perpetually be supported by the German colony. [1927]

ᴇ 3. *Wages in Buenos Aires (Except Where Noted) (cont'd.)*
aper Pesos per Month Except Where Noted)

	1932	1933
–6 per day	75–150	
₅ per week; ‚o for some ‚ialized trades	120–250	
–300 (tech) –300 (prof)		200–350 schoolteachers; 375–500 for academi- cally trained teachers; 200–250 for beginners
₃00		300–800 for engineers and "leading business- men"; 80–300 for clerks
		60–150, rm/bd for gov- erness; 40–120, rm/bd for cooks and serving girls

As the last quotation suggests, the DWG took responsibility for meeting the financial demands occasioned by the immigrants and, in particular, for suppressing "house-to-house begging," which was not only
an annoyance to the established Buenos Aires Germans but also another
blow to German prestige in the eyes of the *criollos* as well. In the 1921
German-Argentine Address-Book, the DWG exhorted readers not to
extend private charity; it insisted that all relief efforts be channeled
through itself. Undoubtedly the German panhandlers were irritating to

TABLE 4. *Cost of Living, Buenos Aires, in Pesos*
(German-Style Levels unless Otherwise Noted)

1919: 40 pesos gold (about 91 paper) the absolute minimum per adult workingman.

1920: Sample budget: white-collar worker, married, one child, 200 pesos per month income:

Rent (suburb)	50
Fares	5
Lunch	25
Milk (30 l.)	5.40
Meat (15 kg.)	15
Bread (30 kg.)	12
Heat and light	15
Other food	30
	157.40

Remainder for clothing, washing, medical expenses (high), etc.

1921: Single man: very poor conditions   125–150
Modest conditions   175–225
Lower-middle-class standards   250–300 per adult

1921: *Conventillos*:

Room with window to court, city center	40 per month
Room with window to court, elsewhere	25
Furniture	10–25 extra
Room on street, city center	80
Room on street, city center, furn.	90
Room on street, elsewhere	50
Room on street, elsewhere, furn.	70
Board	30–60 additional
Furnished room, city center, middle-class	100–150 plus 50 for bath, 100 for board
Houses, 2–6 rooms, older quarters	150–300
Houses, 2–6 rooms, better neighborhoods (Belgrano)	400–1000
Houses, 2–4 rooms, suburbs	40–100 plus 10–25 carfare
Furn. room with kitchen priv., suburbs	30 plus 10–25 carfare

TABLE 4. *Cost of Living, Buenos Aires, in Pesos (cont'd.)*
(German-Style Levels unless Otherwise Noted)

1922: Monthly income required for:

Single blue-collar worker	70–120
Single white-collar worker	80–150
Married blue-collar worker, no children	100–170
Married white-collar worker, no children	100–170
Blue-collar family, 4 persons	120–225
White-collar family, 4 persons	180–350
A man's suit cost	40–90
A man's shirt cost	3.50–6
A pair of men's shoes cost	8–14

The Dirección de Trabajo reported that the cost of living had risen from the 1916 index of 100 to 149 and calculated that a working-class family of 4 required a minimum income of 167 pesos; to which the Reich Bureau for Emigration observed that this sum provided a very modest existence by German standards.

1923: (September) monthly income required for:

Single blue-collar worker	75–150
Single white-collar worker	120–200
Married blue-collar worker, no children	150–300
Married white-collar worker, no children	200–350
Blue-collar family, 4 persons	200–400
White-collar family, 4 persons	300–400

Living expenses in the Comodoro Rivadavia oilfields were reported to be double those elsewhere. Nevertheless, for the thrifty, Patagonia was a good bet. No luxuries were available there, but most workers could not afford them elsewhere anyway.

The Volksbund, in one of its more fatuous pronouncements, exhorted immigrants to save money and buy a plot of land; it offered a short sample budget which demonstrated that a truly self-denying worker could put away 80 centavos a day.

1926: The new chargé d'affaires of the German embassy reported that a house appropriate for diplomatic functions could be had for 800 pesos a month in Belgrano.

1928: Sample budget (reported by the same business employee who

TABLE 4. *Cost of Living, Buenos Aires, in Pesos (cont'd.)*
(German-Style Levels unless Otherwise Noted)

had been threatened with shooting by discharged *criollos*):	
Rent and electricity	70
Railroad fare, suburb (unnamed) to Retiro	18.30
Streetcar fare	6
Lunch	30
Groceries	50
Bread, meat, and milk	45
Washing	18
Monthly payment, furniture	10
Monthly payment, sewing machine	10
Monthly payment, doctor	10
Monthly payment, burial expenses, 2 children	10
Monthly payment, school fees, 2 children	11
Newspaper	6
	294.30

1929: The Dirección Nacional de Trabajo reported the findings of a survey of 1198 working-class families in Buenos Aires (4 persons per family, average; 2 persons working, average):

Yearly income	2043.63
Yearly expenses	2035.87
Yearly surplus	7.76

1930:

Single blue-collar worker	120–150
Single white-collar worker	150–200
Married blue-collar worker, no children	150–200
Married white-collar worker, no children	220–300
Blue-collar family, 4 persons	250–300
White-collar family, 4 persons	300–500

1933: Single academically trained professional: 300 minimum

Sources: *NDZ*, 9 September 1919; *Nachrichtenblatt RA* 2, no. 2 (1920); 3, nos. 6, 18, 21 (1921); 4, no. 18 (1922); 5, no. 12 (1923); 7, nos. 21, 22 (1925); 11, no. 18 (1929); 12, no. 9 (1930); 15, no. 10 (1933); *Bund* 5, nos. 8, 11 (1922); 8, no. 11/12 (1925); Blücher, *Rande*, p. 131; *Auslandsdeutsche* 11, no. 20 (1928); Rohmeder, "Wirtschaftliche Lage"; *Lateinamerika (A)* 4 (April 1920): 169.

the well-off of the community, especially at the onset of cold weather when they returned to Buenos Aires from the countryside.[20] And, as the DWG shrilly reminded its neighbors, it stood as the community's only sword and buckler against them.

To give them their due, the DWG's officials could only feel that they were being asked to perform a task which grew more intractable by the year, with financial resources which were never adequate and which, in fact, declined markedly after the armistice. Contributing members of the society declined from 939 in 1919 to 462 in 1924, after which membership figures were no longer published. Similarly, annual receipts fell from 85,000 pesos in 1919 to some 16,800 pesos in 1932. In 1927 the DWG announced that for the first time it was in the red and warned that, should the DWG go under, "the army of beggars will be turned loose on individual business houses and private persons, and the conditions of which we earlier had our fill will again arise." In 1931, in the midst of an even deeper crisis, the DWG again announced impending bankruptcy and bitterly denounced the community's lack of support. Sir Thomas Browne's dictum, "Afflictions induce callosities," may be true; but, as it was, even the regularly employed among the commonality had little to spare.

The major portion of the DWG's annual budgets went to the support of families which might otherwise have broken up. In 1919 it provided funds to 650 families and expended a total of some 55,000 pesos on them. The number of families receiving some sort of relief rose to 800 in 1920 and 900 in 1921, after which there are no further figures. Each year thereafter into the early 1930s, however, the DWG continued to devote at least one third of its increasingly exiguous annual budgets to family support. A second category of recipients was the "unaccompanied businessmen and technicians"—this, at least, was how they were described during the war and early postwar years; but by 1922 the designation was changed simply to "unaccompanied men." This type of expenditure was of course much smaller than that for families, for the men were supported at minimum levels. The floating dormitory, *Granada*, was closed down in 1919, and thereafter until 1928 the men were given cards for soup and lodging at the Salvation Army. In 1928 the DWG opened its own Night Asylum. The men thus lodged were permitted a maximum of ten nights under cover in summer and fifteen in winter; no known drunkards or "work-shy" persons were allowed in. The DWG acknowledged that these were harsh policies but held that in the circumstances they were the only ones possible.

The DWG also made funds available for medical expenses and remission of fees at the German Hospital, for the support of old people (it operated the Wencke endowment), and for loans, principally to persons who needed to travel to jobs promised them in the interior. By 1924 its officers had concluded, apparently over opposition, that funds spent on repatriation of the totally unfit would result in long-term savings to the society and the community at large, and it began to subsidize passage back to Germany for persons considered "unable to work." This was apparently a convenient fiction with which to align DWG policy to that of the consulate, for under consular regulations public monies could be spent only to repatriate those certified medically unfit. The numbers shipped back to Germany were fifty-seven in 1925, sixty in 1926 (exclusive of the Danzig contingent, whose "ill-considered, senseless" presence in Buenos Aires had cost the DWG much trouble and expense), seventy in 1927, fifty-nine in 1928, forty-two in 1929, twenty-nine in 1930, forty-seven in 1931, and thirty-two in 1932.

In the "official" histories of Argentine *Deutschtum* and the historical essays included in the *Festausgaben* now and again published by the German language dailies of Buenos Aires, the social dislocations, bitter political conflicts, and general misery of the 1920s go virtually unacknowledged. Much of the descriptive writing of the time was also devoted to beautification of the reality. To cite only one apparently well-informed observer, Dr. Warhold Drascher of the Auslands-Institute surveyed the German-speaking communities of South America and, in particular, that of Buenos Aires, in 1925. He noted that the Buenos Aires community had surpassed in size that of Rio de Janeiro, which had been the largest in the area since the mid-nineteenth century. He observed happily, however, that it was still very much a small-town community, on the order of the Hanse towns or other small German preindustrial cities. The hierarchy of status-occupational groups, or *Stände*, was well marked, but "within the rather tightly closed circle, everyone knows everyone else." At the apex of the social order stood the big businessmen, the *Kaufmannsstand*, whose attitudes and values were "predominant" for the entire community. The elite of the *Kaufmannsstand* consisted of the heads and associates of the banks and great investment firms; beneath them, the heads and managers of the more important retail establishments formed a separate though still very superior layer. The white-collar workers belonged to a lower *Stand*; with them Drascher also placed the ex–military officers. The third major *Stand* was that of manual workers. According to Drascher, they participated less than the others in the life of the community, both because the predominantly male laboring immigrants were regrettably prone to marry "daughters of the land" and also because many could not afford *Verein* dues. His mild reservations about the health of the community concerned the underrepresentation of the free professions and also the relatively little social contact between the community's schoolteachers and pastors and its big businessmen.[21]

Drascher's nostalgia-tinged and fatuous view accorded well with the psychological needs of the community, but it should be pointed out that other more perceptive writers did not pander to its illusions. At about the same time, for example, Karl Thalheim wrote of the processes that had brought about the great distention of the social hierarchy and the growing antagonisms among class levels:

> [In the overseas German communities] the social tension will grow in direct proportion to the strength of the [migratory] movement into regions in which Germans have held an economically privileged position. The receptivity of the proletarian toward radical social tendencies is all the greater to the extent that he is torn out of all organic relationships. . . . Even in a country like Argentina, where the German population consists of all social classes, without any sharp disjunctures, from manual workers to a wealthy commercial aristocracy, but where the center of gravity lies in a numerous middle class, the political upheavals in Germany have led to severe and profound conflicts within the German community, which to this day have not been smoothed over.[22]

Although Thalheim seems to ascribe much of the conflict in Buenos Aires to the influx of proletarianized and radicalized Europeans and does not emphasize its indigenous sources, he is undoubtedly correct in underlining the historical privileged German position there. For the latter served as a reference point, a psychological datum, prized and defended by the minority who continued to enjoy high status after the war, generative of complex resentments and frustrations for the many who did not.

Other contemporary observations have the ring of austere candor. An anonymous correspondent of *Der Auslandsdeutsche* reported in 1925 that, although it had been a good year for the harvest and the Argentine economy in general, the German-speaking commonality (*Allgemeinheit*) had not thereby prospered, except insofar as work itself was somewhat easier to find. "The commercial and small-business middle class has, in recent years, unfortunately felt nothing of an improvement in general business conditions in Argentina. Only with great difficulty does it continue to hold on and to hope that finally the Argentine economic situation, and thereby also its own, will get better."[23] Similarly, the diplomat Wipert von Blücher reported an "expert" estimate of thirty German millionaires in the German colony, but he pointed out that the latter represented only one per thousand of the total. "The few successful men stood everywhere in the foreground, and the entire world spoke of them. Of the tens of thousands who in hard struggle with an adverse fate received only a scant return, nothing was said. In this fashion a false picture of the true conditions arose."[24]

In the early 1930s several of the contributors to the sections "Argentina" and "Buenos Aires" of the *Handwörterbuch des Grenz- und Auslands-Deutschtums*[25] showed themselves well aware of rapid social change within the Buenos Aires community and its relation to political conflict. One H. Kloss stated flatly that "the situation of the urban German population in Buenos Aires is determined by the strong tension between upper and lower social classes. . . . The critical situation of the Germans during the world war brought about a first bridging-over of the splits within the community, but following the war the change in form of the German government in 1918 and the conflict over symbols had especially strong effects in the milieu of Buenos Aires —which in any case was full of tensions—and led to new fragmentation."[26] A. Haas (who had been attached to the embassy in Buenos Aires) also believed that the war years had been a watershed in the affairs of the community, for, with its former close associations with the English and other foreign groups broken, it had been thrown back on its own resources and had had to overcome the great social tensions already present. But:

> . . . the postwar period brought a sharp alteration in the social
> structure of urban *Deutschtum*. In part this is attributable to the
> change in the social composition of the immigration, of which in
> the postwar years numbers of the *Mittelstand* (businessmen, offi-
> cers, academics) formed a strong element. The immigration ex-
> ceeded considerably the capacity of the German firms to absorb
> them. A large proportion nevertheless was able to gain a footing
> in Argentine economic life through entry, as workers or white-
> collar employees, in non-German firms. Thereby, and through the
> immigration of numerous independent petit bourgeois elements
> (small entrepreneurs, artisans and tradesmen, restaurateurs and
> hotelkeepers), a sort of new middle class was formed, one which
> stood in closer relationship to purely Argentine or mixed circles,
> and which participated in the sociopolitical coalescence which
> has marked these latter economic and social classes in the last few
> decades. But despite these alterations the social and ideological

confrontations between the economic elite and the broad mass of the urban German population have not been overcome.[27]

But if on the eve of the depression the Buenos Aires community bore little resemblance to the prosperous, self-confident Germanic enclave of 1914, and even less to the comfortable *bürgerlich* society that had dissolved with the economic boom of the 1880s, it should be emphasized that these gross changes had occurred within the memory of living people. Amidst the increasing social differentiation and class tensions of the 1920s, the sense of a reversal of fortune since 1914 and the frustrations and personal tragedies of the postwar immigration, there were many evocations of the intense sociability and fixed relationships of the Old Colony. Nostalgia and the awareness of change were heightened by the passing, during the decade, of an earlier generation of community leaders—such, for example, as the journalists and publishers Heinrich Kohn (d. 1921) and Theodor Alemann (d. 1925), the banker Gustav Frederking (d. 1924), and the businessmen Friedrich Kozel (d. 1928) and Carlos Rothenburger (d. 1922). Kozel, a pioneer in the sugar industry and president of the German Chamber of Commerce, left a million *Reichsmark* to the German institutions in Buenos Aires (including a fund for a yearly banquet in his memory at the Deutscher Klub). Of Rothenburger, a founder of the Quilmes brewery, A. E. Gross observed that he had been one of the last public men to retain friendships in all quarters of the community.[28]

With the changing of the guard, two tendencies deplored even before the war became clearer. In the conferring of status within the community, the single criterion of wealth (and economic power) had become paramount; respectability and civil involvement were being devalued into irrelevance. And the leadership roles associated with such status were now being exercised by men whose own interests were more closely bound to German and international big business than to the parochial concerns of the Buenos Aires community.

For the *Geld-Aristokratie* succeeded in living in, and having the best of, two worlds, the European and the Argentine. There was still time for languorous sojourns at the fashionable spas and resorts of Western Europe, in their last bloom; there were still gala winter social seasons in Europe's cultural capitals; and the German language newspapers faithfully chronicled the periodic migrations of the local eminences to the rhythms of the stately transatlantic passenger liners of the period. Their Argentine world overlapped that of the Buenos Aires *oligarquía*, whose way of life, centered upon the prestige *estancia*, they emulated and with whom they cultivated business, social, and marital alliances; but it was rooted in exclusive German language social circles and elite clubs. These latter were the German Riding Club and, at a slightly less exalted level, the Deutscher Klub and the rowing club Teutonia. In 1931, after his return to Germany, Emil Hayn described what he blandly assumed to be the way of life of the entire community:

> In South American cities the foreign colonies lead their own sep-
> arate existence. They maintain good relations with the natives and
> officials; otherwise, however, there is little intercourse worth men-
> tioning with the locals except on the occasion of club galas and
> patriotic festivals, to which the upper levels of officialdom, soci-
> ety, and the officer corps are invited—and accept with pleasure.
> If one is able to deal properly with the latter—and we Germans
> are mostly quite skilled at this—then the relationship is a warm
> one. In Buenos Aires, for example, we had especially good con-
> tacts with the elite of the Argentine officer corps; these relation-
> ships were cultivated in particular through the German Riding
> Club. This club and the Argentine Club Hípico, composed of offi-
> cers, often held joint social events and invited each other regularly
> to their celebrations.[29]

It is evident that the Riding Club served as a significant medium for the cultivation of connections with Argentine elite circles—connections that would later have political consequences—but most probably only a minority of Germans were privy to such calculations. For the majority, the Riding Club was the capstone of acceptance into the community's upper class and, beyond it, the Buenos Aires *oligarquía*. In 1923, *Der Bund* wrote of the Riding Club's autumn hunt, to which members of Argentine high society and the army had been invited, "happily, this *Verein* has succeeded in strengthening its good relations with the above-mentioned influential circles, and thus in gaining broader sympathy for *Deutschtum*." The account ended contentedly with the note that the Sociedad Rural, in reciprocal hospitality, had invited the German Riding Club to participate in its forthcoming obstacle race.[30]

Well beneath the *Geld-Aristokratie* in the social hierarchy, but vir-
tually indistinguishable from them in outlook, were the managers and senior technical personnel of the German enterprises; the legally trained agents (usually Argentine born; Carlos Meyer Pellegrini was an exemplar); the *Herren Doktor* school rectors (though certainly not the schoolteachers, as will be seen); the church administrators (though not the pastors); Weimar's diplomatic functionaries (here, however, an aristocratic title could make a large difference); those ex-*Reichswehr*

officers who, unlike many of their brethren, continued to work in some military or administrative capacity; and the newspaper proprietors. The community's political activists, clubmen, and clubwomen (*Vereinsmeier*, in the common, slightly mocking term) were drawn principally from this stratum.[31] As such, they made the community's official history; what is worse, to the confoundment of the present day historian, they also wrote it.

Some statistical estimates are possible for this upper-middle-class stratum. For example, through the postwar decade and a half the number of professional engineers under contract held at about sixty. This was the average yearly membership of the Argentine Society of German Engineers, which provided legal mediation with the Argentines in contractual matters, personal contacts for further professional employment in the country, and a certain amount of jollification as well.[32] The total number of persons at this socioeconomic level can be inferred fairly firmly from the records of the rowing club Teutonia and the Deutscher Klub, the two largest associations identifiable with it. In 1921 the initiation fee of Teutonia was raised to 300 pesos (the monthly wage of a well-established manager); the annual dues were set at 80 pesos. These rates held at the same level until early 1933, when the maximum initiation fee was reduced to 200 pesos. Membership rose from 669 to 722 in 1921; from 743 to 811 in 1928; and reached its peak, 998, in 1931. The economic crisis hit Teutonia especially hard, as it had just built a sumptuous new lodge on its grounds at Tigre at a cost of over 500,000 pesos. It 1933 the fixed rates were cut in half until such time as the membership should again have risen to 700.[33]

Data on fees at the Deutscher Klub are unavailable for the earlier part of the decade. In 1927 a membership drive was begun; initiation fees were waived and yearly dues were set at 60 pesos per year for men under twenty-two, 120 pesos for men under thirty, and 200 pesos for men over thirty. In the following year the initiation fee was set at 100 pesos. As a result of these measures, membership, which had held between 500 and 600 since 1920, rose for a time over 600. But the Deutscher Klub was also hard hit by the depression, and despite a lowering of charges in 1931 membership slowly drifted down below 500. The *Gleichschaltung* to Hitlerism in 1933 undoubtedly cost a further loss of members.[34] By 1936, corporate memberships were being sold to thirty-two firms, which then made them available to their employees; thus, so long as one was "racially" acceptable, exclusivity had been virtually abandoned. In that year the NSDAP held seven functions at the club's premises in Avenida Córdoba.[35]

The available annual reports of the Deutscher Klub also confirm the high incidence of movement at this social level between Europe and Argentina. In 1920, the first normal postwar year, 24 percent of the membership was recorded as being either "absent" or "returned." The proportion was the same in 1923, rose to 31 percent in 1924 and to 32 percent in 1925 and 1926, and declined again, for reasons not apparent, through 1927 to a low of 15 percent in 1928, the last year for which these figures are available. Given the extensive business and professional connections of the men who gravitated to the Deutscher Klub, this incidence of travel is not at all surprising. But it must also be remembered that in the hierarchically ordered community it was precisely this *Stand* which supplied as a matter of wealth and right the great bulk of *Verein* officials and opinion leaders of the community. Thus the cogency of the complaints concerning the neglect of local concerns and the injection of extraneous (that is, European) issues becomes clear.

Since the rowing club Teutonia and the Deutscher Klub memberships included a large, though unknown, proportion of unattached males, the *Verein* rolls need to be increased by only a relatively small factor to account for households (and a handful of nonconformists who joined nothing). At a rough estimate, then, the community's upper and upper-middle classes comprised perhaps fifteen hundred to two thousand persons. A loose estimate can also be made for the stably employed working class. In 1923 a communist colleague told Wilhelm Herzog that, of the seventeen thousand German-speaking immigrants then residing in Buenos Aires, some six thousand were manual workers.[36] As has been noted earlier, the German-speaking proletariat established itself in the city relatively early in the postwar decade, and there is no reason to believe that its proportion of the total rose much beyond one-third thereafter. Undoubtedly, therefore, as all the descriptive materials at hand attest, the petite bourgeoisie of white-collar workers, small business owners, and their families made up by far the largest socioeconomic class within the community in the late 1920s. There is, however, no way to establish a more precise estimate of their numbers. Indeed, amazing as it may seem, in 1933 Dr. Martin Arndt of the Volksbund and the geographer Franz Kühn—both presumably well informed, both ideologically to the right—differed by ten thousand in their estimates of the community's total population: Arndt put it at thirty-five thousand and Kühn at twenty-five thousand.[37]

Not precisely of the community, but ever-present in its consciousness, was the nether end of the social order: the casual proletariat of "derelict existences." It consisted of the detritus of all social classes but principally of the young men of the German middle classes who had come of age during and immediately after the war. They surged out of Buenos Aires at the onset of warm weather and returned with the cold; and the rhythm of their movement was also chronicled by the German language press of the capital—in the form of testy editorials and exasperated appeals for charitable donations.

In this situation of rapid socioeconomic differentiation, the community also lost its geographic cohesion. Although many middle-class families at median levels remained in Belgrano (which has stayed in the popular mind until today the German-speaking *barrio* of Buenos Aires),[38] the more affluent began by the early 1930s to move beyond Belgrano to newer and "better" north shore suburbs such as Vicente López, Martínez, Olivos, and ultimately San Isidro. At the same time, working- and lower-middle-class communities grew larger at points scattered all across the vast metropolis and even beyond: Dock Sud, Barracas, Villa Devoto, Quilmes, Lanús. An entire new settlement, some 3,000 strong, of Swabians from the Banat grew up in the outlying town of Piñeyro.[39]

But the largest—indeed the archetype—of the newer German-speaking neighborhoods was in Villa Ballester, on the city's remote western rim. There, during the war, Germans and many others had begun to buy up cheap building lots on long-term installment plans and to construct their own dwellings, room by room, with whatever building materials came to hand. Even today, the district's highly heterogeneous architecture stands as a monument of sorts to this process. The German-speaking population of Villa Ballester was as diverse as its architectural styles. It was par excellence the settlement of the survivors of the 1920s immigration who had, with great toil, gained a modest foothold in Argentina. Working-class and lower-middle-class households existed cheek-by-jowl to an unusually high degree.[40] Long after the Second World War Villa Ballester would retain its heritage of hardscrabble survival, its folklore and reality of men with murky histories of many adventures and few successes—an environment into which an Adolf Eichmann, for example, could blend with ease.

The centrifugal forces at work since before the war, and accelerated by the events of the 1920s, had eroded many of the elements of community and should, perhaps, on a rational calculation, have destroyed it altogether. As will be shown in the following chapter, assimilation was proceeding apace with social differentiation and reinforcing the disintegrative processes. But there were also centripetal forces at work to keep the community intact, at least in simulacrum. More precisely, there were purposeful people at work to enforce the claims of German nationalism and to hold the community to *Deutschtum.*

8. Assimilation and the School Question, 1918–1933

In an essay written in 1919, one of the shrewdest public figures of La Plata *Deutschtum*, Pastor W. Nelke of the Montevideo congregation, addressed himself to the question, "who are the Germans of La Plata?" Nelke dispensed with the theoretical subtleties that such writers as Alemann and Keiper had brought to the same subject and sought pragmatic definitions. For him, formal legal nationality was a serviceable criterion in only a minority of cases, for he was aware of the diversity of the European sources—the German Empire, the Austro-Hungarian Empire, German Switzerland, Russia—from which La Plata *Deutschtum* stemmed. (He could not foresee that with the large postwar influx of refugees from old Germanic enclaves in Eastern Europe they would grow more diverse still.) With respect to the American-born offspring of immigrant parents, he held, like Keiper and many others, that the *jus soli* principle that automatically made Uruguayan or Argentine citizens of these children was in contradiction to the psychological realities. Unlike Keiper, however, he rejected out of hand "the bearers of German names who no longer understand German, but who have instead sunk into the local population."[1] Rather, irrespective of origins or nationality, the true Germans of La Plata were, for Nelke, those whose social existence was enveloped in German language clubs, societies, schools, and other institutions—in *Vereinsleben*. This associational structure represented, in fact, the only cement of La Plata *Deutschtum*. To Nelke, the preservation of Germanic identity and hence resistance to assimilation were unquestioned imperatives. It therefore followed that the structure of *Vereine* must not only be kept in good repair but must also be expanded purposefully so as to make them available to all potential sectors, interests, and socioeconomic levels of the community.

During the 1920s, holding the German community to *Deutschtum* remained the obsession of right-wing nationalists in La Plata, and Nelke's dictum became their guiding principle.

The fact of assimilation into *Kreolentum* was nothing new. In the absence of any usable quantitative data, one can only conjecture that during the first half century or so of the community, from the 1830s to the 1880s, it had gone on at a rapid pace: German-born women were relatively scarce among the immigrants, and transatlantic communications infrequent. But a significant amount of the assimilation of this period was a function of upward mobility—the reward of judicious business activity, land speculation, and marital alliances with *criollo* families of note. Thus it was that by the 1920s many of the famous founding families—Altgelt, Arning, de Bary, Bemberg, Bracht, Bull-rich, Bunge, Frers, Holmberg, Mallmann, Meyer (the distinct Hanse and Austrian lines), Schlieper, Seeber, Stegmann, Zimmermann, Zuber-bühler—were *criollo* oligarchs in all but patronymic. One may suggest, with only a touch of cynicism, that to assimilation at this level of status there had never been any perceptible objection.

It is further probable that the pace of assimilation slowed somewhat in the newer community that emerged from the boom of the 1880s and lasted until 1914. The founding of the German Empire in 1871 and its swift development as a major industrial and military power gave a new worth to German nationality. Communications and commercial connections with Germany and Europe improved markedly. If, as seems likely, ascent into the *criollo* landed upper class became somewhat less common, the community had by that time created a German language institutional environment—the structure of *Vereine*—that tended to insulate it from the ethnic crosscurrents, pell-mell economic and demographic expansion, and absorptive social processes of the new metropolis.

Before the war, public men of the community had often dilated on the Germans' purported gifts for adaptability, but they maintained at the same time that adaptation was prevented from being merely the first step toward assimilation by the total cultural environment that the community was able to provide. Although they were generally correct in this, there were small but widening holes in their argument. To be sure, until 1916, under the rule of the *oligarquía*, pressures from above for Argentinization had been virtually nonexistent. Rather, the authentic pressure for assimilation had been from below: from the level of language and customs, sports and entertainments, work groups and trade unionization, concubinage, marriage, and the founding of families —and against this pressure middle-class norms, occupations, and voluntary groups, all built upon and perpetuated by German language education, had seemed an effective set of defenses.

But implicit in this proposition is the rule of thumb that correlates resistance to assimilation to high socioeconomic status.[2] Thus even before 1914 it had ceased to have blanket application to a community which, despite the ritual pronouncements of its newspaper editors, churchmen, and school directors, could no longer accurately be described as homogeneously middle-class. After the war, the straitened circumstances of the majority made a far greater proportion of the community's members vulnerable to precisely such assimilative pressures from below. Status decline in terms of the German language reference group, itself a source of generalized anxiety, also thus contributed to the gathering sense of a crisis of cultural identity; and this pervasive unease was aggravated further still by awareness that, simultaneously, significant numbers of urban *criollos* were rising to income and occupational levels that had once been monopolized by Europeans.[3]

There were other, more generalized sources of concern on both sides of the Atlantic. Germany, through the peace of Versailles, had been made a moral pariah among nations. The condemnation of Versailles provoked bitter resentment among many or most of the Germans of La Plata, but it also weakened in many ways their situation vis-à-vis Argentina's other ethnic groups. As during the war, therefore, a sense of persecuted nationalism strengthened in-group solidarity for many, but at the same time it accelerated the drift away from *Deutschtum* for some. Equally to the point, the Germany of Weimar was no longer a great power with imperialistic ambitions; no longer could it work aggressively to export its manufactures, capital, and *Kultur* with the backing of one of the world's most powerful military establishments. For the time being, Germany's remaining overseas dependencies (which was certainly the way the right-wing leadership viewed the Buenos Aires community) were left to their own resources, with only a modicum of hortatory and organizational support from such semi-official groups as the Auslands-Institut[4] and the Verein für das Deutschtum im Auslande (Association for the German Racial Community Overseas) in the Fatherland.

Insofar as the future of La Plata *Deutschtum* would be affected by actions at the official level in Argentina, the situation was ambiguous. The middle-class parliamentary regime of Hipólito Yrigoyen and the Radical party that had taken power in 1916 had shown itself unusually well disposed toward German interests during the war. Yrigoyen's personal attitude during and immediately after the war seemed to indicate a willingness to expand the economic connection with Germany; this would be principally at the expense of Great Britain, hitherto identified with the interests of Yrigoyen's political enemies among the landholding *oligarquía*. (The economic role of the United States was a new, threatening, but as yet largely unknown factor.) As has been shown, German trade with and investment in Argentina increased mightily through the postwar decade, and German businessmen had no need to complain of the cooperativeness of their Argentine compeers. But the apparent triumph of bourgeois democracy in Argentina—its insubstantiality would become apparent only after 1930—was accompanied by an upsurge of *criollo* nationalism, the consequences of which could not easily be foreseen.

In any event, the economic effects would prove to be minimal: the creation of the national petroleum corporation, YPF, in 1922 would be the chief monument to Radical economic nationalism, and an ambiguous one. But in the educational system, including the foreign language schools, requirements for more thorough indoctrination in the symbolism and heritage of Argentine nationality would increase. So also would pressures for greater employment opportunities for schooled *criollos* in the professions, bureaucracy, and foreign-controlled business establishments. As has been seen, these latter developments spelled increasing difficulties for the German-speaking professional and technical caste, which before the war had enjoyed easy access to comfortable positions in the Argentine schools, universities, and public service. In time their repercussions would be felt also in the curricula of the German schools.

The task confronting the German nationalists who undertook to hold the community to *Deutschtum* was therefore formidable. It was further complicated by simple geography—the dispersal of the German-speaking population into *barrios* scattered across the sprawling metropolis—and by the class hostility that had broken into the open at the popular assemblies of 1918 and their sequelae through the early part of the 1920s. The postwar immigrants added another large dimension to the problem, in part because of their many attitudinal conflicts with the old settlers, in greater part because of their economic misadventures. These threw them into intimate contact with the generality of the immigrant and *criollo* working-class population and made it difficult to assimiliate them to the stable social relations and institutions of the old community, which were, in any case, bourgeois and more than a bit archaic. Finally, of course, the ratio of males to females among the German-speaking immigrants remained high.[5]

In the early part of the decade, many of the projects to shunt immigrants into closed Reichsdeutsch agricultural colonies had been dictated by ideological as well as economic considerations—on the commonplace assumption, that is, that cultural identity could better be preserved in isolated communities on the land than in the city. The dismal agrarian disasters of the decade, however, caused a change in thinking by about 1930. It began to be believed that the bitter hardships and reversions to primitive living standards that were the all too common lot of the agricultural *colonos* caused them to lose any cultural identity whatever and merely to swell an already abundant anonymous rural proletariat. By 1931, *Der Bund* was insisting that "settlement in remote jungle colonies has led almost everywhere to a decline to a lower cultural level"; few pioneer families would survive there into the second and third generations, and those that did would no longer be capable of serving as bearers of culture. Only by remaining in contact with established Germanic colonies and by cultivating appropriate "double-form" (that is, German and Argentine) education "can the value of *Deutschtum* for the cultural development of South America be demonstrated."[6] Thus it was imperative that new immigrants settle in, or at least near, the cities.

If the awareness of assimilation and the volume of discussion on the subject were high through the postwar decade, the reality of the matter is much more difficult to examine. One obvious (though, as will be seen, superficial) yardstick is the rate of endogamous marriage. In 1934 the *Handwörterbuch für das Grenz- und Auslandsdeutschtum* announced cheerily that, whereas before 1914 55 percent of the marriages of male Reichsdeutsch citizens in Argentina had been with non-Reichsdeutsch women, the rate since the war had fallen to 37 percent.[7] The latter figure tallies roughly with the *Cuarto Censo General* of Buenos Aires, taken in 1936, which supplies data for amplification. In that year 4,559 households in the city were headed by male Germans; in 2,730 cases the birthplace of the wife was given as Germany and in 225 as Austria. In 795 cases (17 percent) the wife was recorded as other foreign-born and in 809 (18 percent) as *nativa*.[8] Both latter categories undoubtedly include a proportion of women of Germanic cultural background, so that marriages within the cultural group were well in excess of 65 percent. On the other hand, the census data also include marriages contracted in Germany (that is, families that had migrated as units to Argentina); the number of endogamous marriages in Argentina must thus be reduced by the same (unknown) amount. At a loose estimate, therefore, in the immigrant generation two-thirds or slightly more of the marriages contracted by male German immigrants living in Buenos Aires were endogamous, and one-third were exogamous.

By themselves, however, these calculations are not very meaningful —especially in the light of Wilhelm Keiper's observation that, whereas an Englishman who married a non-Englishwoman in Argentina was automatically dropped by his countrymen, the same was not true of a German, provided that the spouse learned passable German, kept a German household, and worked to obtain a German education for the children.[9] Whatever the accuracy of his observation concerning the

English, his point concerning the mores of the German community is of great importance because of its obvious corollaries. The prestige of Germanic culture in general and the derivative prestige of the local German-speaking community were of great weight in diffusing and perpetuating the cultural tradition—through non-Germanic media (thus it is possible that, despite higher rates of exogamous marriage, it was transmitted more effectively before 1914 than in 1930). But it is also clear that Keiper and his colleagues were correct in their insistence on maintaining the institutional structure, particularly the schools, necessary to reinforce the will, desire, and ability of individuals to identify themselves as Germans rather than Argentines.

The 1936 *Censo* data for citizens of the Austrian Republic are approximately the same as for the Germans. In 60 percent of the 2,295 households headed by male Austrian citizens, the wife was either Austrian or German. In 24 percent of the cases the wife was other foreign-born and, in 16 percent, *nativa*.[10] By 1936 just under 8 percent of all German born (1,379 of 17,433) had become naturalized Argentines, and slightly over 7 percent (625 of 8,837) of the Austrians.[11] The fact that the findings for Germans and Austrians are so closely comparable suggests that common cultural factors, which do not emerge from the data,[12] produced common results. Since the Austrians were subjected to far less nationalistic rhetoric and inducement to associate with their countrymen than were the Germans, it also suggests that the tireless organizational work of the German nationalists was, in the end, little more than the rodomontade that their critics had always considered it.

During the 1930s the community continued to receive a small but steady replenishment of Reichsdeutsche, both through immigration from overseas and, especially, through internal migration from the farm colonies and secondary-city communities (the latter point will be considered below). Thus it was that the Buenos Aires community reached its maximum size, some 45,000, in 1938.[13] Even had the destructive after-effects of the Second World War not intervened, however, the future of the community was by this time very much at risk. Surprisingly, no one seems to have been aware of a basic demographic fact: the extremely low fecundity of German-born women in the city. This was a long-term phenomenon. In 1909, 10.4 percent of all married German women had had no children; in this and other indices of fecundity they had been the lowest of the city's ethnic aggregates. In 1936, 35 percent had no children, 26 percent had one, 17 percent had two, and 22 percent had three or more. Again they ranked lowest in this respect among all the city's ethnic collectivities.[14] Among the Germans, limits on the size of families obviously represented a response to the economic reverses since 1914. Given the thinning margins of middle-class existence, concern for the coming generation and its prospects was intense and agonizing. And very complex, as the continuing debate on the nature and purpose of German language schooling revealed.

The geographical dispersal and social differentiation of the urban Germans had required the founding of six new schools between 1893 and 1912. These were Barracas al Norte, 1893; the Belgrano School (later the Goethe School), 1897; the German School of Buenos Aires (the Cangallo School), 1898; Quilmes, 1898; the German School of Belgrano (the Monroe School), 1910; and Dock Sud, 1912. The original Congregational School moved to Calle Ecuador, not far from Plaza Once, in 1903 and, under a secular school association, adopted the name Germania School. The process continued during the war and at an even more rapid pace afterward. In Villa Ballester, a school association was created as early as 1913 by one Dr. J. S. Grimme. It suspended operations during the war, but German language schooling was made available at the home of Karl Bühler. In 1922 the refounded school association arranged to take over Bühler's operation with Bühler as first director. The German School of Villa Devoto was begun in 1917; by 1920 it was in full operation with a kindergarten and the first four primary grades. In 1928, German language elementary schools were begun in two other outlying districts of the urban sprawl of Buenos Aires, Liniers and Munro-Florida. By the early 1930s a constellation of primary schools had developed in small towns lying beyond the urban periphery: Lanús, beginning in 1926; the Hindenburg School in Avellaneda-Piñeyro, 1927; Temperley, 1930–1931; and Valentín Alsina, 1932. The migration to the more prestigious north shore suburbs led to the founding of a branch of the Germania School in Vicente López in 1932 and of a private *Pädagogium* in association with the Goethe School in Olivos in 1933. With the exception of the last, all were under the administration of nonprofit school associations. Two private boarding schools, that of G. Abinet (f. 1924) and the Hölters School (f. 1932), were located in Villa Ballester; and a Home School under the administration of the German Women's Association was in operation in Belgrano.[15]

In the same period, postprimary education developed more slowly. The Belgrano School had begun at the turn of the century as an all-purpose boys' school modeled on the Prussian *Realschule*. In 1906 it began to offer certification for entry as a one-year-volunteer—which could lead to an officer's commission—in the German military. In 1914 it merged with the private German Girls' Upper School that had been operated in Belgrano for the daughters of the well-to-do since 1895 by *Fräulein* Marie Liebau. After the war, its rectors—R. Gabert and, after 1923, Wilhelm Keiper—caused it to be raised to the level of a fully accredited *Oberrealschule*. In 1921, one of its students became the first to pass the state-administered German university entrance exam (*Abitur*) produced by a German school in South America. Its administrators made it the elite school of the community and the most expensive: the average cost per child per year was 300 pesos, though fees rose sharply at the uppermost levels.[16] Where obliged to do so by the new nationalistic legislation, Gabert and Keiper introduced Argentine subjects; otherwise, all instruction was in German, and the curriculum was shaped to prepare students for entry into German universities. Students were permitted, however, to matriculate as "free students," which would permit them to sit exams for the Argentine *bachillerato* and thus qualify for entry to Argentine universities as well. On 1 January 1931 the school adopted the name Goethe School.[17]

Two other schools offered postprimary instruction. One was the Cangallo School in the city center, whose school association had from the beginning emphasized preparation for Argentine careers for the children of German-speaking parents. At least as early as 1914 it had created an ancillary German Evening Business School, tuition at which was free to school association members and nominal to others; this remained active through the postwar decade. By 1919, moreover, the Cangallo School had advanced from a six-class to an eight- and then nine-class program and was offering the Argentine *bachillerato* in conjunction with a *colegio nacional*.

The other postprimary school was the Germania School, which was more closely identified with the traditional community. Like the Belgrano School, it too, from 1906, offered the one-year-volunteer preparation for military service, "on the expressed wish of the kaiser."[18] In the 1920s, it continued to operate as a terminal *Realschule*; an elementary school and a girls' upper school were administered in the same complex. The ubiquitous Keiper was rector from 1921 until his transfer to the Belgrano School in 1923; he was succeeded by Max Wilfert, who held the post through the latter part of the decade. The Germania School was known as the most politically reactionary and socially exclusive of the community's schools. It systematically excluded Jews and continued to be derided as the school at which scholarship students were segregated from paying students.[19]

Aside from its dubious repute on these counts, the Germania School's commercially oriented curriculum duplicated many of the offerings of the Argentine *liceos*, which were, of course, less expensive and at which immersion in a Spanish language environment was total. Student enrollments began to decline, and by 1926 the school was suffering a budgetary deficit of 300,000 pesos.[20] The financial position worsened to critical proportions by 1929; therefore, at the beginning of 1930 the secondary levels of the Germania School and the Cangallo School were merged into the Colegio Incorporado Burmeister on the Germania School premises at Calle Ecuador 1162. The Burmeister school thereafter followed the full Argentine *liceo* curriculum with the addition of certain subjects in German; it was "incorporated" into the Argentine system with the designation of a *colegio nacional comercial*. The *bachillerato* it offered led, of course, to Argentine university study.[21]

This elaborate school system was grist for the mills of the community's publicists. In 1925 they calculated that the nine German language schools of the time were serving some 2,300 students and declared this to be "the largest German school concern outside Germany." By 1932 Max Wilfert could tabulate seventeen school association schools and three private schools in the greater Buenos Aires area, with a total enrollment of 4,525 students; and he repeated the boast.[22] But obviously by 1932 the term "German school" required some qualification.

During the war, the student population of the German schools had risen, reaching a total of approximately 1,700 in 1918.[23] Part of the growth was due to increased enrollment of children of non-Germanic background. This represented a vexing question. On one hand, German educators acknowledged the value of creating good will among influential *criollo* parents; more important, they were also quite aware that the fees paid for these children often spelled the difference between red ink and black on yearly balance sheets. They also felt, however, that some indeterminate number of these children began to dilute the Germanic character of the schools. Only fragmentary statistics are available. In 1919, for example, the Cangallo School had a total of 360 students: 50 of these were of Reichsdeutsch origins (both parents), 10 of Austrian, and 9 of Swiss; 177 others were of partial Germanic background, and the remaining 114 apparently had none at all. In that year, 85 students received full or partial remission of fees. The *Annual Report* does not make the point explicitly, but the school association—like all the German school associations in the city at that time—clung to the principle that no child of Germanic origin should be denied a German language education by its parents' unfavorable economic situation. One may thus presume that most, perhaps all, of the scholarship students were of Germanic origin and that they were in effect subsidized by non-Germanic parents.[24] In the more prosperous year of 1925, at the opposite end of the socioeconomic scale, Wilhelm Keiper noted that 428 of the 501 children attending the Belgrano School came from German households (that is, German male head) and that this was an unusually high percentage for the German schools of Argentina.[25]

The greater part of the increase during the war, however, was due to the physical impossibility of sending children to Germany for their schooling. Nor did this practice revive to any degree after the armistice. The unsettled political and economic situation of Germany until about 1924 provided little incentive, and by the middle of the postwar decade the German middle class of Buenos Aires was generally in no financial position to consider the idea anyway. In 1924 Theodor Alemann, long a vigorous exponent of coming to terms with the Argentine realities, offered an interesting rationale for sending children to local schools as a matter of course. If they were sent to Europe, he observed, the bonds of family were weakened too early. Further, through long absence children schooled in Europe became alienated from local conditions and lost contact with local comrades. Professional degrees would of course have to be revalidated by Argentine officials, a time-consuming and annoying procedure. All this would cause them "great difficulties in obtaining a position."[26] Alemann, it appears, had a clear sense of the importance of *relaciones—la cuña*, the "wedge," the "in"—in making one's career in German Argentina.

The populist agitation of 1918–1919 included demands for educational reform, particularly eradication of the naked class basis upon which the schools of that time had been founded. As one O. Geffers put it in a letter to *Der Bund* in April 1919: "Our social institutions still stand on bases that provide a fertile ground for a vigorous flourishing of class contrasts. We have here in Buenos Aires schools in which 'Junkers,' 'well-to-do bourgeois,' 'petits bourgeois,' and 'proletarians' are educated—or one might better say 'manufactured.' . . . In these schools class consciousness is in full bloom; that is, the students of one or another of these four classes sense their social superiority or inferiority, and group themselves more or less accordingly."[27] The more thoughtful protests took the form of proposals for reorganization of the community's schools on the "unitary school [*Einheitsschule*]" model, which was also under intense discussion in Germany at the time. This was Geffers' solution. It was also the solution proposed by Karl Jesinghaus, sometime member of the faculty of the Instituto Nacional del Profesorado Secundario, later of the Education Faculty of the University of the Litoral in Paraná. Jesinghaus believed that the unitary school should consist of a six-year lower school, culminating in the *sexto grado* cer-tificate (the basic Argentine school-leaving document), plus a two-year technical or commercial middle school. He pointed out that the two existent middle schools on the German *Realschule* model (that is, Germania and Belgrano) were losing students rapidly, as most of the German students who went beyond *sexto grado* were choosing to at-tend Argentine *colegios nacionales* instead. He rejected the idea of a German *colegio nacional* incorporated into the Argentine system; he proposed, rather, the creation of a six-year upper middle school (*Ober-realschule*) which would offer the European *Abitur* exam, with facili-ties for study toward the Argentine *bachillerato* for those who chose it. He here adumbrated the structure that the Belgrano School would adopt under Wilhelm Keiper after 1923.[28]

Hugo Dörsing, who for most of the postwar decade was director of the Quilmes School, was also in 1919 an advocate of the unitary school. His goals were liberal, for he too believed that a unitary curriculum would help reverse the development of class divisions. But he pointed out that the unitary school implied further-reaching educational re-forms. It would require the creation of a single teaching corps of uni-formly qualified academics and normal-school graduates; and this implied in turn the unification and rationalization of the entire con-geries of Buenos Aires schools into a single system. At the same time, however, he insisted upon greater financial and administrative auton-omy for the several school associations. In doing so, he posited a di-lemma which in the end would prove insoluble.[29]

For in practice the local autonomy of the school associations bore several kinds of defects. They competed with each other for teachers and also for students, especially after the war. The more intense the competition became, the more prone they were to accept non-German children, as has been seen. Aside from fees and minuscule contribu-tions from the Reich and from charitable funds, such as that left behind by Ambassador Waldthausen before the war, financial support came entirely from school association members: their annual dues plus the receipts from bazaars and so on, plus their own gifts and bequests and those they were able to cadge from wealthy personal contacts. The wealthier and better-connected members, therefore, acquired dispro-portionate influence in the executive committees of the school associa-tions and in the policies that the committees set. Such persons, more-over, were not always identified with the locality or constituency served by the school. In 1923, A. E. Gross (who else?) pointed out that the community's lesser schools—the Monroe School, Quilmes, Barracas, Villa Devoto, Villa Ballester—continued to adhere to the monarchy and to ignore the German Republic—or at least their executive committees did. In the case of the older working-class Barracas and Quilmes schools, he ascribed this to the fact that from the beginning "a gracious fate" had permitted them "to number among their benefactors disinterested great men of the *Mittelstand*, who—together with their *Damen*—had most kindly lifted the burden of administering a school from the overworked and disorganized workingmen." Thanks to these gentlefolk, therefore, the Quilmes and Barracas schools "could show their heels to any competitors in the matter of black-white-red patriotism."[30]

That the schoolteachers played a leading role in the shaping of such attitudes scarcely needs saying. In the wartime absence of schoolbooks imported from Germany, the German Teachers' Association produced a complete set of primers for the elementary schools. The statement of purpose of the *Reader for the German Schools in South America, Sixth through Eighth Grades* gives some sense of the mentality that the schools sought to inculcate:

> The *Reader* is designed to provide the concept of Home, such as German life demonstrates it in contrast to the unquiet, unstable life of others. The magic of quiet domesticity, in which sacred memories attach to every stick of furniture, the pure fundamentally German [*urdeutsch*] family life with its high standard of family awareness form a strong counterweight to the shallow norms of exaggerated personal worth and the consequent failure to give others their due. In particular, profound respect for the Father is the preparation for loyal performance of duty; love of the Mother is preparation for the high respect due to women and to a philosophy of life in accord with the highest social standards. . . . Render unto others what is due unto others, and to the State what is due to the State.[31]

In any event, in the decade and a half following the war, the German language school system of greater Buenos Aires was unified and rationalized—though not precisely on the lines envisioned by the reformers of 1918–1919. The principal architect was Wilhelm Keiper. In Keiper, an extraordinary energy was joined to an equally remarkable ability to land on his feet. His position as head of the cadre of German pedagogues at the Instituto Nacional del Profesorado Secundario had been phased out in 1916, but by that time he was deeply involved in wartime propaganda work through the German Scientific Society, of which he had been president since 1912. He was also highly active in the founding of the Volksbund from 1916 through 1919; simultaneous-

ly, he served as the first editor of *Der Bund* and, for six months in
1917, as an editor of the archmonarchist *Deutsche La-Plata Zeitung*.
Reputedly he continued to draw a salary for his propaganda work
until 1921. Before that assignment was terminated on the arrival of the
first ambassador of the Weimar Republic, Dr. Adolf Pauli, he began a
two-year term as rector of the Germania School. In the same year, he
reappeared on the republican embassy's payroll as school counselor
and *Reichs-Komissar* (that is, inspector) for the German language
schools, a position he held for five years. From 1923 until 1932 he was
rector of the Belgrano School, and from 1929 to 1938 he served as adjunct counselor for culture at the embassy—and then, at the age of
seventy, retired to Germany. He died there in his tenth decade in
1962. In addition to his services to three German regimes in Argentina,
his writings ran into the dozens.[32]

Already in 1919 Keiper was proposing a central office for the collection of funds for education; the funds would then be distributed by a
committee of three—two big businessmen plus Keiper. He later claimed
that he was supported in this and subsequent efforts by the heads of
the larger German concerns, who had grown thoroughly exasperated
by constant badgering by "women's commissions."[33] The year 1919 was
an unpropitious one for such a project, however, for, although the
populist factions acknowledged the desperate financial situation into
which the schools were falling, they vigorously opposed the upper-
class domination that Keiper's proposal implied. According to the *Neue
Deutsche Zeitung*, it was also opposed by most of the school associations of the time.[34] In any event, the project was abandoned for the
time being, and the old system was retained, through one minor financial crisis after another, during the 1920s. In his position with the
embassy, Keiper advised upon the distribution of Reich school subsidies within Argentina. However, as these amounted to no more than
ten to twenty thousand *Reichsmark* per year for the entire republic,
whereas the combined annual budget of the city's schools was running
to half a million pesos by 1925,[35] his ability to extract quid pro quo's
in pursuit of his objectives remained minimal.

But after 1929 the situation became intolerable, and finally in 1931
a School Finance Committee was founded. It had three members: the
embassy's adjunct counselor for culture (Keiper), a representative of
the Chamber of Commerce, and a representative of the Volksbund. In
July of the following year, there was formed around the finance committee the German School League of Buenos Aires (Deutscher Schulverband Buenos Aires), and before 1932 was out fifteen of the twenty
German language schools of the greater Buenos Aires area had affili-

ated themselves with it. In that year total expenses (which did not include capital costs) of these fifteen schools amounted to 668,359 pesos, and their combined income from conventional sources amounted to 632,206 pesos. The school league made up the difference. It requires little imagination to appreciate the pressure on the remaining schools in Buenos Aires to join the school league and thereby accede to policies set by the embassy in conjunction with the local *Geld-Aristokratie.*[36]

The work of unification enjoyed the enthusiastic support of the German Teachers' Association. In 1918, the schoolteachers, too, through their president, Max Wilfert, put forward proposals for reform. But reform, so far as Wilfert was concerned, was equivalent to measures for holding the Germans to *Deutschtum*, and these, in turn, were virtually synonymous with concern for the status and material situation of schoolteachers.

Wilfert was not overly optimistic about the future of La Plata *Deutschtum*. In effect, he wrote off the rural German population. The primitive, wretchedly supported camp schools could do little to combat the effects of isolation, poverty, and, in many rural districts, ethnic mixture, and he assumed that in the third generation most of the Germans would "become locals." In the cities, a crisis was developing from the interaction of two factors. One was the rise of nationalism: "over the decades, the more the local nation becomes able to meet the need for scholars and teachers through its own efforts, the more it will feel the desire to free itself from the annoying *gringos*, and to the same extent it will begin to place pressure on the foreign educational institutions." The situation of the Germans, for their part, was being undermined by a defect in the national character: their great "adaptability" led many of them not only to "cozy up to [*anzuschmiegen*]" the customs and uses of the host country but even to give up their own Germanness, "if only we can thereby make ourselves pleasing to the locals."[37]

But all was not lost, for the school was the "defender of the German linguistic and racial community." With which Wilfert came to the point. The urban German schools must be expanded, especially at the secondary level. If necessary, local auxiliary teachers could be hired—as indeed they would have to be, for Argentine citizens were required to teach the Argentine history, civics, and geography made obligatory during the 1920s. But dedicated teachers "German to the core [*kerndeutsche*]" must "learn how to secure the upper hand for the German spirit." And the strengthening of the teaching corps required, above all, money—money for higher salaries and for regularization of the salary structure throughout the local systems, money for full sabbatical leaves, money for pensions and survivors' benefits. For relief, Wilfert looked principally to the Reich government rather than the local community. He gratefully acknowledged the generosity of the local big businessmen, but only the German government could provide the great additional sums of money he had in mind. It would be the responsibility of Reich officials, moreover, to make overseas teaching service equivalent to domestic teaching service in career dossiers and thus to offer incentive to German teachers to come out to Argentina on a short-term basis. By the same token, teachers who had made their careers overseas would be enabled to qualify for the German educational bureaucracy's pension and survivors' funds. All this implied a much more centralized and purposeful control of the German language schools in the hands of Reich educational officials working through the embassy. Such a development would be quite agreeable to Wilfert; among other things, it would then be possible to ostracize, financially and otherwise, certain "pseudo-German *colegios*"—by which he meant the more derelict camp schools and perhaps the Cangallo School as well.[38]

These "reforms" did not prosper in the 1920s either. Through Keiper's efforts as *Reichs-Komissar*, the Belgrano School became the second local school—Germania had been the first—to affiliate with the German government's pension fund; but the others remained without. Wilfert had termed the imperial government's educational subsidies "ridiculously small," but under Weimar they became smaller still.[39] The Teachers' Association persevered—in 1927, still under Wilfert, it had 130 members, all with German, Austrian, or Swiss degrees; and it continued to hammer away at bread-and-butter issues[40]—but the postwar immigration brought a gross oversupply of schoolteachers, and, except for senior administrators and the faculties of the elite schools, their situation was unenviable. In the early 1930s they were among the most poorly paid of the white-collar class: a beginner with a normal-school degree received 200 pesos per month; according to Keiper at the embassy an experienced teacher with an academic degree could receive as much as 500. Few teachers had contracts; the usual practice of the school associations was to release a teacher at the end of the school year in December and to rehire (or not rehire) in March. In this way they were spared the expense of a paid holiday. Most teachers, and all married teachers, had to hold additional jobs. Loss of a position meant, normally, banishment to one of the camp schools. The Teachers' Association could occasionally provide small subventions to retired teachers without pensions.[41] Thus the founding of the finance committee in 1931 and of the German School League of Buenos Aires in 1932 could only bring improvement of the material situation of the schoolteachers. Under the Nazi Teachers' League, Argentine Branch, which replaced the Teachers' Association soon thereafter, it improved still further.[42]

The centralizing reforms of 1931–1932 promised relief from long-standing organizational and financial problems, but of themselves they did not provide means of coming to grips with the more profound issues that had been raised in 1918–1919 and ignored uneasily ever since. The community's class hierarchy had become more distended in the intervening years. The schools not only reflected and perpetuated this faithfully, but it was clear also that most of them—the working-class schools especially, but also the Burmeister School—were becoming "German schools" in little more than name. In 1932, W. Rohmeder described the Cangallo School and the Barracas School as decaying relics—in Germanic terms, obviously, as both schools had increased their enrollment since 1919, from 360 to 578 and from 172 to 315 respectively. He wrote that he expected the outward dispersal of German *barrios* to continue, and he made it clear that he was quite aware of the socioeconomic differentiations involved. Particular effort, he felt, should be placed on strengthening the Germanic character of the two Belgrano schools and those developing in the wealthier suburbs just to the north of Belgrano. The large remainder of the greater Buenos Aires schools he considered more or less working-class; he was not optimistic about their future—or, apparently, even very interested in it.[43]

The obeisances toward Argentine nationality required by law had not, in any event, proven especially bothersome: they could easily enough be reduced to perfunctory ritual and routinized teaching. One still hears the anecdote, which dates from the later 1930s, of the two-sided portrait which (according to legend) hung in the office of the rector of one of the German schools. On one side, displayed when Argentine school inspectors were expected, was Domingo Faustino Sarmiento; on the obverse was Adolf Hitler. The deeper issue was the commitment, voluntary or otherwise, of most of the community to a life-long stay in Argentina. For, like it or not, their children were not only legally Argentines (in most cases), they were also de facto Argentines. The language of the streets, of their peers, and increasingly of the schools themselves was Spanish. From the pessimism that darkened his last years in Argentina, Wilhelm Keiper wrote: "for the child, this is *his* world. That German world, in which the teacher would dearly love to immerse him, is in the best case a beautiful but unrealizable ideal."[44] And he added dourly that, should the child by chance reenter the German world, he might well be disillusioned.

Understandably, parents were concerned to insure that their children's education was appropriate to Argentine conditions. Hugo Dörsing observed in 1933: "Among employers as well as among employees it has become obvious [since the war] that, by itself, being a 'vivo' is not sufficient for rising in life. It must be joined to a solid school education; so that today applicants with a broad school-acquired knowledge are given preference."[45] Dörsing declared himself satisfied, in general, with the German elementary schools in Buenos Aires, for he believed they accomplished in six years what the Volksschule in Germany accomplished in eight. They were versatile: from the beginning instruction was in both German and Spanish; the curriculum was appropriate for the Argentine sexto grado; those that had a seventh year used it well to permit their students to review and internalize in Spanish all their previous studies. To be sure, by a "solid school education" Dörsing had principally in mind such subjects as shorthand, accounting, and typing. Some improvements could be made, he felt, by emphasizing these subjects at the upper levels or in a German intermediary business school—since by law children could not go to work anyway until the age of fourteen.[46]

It is perhaps best to give the last word to Wilhelm Keiper. In 1928 he had acknowledged that year by year pressure had grown to carry out more teaching in Spanish—Argentina was, after all, a land of the future, and time was working for it. It was fortunately true that Argentine custom and law respected the inviolability of personal and family life, and it was therefore possible for the schools to encourage "duality" in their students: to make them Argentine citizens but German culture bearers. But by 1932 his gloom had deepened: "Deutschtum, and with it the German schools here, as everywhere outside the Fatherland, must probably of necessity disappear into foreign cultural communities. Thus it is probably not worth the trouble to expend any further strength and effort."[47]

Behavioral acculturation was thus proceeding in infinite particulars— one is almost inclined to say, inexorably. This is the all-embracing phenomenon in the context of which the frenetic organizational work of the German nationalists of the 1920s and early 1930s must be understood. For in terms of tables of organization, and in terms of the capacity to enforce the appearance of political conformity, they had been remarkably successful in holding the Germans to Deutschtum.

Much of the proliferation of German associations during the latter 1920s was simply a function of the dispersal of the German-speaking population throughout the vast metropolitan area. From the existing matrix of *Vereine*, new schools, religious congregations, occupational associations, musical, sport, and general-purpose social clubs were spun off into the new outlying *barrios*. But the altered social hierarchy of the 1920s necessitated other adjustments as well. The Riding Club, the Rowing Club, and the Deutscher Klub had evolved into the community's upper-crust sanctuaries; and most of the remaining pre-1914 *Vereine* retained, however vestigially, their original bourgeois norms and exclusivity. They were therefore beyond the financial grasp and/or social pretensions of the majority of postwar newcomers. This *lacuna* was filled by so-called *Landsmannschaften*, or regional associations—the Donau-Schwaben, the Siebenbürger-Sachsen, Banat-Deutschen, and so on—that began to appear rather suddenly in the late 1920s. Wilfert's listing of 1932 includes 12 such regional associations, not including the old-line Swiss and Austrian organizations; by 1936, there were 17. The great variety of sport clubs that appeared toward 1930 also served as nuclei for a Germanic population of heterogeneous origins and largely lower-class social status. By 1932, the number of German-speaking associations of all types in the greater Buenos Aires area reached the impressive total of 119.[48]

But it is important to note also that this proliferation was accompanied by centralization under high-level coordinating agencies—the so-called *Dachverbände*—which were both city-wide and, increasingly, national in scope. The creation of the German School League of Buenos Aires, discussed earlier, was typical of this process; not surprisingly, under the nazi regime an attempt was made to create a nation-wide school league, but this was unsuccessful.[49] Several important *Dachverbände* were, of course, older: the German Welfare Society, the German Chamber of Commerce, and the Volksbund all dated from 1916. Under Hitlerism the Chamber of Commerce would become the single directive agency of the German economic establishment in Argentina, and membership for German firms doing business in the country would cease to be voluntary. The Volksbund, particularly after it came under the direction of Dr. Martin Arndt in 1928, provided social services, occasional financial assistance, and educational materials to the scattered and financially strapped Germanic communities of the interior. Its nationalist propaganda became more specifically national socialistic after 1931; after 1933 it would serve as the principal organizer of the pageants and rituals of nazism in Argentina. The work of these organizations in the interior was paralleled by that of other *Dachverbände*—religious, sport, musical, occupational—all of which had their headquarters in Buenos Aires.

The emerging preeminence of Buenos Aires among Argentina's German language communities was further strengthened by its educational advantages: the Goethe and Burmeister schools afforded the only secondary-level German education available in the republic. And it was strengthened also by the tendency after World War I of German firms to close down unprofitable branches in secondary cities. Buenos Aires was the point of reference and ultimate goal of innumerable immigrants who had been unable to establish themselves there on first arrival. It was where bright young people from the interior would attempt to make their careers. In consequence, once-flourishing German communities in such cities as Rosario,[50] Córdoba, Tucumán,[51] Santa Fe,[52] and Bahía Blanca subsided into stagnation. In all this, of course, the Germans were merely reproducing in miniature a generalized Argentine phenomenon. Some writers, notably Elsner and Keiper, did not view this process with unrelieved enthusiasm. However, the geographer Franz Kühn, a resident of the republic since 1909, took the more common yea-sayer's view: in 1933 he wrote that the entire Germanic population of Argentina stood in the shadow of the Buenos Aires colony, which he apostrophized as "a cultural factor of the greatest importance as a crossroads and defender of *Deutschtum.*"[53]

Even as Theodor Alemann had foreseen in 1920, the Reichsdeutsch nationalists had systematically driven their opponents from the executive committees of the community's associations. In 1927 a partial list of the *Vereine* sending greetings to Field Marshal von Hindenburg on his eightieth birthday included all the school associations, the Evangelical and Catholic congregations, the Bavarian and *Plattdütche* regional associations, the Football Club, the Philatelists' Club, the several choirs, and the Mandolin Club.[54] These executive committees were in turn represented in the Council of Executive Committees, which remained after the war the supreme organ of community self-government. By 1929, the expanded associational structure and the increased demand for social services combined to drive the council's aggregate annual budget over one million pesos.[55] In the same period, however, the ability of the commonality to support these private institutions at prewar levels had declined sharply. The principal financial support therefore came from the great trading houses, investment consortia, utilities, and manufacturing concerns. Until early 1933, the leverage provided by organizational adroitness plus money was more than sufficient to maintain the sway of the *Geld-Aristokratie*'s traditionalist, vestigially monarchist, ideology in the community's associations. After 1933 it would suffice to enforce outward conformity to Hitler's New Order.

9. Cultural Despair, Perceptions of Nazism, and the Gleichschaltung of 1933

Field Marshal von der Goltz, whose laudatory though superficial description of Buenos Aires during the centennial celebrations of 1910 was widely known on both sides of the Atlantic, was, in the words of the *Geschichte des Deutschtums in Argentinien*, "the last visitor who could say of the German colony in Buenos Aires that it was a truly happy place."[1] The authors have grasped the community's overriding mood from the reversal of fortune it suffered in 1914 down to its final dissolution in the aftermath of World War II. What has been written here of the period until the early 1930s should make it unnecessary to belabor the point. The sufferings of the First World War were compounded by the repercussions of German defeat. In the postwar decade the community was beset by interrelated anxieties over socioeconomic status and cultural autonomy and was further racked by political conflict and the social disorganization that attended the inundation of newcomers, most of whom could be assimilated into the community only with the greatest difficulty.

Strange ideas and passions, and passions masked as ideas, circulated abroad in this community. Through most of the postwar decade cynicism and despair dominated the community consciousness. Its intellectuals, such as they were, cultivated such attitudes in more or less deliberate imitation of European fashions; but they were also current, if less polished, far beyond the ambit of literary salons and their doyennes. It is equally clear that for a time the appeals of national socialism overmastered these moods and replaced them with excitement and hope—hope of purposeful work and recognition of the common people, the *kleine Leute*, of the community, of—to put it in slightly grander terms—moral renewal and regeneration of the Germanic cultural bond. In the context of Buenos Aires *Deutschtum* renewal and regeneration implied, of course, a restructuring of authority and the supercession of hierarchs whose arrogance had failed to conceal their tiredness and moral bankruptcy—but these objectives had been nurtured, after all, by the community's dissidents since 1918.

In a time of mass bewilderment and unease, of erosion of traditional authority and paralysis of traditional institutions, national socialism's reliance on activism, visceral dynamism, and sheer will evoked highly positive reactions. But precisely because it operated less on the intellect than upon the will to act, and the will to believe antecedent to it, national socialism succeeded in being very different things to very different people. This was as true in Buenos Aires as elsewhere and thus, even within a relatively small population, the psychology of the reception of nazism was most complex.

On the other hand, the manipulations that caused the community, by the end of 1933, to give the appearance of enthusiastic conformity to Hitler's New Order were quite straightforward. Therein lies abundant irony, for all available evidence indicates that, whatever the intensity of the commonality's response to nazism, and whatever the motives behind it, the conversion (*Gleichschaltung*) of the Buenos Aires community to nazism was an arrangement acquiesced in by the traditionalist elite, one which served to maintain their hegemony.

A conventional sort of anti-Semitism—social anti-Semitism—had been present in the community from its beginnings, but little written evidence survives to permit generalizations concerning its scope. As noted earlier, it had figured in the snubbing of Albert Einstein by the socially prominent circles of the community in 1925 as well as in the harassment of Alfons Goldschmidt two years earlier. For a time at the end of the war it had emerged to the public view in a more virulent form in the pages of *Die Wacht* (later the local organ of the racialist Deutsch-Nationale Volkspartei) and in fugitive pamphlets put out by one Merzbacher entitled *Deutsche Blätter*.[2] One must assume that it was these same ultrareactionary circles which were in contact with *criollo* groups such as the Liga Patriótica which were simultaneously cultivating indigenous reaction and anti-Semitism.[3] Among the Germans, however, the attempt to excise German-speaking Jews from the (informal) body politic would come only in 1933 and after.[4]

The related doctrines of Nordic racial superiority were also in the air. They received a full-dress exposition in *Phoenix*, the prestigious journal of the German Scientific Society, in 1926. In a long essay entitled "Races, Heredity, and Eugenics," one Dr. Rauenbusch[5] summarized the theories of Gobineau, Chamberlain, Madison Grant, and others and developed their implications for Argentina. To meet the need for a "sane race policy," the developing science of eugenics was providing means for identifying and dealing with the feebleminded and other undesirables. But the menaces were much greater and time was short. Rauenbusch observed that the Protestant peoples of Northern Europe and North America were following a policy which would,

in a few generations, lead to "race suicide." These peoples were limit-
ing the number of their progeny in each generation whilst the inferior
races surrounding them continued to multiply like fruit flies. To be
sure, in Catholic Argentina prospects appeared somewhat brighter, for
there the natural elite did continue to reproduce itself at a satisfactory
rate.

But there also existed the danger of creating an "inferior mongrel
population," and Argentina was far from immune to this. Italian influence was visibly growing in Argentine intellectual and cultural life,
Rauenbusch pointed out, while that of the Germans was in retreat; nor
was it likely that this degenerative tendency could be ameliorated by
other superior people: the Scandinavians, the English, the *criollos*
themselves. Argentina was perhaps the "whitest" country in the New
World, but purposeful work would be required to keep it that way.

The same year Rauenbusch's jeremiad was seconded, in a rather
more earthy way, by one Otto Steininger of Bahía Blanca, a philoso-
pher more of the beerhall variety. For Steininger also, Argentina was
the whitest country in the New World; whatever else one might say
of them the Argentines did not run the same danger as the Brazilians
and other South Americans of becoming "totally niggerized [*volkom-
men zu verniggern*]."[6]

A fashionable Spenglerian sort of despair also found its practitioners
in Buenos Aires. One of them, as one might expect, was A. E. Gross.
Early in 1924, in an extended piece of doggerel sardonically entitled
Al gran pueblo argentino salud, he wrote of:

> The well-known ease with which the Teutons as individuals allow
> themselves to be denationalized and, in particular, to become
> Latinized. It is really questionable whether . . . the remnants of
> the German racial community will leave behind, for future mil-
> lennia, any evidence of one-time German brilliance, might, great-
> ness. . . .
>
> Once the Germans were the only energetic people in Argentina.
> Today the workingman swaggers by with walking stick and
> patent leather shoes. The stableboy, when he is not at the beck and
> call of the "noblesse," lounges about smoking. Everyone is at home
> around the beer tap. Even the least flunky now passes out tips with
> a grand gesture. The serving girl imitates Madame—for better or
> worse. . . . In these enormously miserable times—today.[7]

The usual objects of Gross' bile were the local elite and their supporters among the well-to-do business and professional people; this
attack on the working classes is a rare departure. It is not clear to what

"these enormously miserable times" refers: events in Europe (the Franco-Belgian occupation of the Ruhr and the inflation) or the wretched situation of the white-collar German immigrants who inundated Argentina in 1923–1924. Certainly, however, his sensibilities were outraged by the sight of apparent working-class affluence and perhaps even more by the insouciance with which it was displayed. For an educated man like Gross, whose many qualities had long gone unnoticed, the times were really out of joint.

At somewhat higher social levels of the community a more raffiné existential nausea was a common reaction to its pervasive materialism and philistinism or to the suspension of affective life necessitated by living in or for the future: "Everyone newly arrived here asks himself the same question: does the entire sense and purpose and content of life of the Germans here consist of only one thing—the leave-trip back to Germany after ten years? Or, if one has been really lucky, only five?" The same writer observed that, if anything, this existence was harsher on women than men; he described "the colony women who have forgotten how to laugh . . . even face powder and cosmetics do not conceal this in the woman-about-town."[8] Else Jerusalem gave a more extended version of the situation of the well-to-do woman:

> The foreign atmosphere lies like a thick fog layer around mind, nerves, soul; it produces a certain impressionability of the entire organism. How many women who return to the Homeland in high spirits come back again bearing the painful discovery, "I don't know what's happening"—"but I don't understand people anymore"—"everything has become strange." [The pathological symptoms grow clearer]; the richer and worthier the [human] material, the greater the damage done by the germs of indulgence and boredom. . . . Perhaps nowhere on earth are there colder, more hostile, more indifferent onlookers than those who in a colony observe the life and struggle and death of a soul. . . .
>
> One is imprisoned in class distinctions: "this is what is done"— "that is what is not done" are written in flaming letters over the lintel of every household. For one's social classification, and hence what is permissible and what is not permissible, depends for the most part on the material income of the head of the family. . . .
> In North America the women of the foreign communities join in the general intellectual life; not so here in the provinces. . . . In order to grow, the human soul has one great need: the feeling that "I belong to this; everything that happens here has to do with me." This does not occur on foreign soil.[9]

An earthier evocation of immigrant existence was provided by Peter Harold-Hatzold. Objectively, perhaps, Harold-Hatzold rose far above his origins as an illegitimate child in Franconia, one of the poorer regions of Germany, but he never betrayed any awareness of what he had accomplished, much less pride in it. It is evident from his own account that he never overlooked an insult nor forgave one. Unquestionably he would have been a difficult person in any environment—as is in fact clear from his escapades in Germany and Switzerland even before he migrated to Argentina in the 1880s with his English wife. (She later returned to England—for health reasons, according to Harold-Hatzold. They were never divorced. He later lived *a la americana*, as he put it, with a number of women who at least satisfied his instinct for strife-filled relationships.) He was evidently a hard worker, and the *recreo* that he built up on an island at Tigre ultimately prospered. In 1925, at the age of sixty-eight, he sold it for 100,000 pesos. By 1933 he had gone blind and—as a result of a poor investment in a *quinta* in Morón, the greed of his common-law wife, medical bills, and living expenses—was virtually destitute. His only "purpose in life" was to complete a "little book"—his memoirs.

Making all allowance for his peculiarly abrasive personality and the vengeful bitterness of his last years, Harold-Hatzold still succeeds in re-creating a lower-middle-class social landscape—one pervaded (if your sensibilities run that way) by the smell of sweat and boiled cabbage and the squawking of chickens in a muddy back yard. He paints a social landscape of rattlebrained small businessmen one short jump ahead of the bailiff, picaresque young immigrants on the make, sodden gone-to-seed exschoolmasters and exofficers, leathery tightfisted widows and the embattled dwellers of the *pensiones* they kept, aging prostitutes with a sharp eye out for material security in their declining years; of mistrust, petty swindles, and betrayal; of endless gossip, fleeting unstable relationships, and existential loneliness; of tradition-encrusted ethical norms which rarely, in the anarchic Argentine environment, inhibited extremes of predatory or self-indulgent or self-destructive behavior. Harold-Hatzold did not believe in God—otherwise, he said, he might have taken comfort from the biblical injunction: "revenge is mine, saith the Lord." As it was, his last strength, and last pesos, had to be devoted to trying to accomplish the task himself.[10]

The failure of traditional social restraints to operate more than fitfully in the Argentine environment did not silence the moralism of public discourse—if anything, perhaps, it heightened it. Gross and the socialist press had played an important role in exposing the wartime profiteering of the respectable business houses, the more noisomely fraudulent postwar colonization schemes, and the hypocrisy of the leading members of the Chamber of Commerce who, although publicly committed to the most strident German nationalism, were in practice free of any rigidity when it came to cultivating profitable business connections. The dissident press also belabored the alleged involvement of well-placed German businessmen in Buenos Aires' notorious organized prostitution and white-slave traffic. It repeatedly warned women immigrants against the more dubious types of employment offered through the German agencies and denounced the respectable German language press (especially the *Deutsche La-Plata Zeitung*) for accepting large numbers of euphemistically worded personal advertisements placed by prostitutes or procurers.[11] When in 1930 the Jewish Zwi Migdal organization, the cover for one of the largest white-slaving operations, was broken up, it was reported that a thrill of fear ran through much of the business community—for it was not known how far the reformers' net might be cast.[12]

The most savage indictment of the local elite, however, was produced by a man who lived in its midst for nearly two decades. He was Max René Hesse: member of the staff of the German Hospital, society doctor, erstwhile member of the Committee of Fifteen and the Republican Association, and, beginning in his forties, successful popular novelist.[13] He had earlier published a number of innocuous short pieces; the community was far from prepared for the explosive appearance of his two novels, *Morath schlägt sich durch* (*Morath Struggles Ahead*) and *Morath verwirklicht einen Traum* (*Morath Realizes a Dream*), published simultaneously in Berlin in 1933.

They are not impressive as literature. The prose is pedestrian and cliché-ridden; the structure is distorted both by bizarre anecdotes drawn mainly from Hesse's medical practice and by excursuses on Argentine customs which Hesse or his publisher apparently thought necessary for a European readership. The novels' great impact at the time was due chiefly to the fact that they are lengthy (more than thirteen hundred pages) and detailed romans à clef set in the German high society of Buenos Aires. Most of the main characters were easily recognizable and almost no one came away unscathed. For us, nearly half a century later, their interest lies in their exposition of the movement of a particular sort of psyche (the unfulfilled little man) within a particular social milieu (the materialistic German upper middle class of Buenos Aires) toward the mythos of nazism.

The protagonist, Jakob Morath, is a physician; it seems apparent that Hesse put much of his personality and personal history into the character. If so, it is a remarkable exercise in self-flagellation. The sole physical attribute that the author establishes for Morath is the "wooden smile" with which he responds to virtually all social contretemps. Otherwise, Morath strikes the reader as a complaisant cuckold and a prig, and it is difficult to accept Hesse's attempts to make of him the most extreme kind of idealist, a Dostoyevskian "holy fool." He is merely tiresome.

The two novels form a linked narrative that covers a span of perhaps ten years. The first, *Morath Struggles Ahead*, begins with Morath's arrival in Argentina, his first months as the most junior physician on the staff of the German Hospital, and the launching of his social career (which, it is understood, is to lead to a lucrative private practice) in upper-middle-class circles. In passing, there are satirical treatments of the ethics of the medical profession and the hypocrisy of the community's "salon-Bolcheviks." Morath becomes infatuated with Haidée Tucher, daughter of a German father (deceased) and an Argentine mother. Since mother and daughter, although acceptable in the best circles, have been left with little income, it has become necessary to find an advantageous match for her; and Morath becomes dimly aware of the machinations through which her circle arranges the match between them. The most important wire puller is her uncle, Ricardo Erdmann (Emil Hayn), whose relation to his beautiful niece is tinged with eroticism throughout. Erdmann uses his influence with *criollo* associates to permit Morath to pass easily through his revalidation exams. On another occasion, when Morath has stupidly trodden on the prerogatives of medical colleagues, Erdmann uses his power as a member of the hospital board of governors to save Morath from reprimand. Morath "should by now have gotten the idea of how the game is played: it is simply politics—whose power is behind you?" (p. 454). The novel ends with the civil marriage of Morath and Haidée in Montevideo (where—conveniently for Hesse's plot structure—divorce was and is legal).

The first volume, in which Morath is meshed into the system, is in effect a denunciation of that system:

> In this country one has only two things in mind: to get rich and to draw attention to oneself. Of the things that go together with getting rich, you simply have no idea. To be noticed in the colony, one must be as strongly and visibly active as possible in the not always good-smelling stew of a *Verein* or club, so that the colony says, "There! See him! That man busies himself for the general good!" (p. 51)

And the most eminent members of the colony here—what are

they outside business hours? Totally ignorant, superstitious neu-
rasthenics. Many rich men are scarcely able to compose a letter of
any length in good German. They came into the country with
patches on their behinds; most of them have come up in the world
by means of business dealings they would be unwilling to admit
to. In wartime, even before, they were ready, at the slightest
whisper of business advantage, to change their nationality—to
make available to the enemy their wolfram ore, their alcohol, their
wool and grain, their shipping—just so long as it was well paid-for.
That is the cruel reality, which no one who wishes to belong may
acknowledge, let alone try to change. For the little guy, the employee, who is on the outside, a curtain is drawn—perhaps one
does this even for oneself and one's conscience (should such a
rare commodity happen to be present). [The curtain consists of]
the flags of the Homeland, patriotic speeches à la Fichte, money
collections for the needy Fatherland (naturally always noted in
lists published in the [DLPZ]). (pp. 292–293).

Who is the influential, determinant German colony? Without
question, a conglomeration, accidentally thrown together, of businessmen and technicians of all sorts, all of them entirely one-sided
in their training and active life. Often—in most cases, in fact—
they came out here as young men with small incomes or as out-
and-out adventurers. They have made it on ability or luck—or, let
us say, taking the opportunities as they came. They have made
fortunes, some of them giant fortunes, and have attained the corresponding social position; but intellectually they are narrow and
dried out. At bottom, they believe only in money; and thus, without knowing it, they are ready to believe in anything magical, oc-
cult, even absurd. They consult graphologists; they have their
palms read and their horoscopes cast. Such a society will always
have a nagging fear of illness and death. The little that the physician can [honorably] promise, they cannot accept. . . . Basically
they only want to be allowed to believe in sorcery. . . . Spiritually
we still live, or live again, in the same landscape as Central African
Negroes or Brazilian headhunters. (pp. 254–255)

The action of the second volume, *Morath Realizes a Dream*, consists of Morath's rejection of the role that the community has assigned
him and his fumbling search for a more satisfying existence. It begins
a couple of years later. Morath has become prosperous through his
private practice as well as his affiliation with the German Hospital. His
domestic situation, however, is disastrous. He and Haidée have had no

children. She has, in fact, banished him from her bedroom—ultimately from the house—and is carrying on an affair with the German ambassador, von Rutlitz, whom she intends to marry as soon as she can divorce Morath. In the meantime she continues to extort financial support from Morath, a process which Hesse describes in what seems ruefully well-informed detail. Toward the end of the novel, Morath saves von Rutlitz's life during a hunting trip on an *estancia* in Santa Fe and then agrees to divorce Haidée.

In the interim the opportunity to create a new life has appeared when Morath is offered the post of medical officer to a small revolutionary force then being organized by one Colonel Jara to overthrow the Paraguayan government. His spirits are further raised by friendship with his sister's husband, Dietrich Uhlenkamp, once (in 1918) a Communist, more recently a storm troop *Führer*. Uhlenkamp persuades Morath: "You don't know what I know. The world is finally once again full of adventure and possibilities" (pp. 206–207). But Uhlenkamp is uncomfortable in the social circles to which Morath introduces him in Buenos Aires and Morath discovers why: Uhlenkamp had been forced out of the storm troopers because of his unacceptably radical views: "industry, landed estates, nobility—these things are all right, but they must take a second place in the coming Reich. We workers, peasants, ordinary citizens are the salt of the earth; with the masses, we will be the bearers of ideology and the leaders. The unknown little man was always Germany's best, most loyal son" (p. 210).

The expedition to Paraguay is routed (the Paraguayan loyalist forces are also led by German officers) and Uhlenkamp is killed. During the campaign Morath spends much time with the other German free lances whom Jara has recruited and conceives a deep admiration for them (evidently Hesse had been reading Ernst Jünger). In the end, however, Morath refuses to accept their willingness to sacrifice themselves for future generations of the *Volk*. Rather, he senses a rising imperative to use his own time, to throw his own life into the balance—the balance between the only two remaining valid value systems of the European order: communism and the nation. His self-discovery and conversion to activism are buttressed by a contrived piece of symbolism. During his career in Buenos Aires he had continued (rather improbably) to read theology in his spare time. He had considered himself a follower of Saint Francis (and also thereby justified his meek reaction to the abuse heaped on him by Haidée and others). Following his Paraguayan experience, however, he put Saint Francis behind him: "he is only a model for politicians and reconcilers. Saint Augustine is my man" (p. 403). His commitment to Augustinianism is, in fact, the key to the fulfillment that Hesse eventually provides for him: "With what God-filled certainty this holy man [Augustine] planned to build the City of God with force and power. . . . It was not as though he [Morath] dreamed of building it himself, or even of being able to plan it; but at least—well, what was his part in it? Where was the other, the saint or demigod, for whom he, Jakob Morath, might carry the mortar, drag the stones, perhaps even shape them; so that the utmost, the greatest thought at the end of his life might be that he was a pillar within [the City]!" (p. 394).

At any rate, toward the end of the novel Morath discovers his "saint or demigod" (or what, in the circumstances, had to pass for such) in General Uriburu, leader of the 1930 coup, and his minister of the interior, "Dr. Ezcurra" (Matías C. Sánchez Sorondo). In Argentina's Northwest he finds coreligionists among the idealistic nationalists of the Liga Patriótica, young men who, like Morath, have hitherto been stifled by the conformism of their elders. On this upbeat the saga ends.

Hesse, according to legend, was rather surprised on the appearance of the novels to find himself hailed as a nazi thinker such as Hitler could have wished; but the more he thought about it the happier he was to accept the acclaim.[14]

In late 1929 and the first part of 1930 the Yrigoyen administration showed itself quite unequipped to deal with the growing economic debacle; when it was overthrown by General Uriburu's troops in September 1930 it left power unmourned. But the following year Uriburu's vaguely defined right-radical and nationalist policies were aborted when he himself was eased from power by a rival clique under retired General Augustín P. Justo. In 1932 Justo won a full six-year presidential term in elections which were a reversion to the worst abuses of the pre-1916 era; his administration, and those that succeeded it, rested upon fraud and ultimately upon force. In the Justo regime the traditional landholding *oligarquía* found an agent with which to try to set the clock back. As the trading nations of the Atlantic world turned increasingly to bilateralism and experiments in autarchy, the government's prime economic objective became that of maintaining the position of Argentina's traditional exports in overseas market-places, particularly the most important of them all, Great Britain. Its success in doing so insured the continuing prosperity of the country's great agrarian and pastoral interests; the quid pro quo's exacted by the British, however, in the form of preferential treatment for their manufactures and capital investments, fell heavily upon Argentina's nascent industries and Argentine consumers generally: Argentina became Great

Britain's "sixth dominion." Although civilian middle-class factions found it possible to work within the system (through the so-called *Concordancia*), resentments flourished among nationalists at all points along the political spectrum; and on the right admiration for the authoritarian solutions of Hitler, Mussolini, Salazar, Franco, and their like grew in military and civilian circles. This period of political cynicism and immobilism—the *década infame*, as it came to be known—would end only in June 1943 with the confused military coup that was the immediate prelude to Peronism.

The Argentine political overturn did not occur in isolation, of course. The onset of the depression placed immense strains on liberal parliamentary institutions throughout the Western world. The Buenos Aires Germans were familiar not only with the demise of an ineffectual and corrupt parliamentarism in Argentina; they could not fail to be aware of economic collapse and mass unemployment in Germany, the erosion of support for Weimar, and the polarization of political society into bristling camps of extreme Left and Right. As noted in Chapter Four, much of the capital that fled Germany at this time was placed in Argentine holdings and many new business establishments were founded. New political currents circulated in the community as well.

The rightist propaganda directed at the German Argentines became more stridently nationalistic and more assertive of Germany's revisionist claims. This was especially true of the Volksbund's publications. *Der Bund*, for example, began to devote less attention to the tribulations of German immigrants on La Plata and much more to the oppressions weighing on German minorities in such countries as Poland and elsewhere. One single edition, that of May 1931, gives an idea of this new orientation: it included essays on "Germany and Disarmament," "Possibilities of Revision of the Versailles Treaty," "The Suppression of South Tyrol," "Alsace-Lorraine under the French," and "Poland's Campaign against German Science." Much of this material was supplied by the Association for the German Racial Community Overseas (Verein für das Deutschtum im Auslande) in Germany, but the Volksbund's president, Dr. Martin Arndt, also mastered the paranoid nationalist style, as the following excerpt from the Volksbund's 1933 *Yearbook* suggests: "A glance at the world and our Fatherland suffices to show that the seeds sown by the enemies of our Homeland during and after the war have begun to sprout; that the powers have remained at work to shake and annihilate our racial unity and economic strength."[15] By this time, too, Arndt had taken to signing his effusions not only *mit deutschem Grüss* but also *Heil Hitler!*

With the new influx of German capital and a renewed bombardment of revanchist propaganda came the first cadres of national socialist organizers. A Nazi Association (*Vereinigung*) with fifty-nine members was organized in Buenos Aires in February 1931. By April of that year it had become the Buenos Aires local (*Ortsgruppe*) of the NSDAP. By September 1932 an Argentine Country Organization (Landesgruppe Argentinien) was in existence with one local, seven "strongpoints" (*Stützpunkte*), and a total of 287 NSDAP members. The work of nazi agents-on-mission was supplemented irregularly by that of party members among the officers and crewmen of the Hamburg-Süd and HAPAG liners touching at Buenos Aires.[16] No evidence has been discovered of agreements between nazi officials and the traditionalist leadership of the Buenos Aires community between 1931 and 1933—nor is it likely to be—but the circumstantial case for such a rapprochement seems overwhelming. In view of the *Geld-Aristokratie*'s proven capacity to harass or stifle political tendencies of which it disapproved, and in view also of the way in which the community would nominally be assimilated (*gleichgeschaltet*) to the New Order in 1933 through the adhesion of its voluntary associations—associations almost totally dominated by the community's moneyed elite, as has been seen—the nazis were simply not free to set about their organizational work without the acquiescence of the community's traditionalist, erstwhile monarchist, holders of power.

Whatever the circumstances of the rapprochement, it is clear that at this time the German-speaking commonality was highly susceptible to the appeals of national socialism. Unemployment had again reached intolerable levels and social agencies, exiguous at best in Argentina, were overwhelmed by the crisis. The 1931 report of the German Welfare Society makes this somberly clear: "The army of the unemployed has grown to shocking proportions. . . . The conditions for temporary work in the countryside are bad, and everyone knows that more help is available in Buenos Aires than there. . . . Not only men without dependents but white-collar employees of long tenure have lost their positions, and wives and children have been dragged down into misery with them. . . . Day by day the troop of unemployed camping out in Calle Azopardo [around the DWG offices] grows. [Many are reluctant to come]: there is more concealed misery among us than one might think."

The DWG's officials claimed that the situation was as bad as it had been in 1915, the worst year of the war, but that now, unlike the war years, its resources amounted to little more than 18,000 pesos. "The need has grown so great that our means are at an end."[17] In November 1931 an ad hoc group headed by the Masonic Johannis Lodge set up a soup kitchen in the Seamen's Home for the several thousand German-speaking unemployed. Early the following year the NSDAP supplemented this with a vigorous and well-financed aid program—for which display of will and initiative the party won, it goes without saying, much general approval.[18]

In January 1933 one Willi Köhn arrived in Buenos Aires from Chile, where he had been serving as NSDAP country organization leader (*Landesgruppenleiter*); he would later serve in Germany as the NSDAP's overseas commissar for South America. His major task in Buenos Aires was to organize, in conjunction with the Volksbund, a mass rally in support of Adolf Hitler's accession to the chancellorship of Germany on 30 January 1933. This was duly held on 5 April in the Teatro Colón with some 2,500 persons in attendance. The auditorium was decked with the imperial black-white-red colors; Köhn, Arndt, and one Leo Schäfer spoke; and fifty-one massed *Vereine* sang the "Horst Wessel Lied." Arndt praised the nazis for their work in reawakening hope and belief in the German future; nevertheless his appeal was essentially nationalistic: "Keep in mind that you are a German!" Standing together for the Fatherland was not necessarily the same as affirming a political party affiliation, he reminded his listeners: "standing together" meant support for German language and German customs, German churches, schools, and charitable institutions—and not speaking disparagingly of Germany in front of foreigners.[19]

Köhn left thereafter, apparently satisfied with his efforts, but the process of *Gleichschaltung* continued in Buenos Aires. Nazis were accepted into the executive committees of the various associations and proposed motions of adhesion to the New Order, which were duly ratified by the membership. The procedure was even simpler for *Vereine* that considered themselves merely branches of German parent organizations. The largest organization of white-collar workers, for example, the German National Business Employees' League on La Plata, construed itself to be technically a local of the league in Germany. In mid-1933 the latter was incorporated into Robert Ley's NSDAP Labor Front, and one A. Haid was named by Ley as its head. It followed therefore that the Buenos Aires branch was also incorporated into the Labor Front, and a party member, Alfred Miller or Müller (who was also to be publisher of the Buenos Aires edition of *Der Trommler*), was named trustee (*Vertrauensmann*)—in effect, the Labor Front's deputy—in the executive committee. And that was that.[20]

The Volksbund and the NSDAP country organization leadership called for a second mass rally on 9 November to send a collective message of approval to Berlin on the occasion of Germany's departure from the Disarmament Conference and the League of Nations. The rapidity with which the community's institutions had been brought into line through mid-1933 is indicated by the fact that now the executive committees of 103 associations, clubs, and leagues associated themselves with this gesture of support for the New Order. "Never since the memorable days of August 1914 has the German colony stood together so solidly with one spirit," burbled the Volksbund.[21] Indeed, to appearances this was true, for by this time only Vorwärts, the *Argentinisches Tageblatt,* and a German-Jewish association to aid refugees from nazism (organized in April 1933) remained to offer forthright resistance.

In one sense, therefore, the triumph of Hitlerism among the Buenos Aires Germans was a cynical political deal which turned on the *Geld-Aristokratie*'s control of employment, welfare, clientage, credit, and voluntary associations and the docility of the community's lesser members. But it would be simplistic to see it as nothing more than that, for the imposition from above of the trappings of Hitlerism was but one aspect of the social dynamics of fascism. The threatening or real decline of social status among the community's numerically predominant middle-class component, concurrent anxiety concerning the community's ability to retain its cultural identity amidst the absorptive processes of Argentinization, smoldering hostility toward the hypocrisy, ruthlessness, and corruption of the German business elite, and the ignominious end of Argentine liberal democracy in 1930 (as well as the return after 1932 to a more authoritarian form of political chicanery) all combined to generate for a time a positive response to the nazis' promises of change and renewal.

To be sure, the commonality remained, as it had always been, mostly voiceless. The responses that have been preserved, however, lend weight to this interpretation. The movement of Max René Hesse from a populist and more or less socialist position in 1918 to all but overt acceptance of "left-wing" nazism by 1933 has been noted. The case of Hans Schmidt is rather different. Schmidt began as a knockabout in Argentina in 1912 and first wrote an account of his adventures in 1921. His fortunes did not much improve, but in 1938 he published an updated version, this one dedicated to the Nazi Labor Front. He wrote passionately of the resurgence of hope he had felt, after so many lost years, when he participated in the mass meetings organized by the Volksbund in Buenos Aires in 1933. Still a third version, even more fulsome in its praise of nazism, was published by Hermes-Druckerei in Buenos Aires in 1942.[22] A third case, that of Emil Ruth, is touched by both the comic and the pathetic. Between 1932 and 1934 Ruth published, at his own expense, no fewer than five pamphlets, which bore such titles as *National Socialism! I Seek Thee!* and *Two Years in the Service of National Socialism in La Plata.* All had to do with an immensely complicated struggle for control of the school association of the Temperley School, which Ruth had helped found as an offshoot of the Barracas School in 1930. Ruth sought the aid of NSDAP officials in preferring charges of corruption against several of his colleagues, especially one P. Günther. His most serious charge was that Günther had falsified accounting of the amount of beer consumed at a school picnic and had thereby made off with two to three thousand pesos. Whether the local NSDAP officials found adjudication of this matter within their *Weltanschauung* is unknown.[23]

And then there was A. E. Gross. Early in 1934 Gross opened *Die Neue Zeit* for the third (and apparently last) time. The immediate cause was the appearance, shortly before, of a pro-nazi satirical journal entitled *Der Djinn (The Genie).* The editorship was pseudonymous but the style was imitative of Gross'; and Gross felt compelled to disavow any connection with the new journal. By July of that year Gross was willing to acknowledge that his earlier populistic essays had been congruent with Goebbels' position (also of an earlier period). However, he held himself aloof from the local nazis, who he felt were already being corrupted by Argentina. But in the August and September 1934 numbers of *Die Neue Zeit* he proclaimed his faith that the decadence of the German Argentines could be eradicated by Hitlerist methods. Liberalism and socialism, he had come to believe, were merely means by which the "strong and worthy" were reduced to the level of the degenerate and were thus driven along amongst the "herd of sheep—the majority." Hitlerism, on the other hand, would make it possible for the "capable, the effective workers of arm and brain, the truly talented and energetic, finally to receive the honor due them as *model Germans [vorbildliche Volksgenossen].*" He embraced the anti-Semitism he had earlier, and often, denounced; and he urged his readers to take part in the "great work" of Adolf Hitler.[24]

Notes

1. Before 1914: the Old Colony

1. Bachmann, *Jahrbuch*, 1: 1–2, 10; 1: 57; *Buenos Aires Handels-Zeitung* (hereafter *BAHZ*), 15 January 1893 (Bachmann's obituary).

2. Wilhelm Lütge, Werner Hoffmann, and Karl Wilhelm Körner, *Geschichte des Deutschtums in Argentinien*, pp. 92–174; *Freie Presse* [Buenos Aires], *Mai-Festschrift*, 25 May 1960; *Freie Presse, Das Deutschtum in Argentinien* (special supplement), December 1951; Hermann Schmidt, *Geschichte der deutschen evangelischen Gemeinde Buenos Aires, 1843–1943*, pp. 34–36, 59.

3. Schmidt, *Geschichte*, pp. 34–36; Karl Kärger, *Landwirtschaft und Kolonisation im spanischen Amerika*, 1: 605; *Freie Presse, Mai-Festschrift*, p. 52; Lütge, Hoffmann, Körner, *Geschichte*, pp. 104, 131, 151–155, 249–251.

4. Bachmann, *Jahrbuch*, 1: 4–13; Ruhland und Reinhardt, *Deutscher La-Plata Kalender für das Jahr 1873*, pp. 164, 210–219; Lütge, Hoffmann, Körner, *Geschichte*, pp. 185–186; Adolfo Dorfman, *Historia de la industria argentina*, p. 305; *La Nación* [Buenos Aires], 25 May 1910, p. 128.

5. Carlos von der Becke, "Von Utz Schmidl bis von der Goltz," in *Freie Presse, Mai-Festschrift*, pp. 117–128; Lütge, Hoffmann, Körner, *Geschichte*, pp. 92–98, 122–133, 145, 204–205; Leopold Schnabl, *Buenos-Ayres: Land und Leute am silbernen Strome*, p. 175.

6. Lütge, Hoffmann, Körner, *Geschichte*, pp. 144, 146–147, 178–180; Kärger, *Landwirtschaft*, 1: 475–478; Juan Schobinger, *Inmigración y colonización suizas en la República Argentina en el siglo diécinueve*, p. 54; *Freie Presse, Deutschtum*, p. 13; *La Nación*, 9 July 1916, p. 593.

7. *Deutscher Kalender 1873*, pp. 189–190, 210–219; Bachmann, *Jahrbuch*, 1: 17.

8. *Deutscher Kalender 1873*, *passim*; Bachmann, *Jahrbuch*, 1: *passim*; *Freie Presse, Deutschtum*, pp. 13, 31, 35, 41; *Freie Presse, Mai-Festschrift*, pp. 116, 132; Schmidt, *Geschichte*, pp. 132–133, 222–223.

9. Schmidt, *Geschichte*, pp. 132–133, 141–143; *Freie Presse, Mai-Festschrift*, p. 132.

10. *Deutscher Kalender 1873*, pp. 151–173; Bachmann, *Jahrbuch*, 1: 64–67.

11. Schmidt, *Geschichte*, pp. 130–131; *Deutscher Kalender 1873*, pp. 182–183; Bachmann, *Jahrbuch*, 1: 6–7; Richard Napp, *1870 und 1871 Drüben und Hier: Zusammenstellung der wichtigsten Ereignisse des deutschfranzösischen Krieges*, pp. 205–209, 213–260.

12. Schobinger, *Inmigración*, pp. 151–152; Bachmann, *Jahrbuch*, 2: 8.

13. *La Nación*, 9 July 1916, pp. 585 *ff.*; *Freie Presse, Mai-Festschrift*, pp. 70–71.

14. *Deutscher Kalender 1873*, p. 205; *La Nación*, 9 July 1916, p. 585;

BAHZ, 8 December 1905; *Freie Presse, Mai-Festschrift*, p. 26; Schnabl, *Buenos-Ayres*, pp. 190–191; Lütge, Hoffmann, Körner, *Geschichte*, p. 297.

15. *BAHZ*, 18 March 1905; [Argentina], *Tercer Censo Nacional . . . 1914*, 8: 47, 135–136, 403; *La Nación*, 9 July 1916, pp. 590–591; [United States] Department of Commerce, *Statistics of German Trade, 1909–1913*, p. 29.

16. *Tercer Censo*, 8: 51; *La Nación*, 9 July 1916, pp. 590–591; U.S. Department of Commerce, *Statistics*, pp. 7–10.

17. *Censo General de . . . Buenos Aires, 1887*, 2: 306; Bachmann, *Jahrbuch*, 2: *passim*; BAHZ (compilations for years 1891, 1894, 1905, 1909, 1914); Lütge, Hoffmann, Körner, *Geschichte*, p. 296.

18. Alexander Jonin, *Durch Süd-Amerika: Reise- und Kulturhistorische Bilder*, 1: *Die Pampa-Länder*, pp. 609–614; Emile Daireaux, *La vie et les moeurs à La Plata*, 1: 267, 273; BAHZ sources, note 17.

19. *BAHZ*, 11 March 1905; U.S. Department of Commerce, *Statistics*, pp. 7–8.

20. *La Nación*, 9 July 1916, pp. 585, 592–593; Lütge, Hoffmann, Körner, *Geschichte*, pp. 296–297; Erich Bähr, "Deutsche Technik am La Plata," *Mitteilungen* des Institutes für Auslandsbeziehungen (IfA) [Stuttgart] 11, nos. 2/3 (April–September 1961; special edition): *Argentinien: Beitrag Deutschlands zur 150-Jahrfeier der Unabhängigkeit Argentiniens*, pp. 162–165.

21. *BAHZ*, 15 April 1905; Kärger, *Landwirtschaft*, 1: 834–847; A. B. Martínez and M. Lewandowski, *The Argentine in the Twentieth Century*, pp. 245–248, 358–363; U.S. Department of Commerce, *Statistics*, p. 10; Lütge, Hoffmann, Körner, *Geschichte*, p. 264; *La Nación*, 9 July 1916, pp. 584–585; Emil Hayn, "Die Entwicklung der deutschen Elektrizitätswerke in Buenos Aires," *Phoenix* [Buenos Aires] 6, no. 1 (1926): 131–176; Bähr, "Deutsche Technik"; Luis V. Sommi, *Los capitales alemanes en la Argentina*, p. 37; V. L. Phelps, *The International Economic Position of Argentina*, pp. 99, 246, 249.

22. Lütge, Hoffmann, Körner, *Geschichte*, pp. 294–295; Kärger, *Landwirtschaft*, 1: 119, 612; BAHZ, 9 December 1893; Bolsa de Comercio [Buenos Aires], *Boletín*, Años 1873, 1886–1890, 1894–1897, 1900; Martínez and Lewandowski, *The Argentine*, pp. 279–284.

23. *BAHZ*, 15 July 1891; *La Nación*, 9 July 1916, pp. 592–593; Dorfman, *Industria argentina*, pp. 116–122, 126–127, 144, 147, 202, 306; Bachmann, *Jahrbuch*, 1: 17.

24. Schnabl, *Buenos-Ayres*, pp. 108–111, 119.

25. Ibid., pp. 195–197; *Buenos Aires Vorwärts*, 16 October 1886 and *passim*; José Panettieri, *Los trabajadores*, pp. 45–87; James Scobie, *Buenos Aires: Plaza to Suburb, 1870–1910*, pp. 135–159. In 1884, 267 individuals and firms were in transport and commerce; 43 were in *Gastwirtschaft*; 168 in retail trades; 216 were professionals of some sort; and 173 were in artisanry or small factories. Bachmann, *Jahrbuch*, 2: 203–242.

26. Lütge, Hoffmann, Körner, *Geschichte*, pp. 102–105, 243; *Freie Presse, Mai-Festschrift*, p. 100.

27. Lütge, Hoffmann, Körner, *Geschichte*, p. 299; Bachmann, *Jahrbuch*, 1: 17; Theodor Alemann, *Die Zukunft des Deutschtums in Amerika*, p. 93;

"Ein deutscher Offizier" [Alfred Arent], *Ein Land der Zukunft: Ein Beitrag zur näheren Kenntnis Argentiniens*, p. 251.

28. *La Nación*, 9 July 1916, pp. 573–574; W. Schulz, "Deutsche Geschicke und Leistungen in Argentinien," *Mitteilungen* des IfA, special edition cited, pp. 117–125; Fritz Ruppert, "Deutsche Gelehrtenarbeit in Argentinien," in F. Schmidt and O. Boelitz, eds., *Aus deutscher Bildungsarbeit im Auslande*, 2: *Aussereuropa*, pp. 401–412; *Zeitschrift* des Deutschen Wissenschaftlichen Vereins Buenos Aires 1 (1915): 182–183, 230–239; 6 (1920): 97–104, 298, and other issues for postings of German academics and obituaries; Karl Kempski, *Argentinien*, p. 26.

29. Bähr, "Deutsche Technik"; Schulz, "Deutsche Geschicke"; Ruppert, "Deutsche Gelehrtenarbeit"; Fritz Graef, "Der Anteil deutscher Topografen an der Forschung Argentiniens," *Jahrbuch 1938* des Deutschen Volksbundes für Argentinien (DVA), pp. 83–86; Wilhelm Keiper, "Die Ausbildung der höheren Lehrer in Argentinien," *Zeitschrift* des DWV 1 (1915): 334–347; Emil Philipp, "Fünf Jahre Mathematikunterricht an künftige Lehrer höherer Schulen in Buenos Aires," in Schmidt and Boelitz, eds., *Aus deutscher Bildungsarbeit*, 2: 395–400; Instituto Nacional del Profesorado Secundario [Buenos Aires], *Memoria, diciembre de 1908*.

30. Von der Becke, "Von Utz Schmidl," pp. 126–128; Alfred Arent, *Argentinien: Ein Land der Zukunft: Jubiläumsschrift zur Hundertjahrfeier der Begründung der Republik Argentinien*, pp. 168–172; Reichs-Marineamt: Admiralstab der Marine. [F5092] II. Arg. 1a. Band I. Krupp von Bohlen to Staatssekretär Tirpitz, 14 August 1908. An attached but unsigned memo—*"auf allerhöchsten Befehl"*—ordered that the connection be kept concealed. Jürgen Schaefer, *Deutsche Militärhilfe an Südamerika: Militär- und Rüstungsinteressen in Argentinien, Bolivien, und Chile vor 1914*, pp. 76–82; Warren Schiff, "The Influence of the German Armed Forces and War Industry on Argentina, 1880–1914," *Hispanic American Historical Review* 52, no. 3 (August 1972): 436–455.

31. *Neue Deutsche Zeitung* [Buenos Aires] (hereafter *NDZ*), 28 February 1927.

32. *Censo General de . . . Buenos Aires, 1887*, 2: 551.

33. Schnabl, *Buenos-Ayres*, pp. 157–159. Order altered.

34. *Argentinisches Tageblatt* [Buenos Aires] (hereafter *AT*), 4 October 1914, 10 March 1920; *Die Neue Zeit* [Buenos Aires] (hereafter *NZ/BA*) 2d ser., no. 18 (August 1923); *Freie Presse, Mai-Festschrift*, p. 161; Schmidt, *Geschichte*, pp. 208–212; R. Gabert, *Das deutsche Bildungswesen in Argentinien und seine Organisation*, pp. 19–21.

35. Schmidt, *Geschichte*, pp. 191–192, 195; [Pater] Johann Holzer, "Bedeutung der katholischen Seelsorge für das Deutschtum in Argentinien," *Der Auslandsdeutsche* [Stuttgart] 8, no. 16 (August 1925): 466–467; *Die Katholiken deutscher Zunge in Buenos Aires: Kurzgefasste Vorgeschichte der Seelsorge für dieselben von 1865 bis 1911, nebst den ersten drei Jahresberichten der Gemeinde deutschredender Katholiken*.

36. Schmidt, *Geschichte*, p. 59; *NDZ*, 7 April 1922; *Buenos Aires Vorwärts* 1, no. 1 (2 October 1886); Verein Vorwärts [Buenos Aires], *Festschrift zur 50-jährigen Gründungsfeier, 1882–1932*, and *Festschrift zur 60-jährigen Gründungsfeier, 1882–1942*, for historical sketches; Bachmann,

Jahrbuch, 1: 82; Schobinger, *Inmigración*, pp. 156, 169–170; *BAHZ*, 11 February 1893; Peter Bussemeyer, *Fünfzig Jahre Argentinisches Tageblatt: Werden und Aufstieg einer auslandsdeutschen Zeitung*, pp. 36–44, 47–48.

37. Lütge, Hoffmann, Körner, *Geschichte*, pp. 300–301; *La Nación*, 9 July 1916, pp. 580–581.

38. Bachmann, *Jahrbuch*, 1: 75–82; Schmidt, *Geschichte*, p. 176; Wilhelm Keiper, "Das Deutschtum in Argentinien: Sein Werden, Wesen und Wirken" (typescript), pp. 65–66; *BAHZ*, 2 September 1910; Argentinischer Verein Deutscher Ingenieure [Buenos Aires], *Jahresbericht 1920*; Lütge, Hoffmann, Körner, *Geschichte*, pp. 300–301; Deutscher Turnverein/ Deutscher Klub Buenos Aires, *Jahresberichte, 1 November 1900–31 Oktober 1901; 1911–1912; 1913–1914.*

39. Waldthausen to Bethmann-Hollweg, 1 January 1910. Reichs-Marineamt: Admiralstab der Marine. [F5092] II. Arg. 1a. Band I.

40. Generalfeldmarschall Colmar Freiherr von der Goltz, "Reiseeindrücke aus Argentinien," lecture, 28 January 1911, before the Deutsch-Argentinischer Zentralverband in Berlin, printed in *Freie Presse*, 1 December 1967; longer version (64 pages) published as pamphlet in Berlin in 1911.

41. H. O. Meisner, *Militärattachés und Militärbevollmächtigte in Preussen und im Deutschen Reich*, pp. 26–28, 38.

42. *BAHZ*, 16 April 1910; *AT*, 19 March 1914; Baron von Holleben, "Capitales alemanes en la República Argentina," *Revista de Derecho, Historia, y Letras* [Buenos Aires] 28 (September 1907): 142–145; Hilmar von dem Bussche-Haddenhausen, "Der Deutsch-Argentinische Zentralverband, seine Entstehung und bisherige Tätigkeit," *Phoenix* 1, nos. 5/6 (February 1922): 65–68.

43. *AT*, 27, 28 January 1914; 10 February; 3, 7 (remark cited; italics in original), 14, 29 March; 4, 8 April; Schmidt, *Geschichte*, p. 227.

2. World War I: Privation and Profiteering

1. In Buenos Aires joint British–German–North American operation of a Protestant cemetery was ended by the war; in Rosario, a joint British–German hospital was dissolved.

2. Deutscher Klub BA, *Jahresbericht, 1 November 1915–31 Oktober 1916*. Figure is as of 31 October 1915.

3. Verein Vorwärts, *Festschrift zur 60-jährigen Gründungsfeier, 1882–1942*, pp. 20–22.

4. *AT*, 5 and 19 December 1914, 20 March 1915; Keiper, "Deutschtum," pp. 62–63.

5. Naval Attaché Moller claimed that the Navy League, founded in early 1914, had 1,300 members busy at war work in Buenos Aires by mid-1915. Reichs-Marineamt: Zentralabteilung. [F7515 PG 69085] *Akten IX.* 9.3.–.14. Heft 1. Moller to Staatssekretär des RMA, 28 October 1915.

6. DWV, *Jahresbericht, 1914 and 1915.*

7. *La Nación*, 15 May 1916; *Der Auslandsdeutsche* 2, no. 11 (November 1919): 426.

8. Keiper, "Deutschtum," p. 73. See also Keiper, *Das Deutschtum in Argentinien während des Weltkrieges, 1914–1918*, pp. 22–28, 59–62.

9. Keiper, "Deutschtum," pp. 78–81; Keiper, *Das Deutschtum*, pp. 62–65.

10. Friedrich Reichert, *Auf Berges- und Lebenshöhe: Erinnerungen*, 2: 333–336, 342–357, 359–365.

11. Alfredo Kölliker et al., *Patagonia: Resultados de las expediciones realizadas en 1910 a 1916*.

12. *AT*, 4 August 1914.

13. *AT*, 24 August 1914.

14. Reichs-Marineamt: Zentralabteilung. [F7515 PG 69085] *Akten* IX. 9.3.–.14. Heft 1. Moller to Staatssekretär des RMA, 11 June 1916.

15. *AT*, 12 and 29 October 1914.

16. Names published in *Foerster's Illustrierter Familien-Kalender für die Deutschen der La-Plata Staaten* 8 (Buenos Aires, 1923), pp. 59–60.

17. E. G. von Jungenfeld, *Aus den Urwäldern Paraguays zur Fahne*, pp. 44–72, anecdote on pp. 47–48.

18. See also von Jungenfeld, *Ein deutsches Schicksal im Urwald*.

19. Keiper, "Deutschtum," p. 63.

20. Deutsches Seemannsheim Buenos Aires, *Bericht* über das Geschäftsjahr 1 Oktober 1913–30 September 1914, *et seq.* through 1918–1919.

21. *AT*, 26 December 1914.

22. *NZ/BA* 1, no. 8 (February 1919).

23. Deutsche Wohltätigkeits-Gesellschaft (Buenos Aires), *Bericht 1916*.

24. [Germany]Marine-Archiv, *Der Krieg zur See, 1914–1918: Der Kreuzerkrieg in den ausländischen Gewässern* (comp., ed. E. Raeder); 1, *Das Kreuzergeschwader*: 176–177. Sir Julian Corbett, *Naval Operations: Official History of the War*, 1: 260–262, 306–308, 325.

25. *AT*, 12 October 1914.

26. *AT*, 29 August 1914, 17 and 30 September, 9 and 12 November, 9 December; 7 January 1915, 8 and 31 March, 19 April, 29 May. DWG, *Bericht 1916*; Verein zum Schutze germanischer Einwanderer, Buenos Aires (hereafter VzSgE), *Jahresbericht 1914, 1915, 1919*; Deutsches Seemannsheim, *Bericht 1913–1914, 1914–1915*.

27. For example, in the month of July, 3,291 persons sought employment through the VzSgE, but only 185 were put upon the "available" lists (VzSgE, *Jahresbericht 1916*).

28. VzSgE, *Jahresbericht 1917, 1918*.

29. DWG, *Bericht 1916, 1917, 1918*.

30. DWG, *Bericht 1916*.

31. Deutsches Seemannsheim, *Bericht 1918–1919*.

32. *AT*, 7 January 1916.

33. VzSgE, *Jahresbericht 1917, 1918*.

34. Keiper, *Das Deutschtum*, pp. 34–36; *AT*, 6 September 1917. Gross claimed after the war that Germans had been stricken from the DWG's welfare rolls because they had refused to work as strikebreakers (*NZ/BA* 1, no. 8 [1919]).

35. VzSgE, *Jahresbericht 1917, 1919*. See also Guido di Tella and Manuel Zymelman, "El desarrollo industrial argentino durante la Primera Gue-

rra Mundial," *Revista de Ciencias Económicas* (April–June 1959): 221–224. The authors hold that the industrial growth of 1917–1918 was felt mainly in large concerns, not in small shops and factories.

36. *AT*, 28 May 1917.

37. Deutsche Handelskammer Buenos Aires, "Jahresbericht 1917" (typescript). See also "Die Vereinigten Staaten und der argentinische Markt," *Lateinamerika (A)* nos. 2/3 (March 1920): 106–108, on U.S. techniques and gains during the war.

38. *Lateinamerika (A)* nos. 2/3 (March 1920): 128. The journal claimed that the wolfram was destined for Germany, but this is contradicted by all other evidence as well as common sense.

39. *BAHZ*, no. 1461, 24 June 1916; DHK, "Jahresbericht 1916" (typescript).

40. DHK, "Einwirkung des Krieges auf den deutschen Handel in Argentinien" (typescript); DHK, "Jahresbericht 1917" and "1919" (both typescript), *Jahresbericht 1922*; Keiper, "Deutschtum," p. 69.

41. Keiper, *Das Deutschtum*, p. 33.

42. *BAHZ*, 9 October 1915; Keiper, "Deutschtum," p. 65.

43. Sommi, *Capitales alemanes*, p. 38; V. L. Phelps, *International Economic Position*, pp. 99, 246.

44. Sommi, *Capitales alemanes*, p. 38, quoting from a 1937 report of the Royal Institute of International Affairs.

45. In 1912 Argentina ranked tenth in the total volume of German trade; in 1913, eighth. Among non-European countries Argentina was surpassed only by the United States (U.S. Department of Commerce, *Statistics*, p. 7).

46. Interview with Colin Ross, reported in the *Tageblatt*, 6 February 1921. In the same year Yrigoyen granted an interview to Mark Neven du Pont of the *Kölnische Zeitung*.

47. *AT*, 1 May 1917. See also *Neue Deutsche Zeitung* [Buenos Aires] (hereafter *NDZ*), 14 December 1919 and 21 June 1926. Attitudes toward the eminent house of Tornquist were mixed: it was alleged against Carlos Tornquist that he had resigned from the executive committee of the VzSgE in 1916 for political reasons and that his pro-Allied (especially pro-Belgian) sympathies remained obvious at war's end (*AT*, 20 November 1918).

48. Keiper, *Das Deutschtum*, pp. 32–34.

49. During the course of his struggle against the boycott of the *Tageblatt* in 1924, Theodor Alemann charged that funds were diverted to right-wing organizations in Germany (*AT*, 28 February–31 March 1924).

50. The account follows the recent study of Klaus Kannapin, "Die Luxburg-Affäre: Ein Beitrag zur Geschichte der Beziehungen zwischen Deutschland und Argentinien während des ersten Weltkrieges," *Wissenschaftliche Zeitschrift* der Humboldt-Universität zu Berlin 13, no. 7 (1964): 879–882. See also Steven Koblik, *Sweden: The Neutral Victor. Sweden and the Western Powers, 1917–1918. A Study of Anglo-American-Swedish Relations*, Chapter Six.

51. *AT*, 16 April 1917.

52. Ernst Alemann, "Im Kampf um die Freiheit: Erinnerungen aus fünf Jahrzehnten," in *75 Jahre Argentinisches Tageblatt* (29 April 1964), Section 2: 2.

53. *AT*, 13 September 1917.

54. Ibid.

55. *NDZ*, 25 October 1926. I have not verified this account.

56. Reichert, *Erinnerungen*, 2: 342; Ernst Alemann, "Im Kampf," 2: 2.

57. *NZ/BA* 1, no. 11 (March 1919).

58. Peter Harold-Hatzold, *Aus zwei Jahrhunderten: Die Tragik eines Menschenlebens, nach Erlebnissen niedergeschrieben*, pp. 97–99.

59. *NZ/BA* 1, no. 1 (September 1918); *AT*, 11 December 1917, 15 October 1918.

60. *AT*, 1 November 1917, 31 December 1917 (on the Liga der aus patriotischen Gründen 2. Klasse fahrenden Deutschen, surely one of the sillier wartime organizations ever founded).

61. *NZ/BA* 1, no. 1 (September 1918).

3. The Political Awakening of the Community, 1918–1919

1. *Der Bund* 2, no. 2 (February 1919).

2. Three issues appeared during 1918, and an unknown number thereafter. Its editor was one Dr. Schreiber, alias Hans Zawitzski. It reputedly obtained material, including anti-Semitic essays, through the German propaganda bureau in Spain.

3. *Die Wacht*'s editors were not otherwise identified. In October 1922 it became *Die Deutsche Wacht: Reichsdeutsches Organ für die La Plata Staaten*, and in January 1923 it became the official journal of the recently founded *Ortsgruppe* of the Deutsch-Nationale Volkspartei. It was printed by the Imprenta Mercur, in which Hayn was said to have a controlling interest (*NDZ*, 10 March 1924).

4. *Die Neue Zeit* appeared in three series: 1918–1919, 1922–1924, and 1934. It was from first to last the single-handed creation of A. E. Gross, whose resemblance to H. L. Mencken is occasionally striking. Unfortunately, beyond the facts that Gross apparently studied for a time at Tübingen and was in 1918 a teacher of English at the Buenos Aires Berlitz School, little is known of him.

5. *AT*, 16 November 1918.

6. *NDZ* 1, no. 1 (September 1919). "Pay up" refers to the pressures exerted upon German employees to contribute to the war fund and other collections.

7. *NDZ*, 2 August 1926, installment of the anonymously authored series "Der Volksbund ohne Volk." During 1917, no fewer than fifty-one German bars, restaurants, and *recreos* advertised in *AT*.

8. *AT*, 12 November 1918.

9. *AT*, 14 December 1918.

10. *AT*, 20 November 1918.

11. The term *Hakenkreuzler* appears to have been first used in Buenos Aires in 1922. See *NZ/BA* 2d ser., no. 3 (September 1922), in connection with the war memorial incident.

12. *NZ/BA* 1, no. 12 (April 1919), for names and descriptions of the fifteen. Dr. Hesse was carried as a member in 1919 but ceased thereafter to be active. A. Simon returned to the fold, however. Bagel reportedly sought admission, unsuccessfully, ca. 1926. *NDZ*, 7 June and 26 August 1926.

13. *AT*, 25 November 1918 and *passim*; Theodor Alemann's signed editorial of 14 December 1918. Keiper ("Deutschtum," p. 88) later claimed that the Committee of Five had "led and advised" the community during the war!

14. *NZ/BA* 1, no. 7 (December 1918), 1, no. 8 (February 1919).

15. *AT*, 12 December 1918; *NDZ*, 7 June and 26 August 1926.

16. Term (*Tummelplatz*) used by Emil Hayn, "Die Gründung und die Kampfjahre des Deutschen Volksbundes für Argentinien," *Jahrbuch 1938* des DVA, pp. 133–135. See also *AT*, 16 November 1918 *ff.*; *Der Bund* 2, no. 1 (January 1919); *NDZ* 1, no. 1 (September 1919).

17. *AT*, 15 January 1916.

18. *La Nación*, 9 July 1916, p. 595.

19. *AT*, 1 June 1916.

20. *Deutsch-Argentinisches Adressbuch, 1917, 1918*.

21. *Der Bund* 1, no. 1 (September 1917); *AT*, 25 October 1918.

22. Keiper, "Deutschtum," p. 74.

23. *AT*, 15 January 1916.

24. Of a total of perhaps 100,000 German-speaking inhabitants of the entire republic, roughly one quarter were Reichsdeutsche. Keiper, "Deutschtum," pp. 107–109.

25. *AT*, 17 June 1916; Theodor Alemann, "Erlebnisse," *AT*, 31 December 1922/1 January 1923.

26. *AT*, 12 August 1918.

27. Keiper, "Deutschtum," p. 102.

28. Ibid., pp. 101–102.

29. *AT*, 29 June 1916. The *Tageblatt*'s sarcastic treatment of Argentine political affairs, and especially of "police news," are also expressions of Alemann's deprecating attitude toward *lo criollo*.

30. *AT*, 25 July 1918; *Zukunft des Deutschtums*, p. 22.

31. *Zukunft des Deutschtums*, p. 20.

32. Theodor Alemann, "Erlebnisse"; *NDZ* 1, no. 1 (September 1919), 1, no. 29 (March 1920) (in which it was said that 1,400 persons had resigned), 18 April 1927. The Rosario local, earlier one of the largest in the provincial cities, recorded only ten members at the end of 1919. *Der Bund* 2, no. 12 (December 1919).

33. *Der Bund* 2, no. 7 (July 1919).

34. *AT*, 9 April 1920.

35. *AT*, 11 April 1920; Hayn, "Gründung."

36. *Der Bund* 2, no. 12 (December 1919).

37. *NDZ*, July 1920.

38. *Der Bund* 8, no. 6 (June 1925); 9, no. 6 (June 1926); 10, no. 6 (June 1927).

39. Keiper, "Deutschtum," p. 191.

40. *Der Bund* 2, no. 3 (March 1919).

41. *Der Bund* 10, no. 10 (October 1927); *Der Bauernbund* [Buenos Aires] 1, no. 1 (December 1927); 3, no. 1 (January 1930); *Auslandsdeutsche* 13, no. 5 (March 1930); 14, no. 14 (July 1931); *Nachrichtenblatt* der Reichsstelle für das Auswanderungswesen [Berlin] 11, no. 22 (November 1929); 13, no. 13 (July 1931) (hereafter *Nachrichtenblatt RA*).

42. *Der Bund* 10, no. 5 (May 1928).

43. *NZ/BA* 1, no. 7 (December 1918); 1, no. 8 (February 1919); 1, no. 9 (March 1919); *NDZ*, 25 October 1926; Reichs-Marineamt: Zentralabteilung. [Akten PG 69085] *Akten* IX. 9.–.14. Moller to Staatssekretär RMA, 3 August 1919.

44. Ibid., Moller to Chef der Admiralität ("persönlich"), 7 March 1920; italics in original. In any case, the Versailles treaty denied Germany the right to maintain military and naval attachés overseas.

4. The Lure of Argentina in the 1920s

1. *Argentiniens Wirtschaft während des Weltkrieges: Ihre Bedeutung für die deutsche Volkswirtschaft und Auswanderung*, p. 125.

2. DHK, "Jahresbericht, 1919" (typescript).

3. Members of both firms participated in the founding of the *Handelskammer* in 1916 and continued to appear in membership lists during the 1920s.

4. DHK, "Jahresbericht, 1919."

5. DHK, *Jahresbericht, 1922.*

6. *Freie Presse, Mai-Festschrift*, p. 72.

7. The latter motive suggested by Friedrich Katz, "Die deutschen Kriegsziele in Lateinamerika im ersten Weltkrieg," *Wissenschaftliche Zeitschrift* der Humboldt-Universität zu Berlin 13, no. 7 (1964): 875–879.

8. *Das Problem der deutschen Handels- und Wirtschaftsinteressen in Südamerika*, p. 4.

9. Carlos Díaz Alejandro, *Essays on the Economic History of the Argentine Republic*, pp. 303–305. See also "Argentinien und Deutschland," *Lateinamerika* (A), no. 1 (October 1919): 1–3; "Entwicklung argentinischer Industrien mit deutscher Hilfe," ibid., nos. 2/3 (March 1920): 79–91; and "Die argentinische Industrie," ibid., pp. 81–82. Also D. M. Phelps, *Migration of Industry to South America*, pp. 13, 325–326; Joseph Tulchin, *The Aftermath of War: World War One and U.S. Policy toward Latin America*, p. 80.

10. "Deutsche Pionierarbeit in Übersee," lecture, Pfingsttagung, 1931, Verein für das Deutschtum im Auslande, reprinted in *Der Bund* 13, no. 6 (June 1931): 50–56.

11. *Lateinamerika* (A) nos. 2/3 (March 1920): 127; nos. 16/17 (April–May 1921): 497; no. 18 (June 1921): 521, 523.

12. Friedrich Wehner, "Hamburgs Beziehungen zu Iberoamerika," *Südamerika* [Buenos Aires] 9, no. 1 (July/August/September 1958): 23. See also *Lateinamerika* (A) items cited in note 9; Werner Pade, "Die Expansionspolitik des deutschen Imperialismus gegenüber Lateinamerika, 1918–1933," *Zeitschrift für Geschichtswissenschaft* 22, no. 6 (1974): 579, 583, 588. GELATEINO was the business office of the German chambers of commerce in all Latin American countries. The Buenos Aires *Handelskammer* controlled all communications between them and Germany.

13. DHK, *Jahresbericht, 1922.* See also "Die Zukunft des Baumwollbaues im Chaco argentino," *Lateinamerika* (A) nos. 2/3 March 1920): 104–106.

14. Sommi, *Capitales alemanes*, pp. 44, 318 *ff.*; Eduardo Alemann, "La co-operación argentino-alemana en el terreno industrial," in *Cámara de Comercio Argentino-Alemana, 1916–1966*, pp. 72–74; Bolko von Hahn, "Beitrag deutscher Industrie an der Entwicklung Argentiniens," *Lasso* [Buenos Aires] 3, no. 6 (December 1935); Pedro Hastedt, *Deutsche Direktinvestitionen in Lateinamerika: Ihre Entwicklung seit dem 1. Weltkrieg und ihre Bedeutung für die Industrialisierung des Subkontinents*, pp. 59–61.

15. *NDZ*, 15 November 1926; *Superusina "Puerto Nuevo" de la CHADE* (pamphlet published for the inaugural of the new plant, Buenos Aires, 1929); Bähr, "Deutsche Technik."

16. Hugo Eckener, *Im Zeppelin über Länder und Meere: Erlebnisse und Erinnerungen*, pp. 286–291, 349–352; *Freie Presse, Mai-Festschrift*, pp. 228–229; Ing. Holzmann, "Beitrag deutscher Flieger an der Entwicklung südamerikanischen Luftverkehrs," *Lasso* 3, no. 6 (December 1935).

17. Max Winkler, *Investments of U.S. Capital in Latin America*, pp. 66–67.

18. Eduardo Alemann, "Co-operación," pp. 72–73.

19. DHK, *Jahresbericht, 1932*.

20. DHK, *Jahresbericht, 1920, 1927, 1931*.

21. Advertisements in *AT* provide the 1917 baseline; they are probably nearly exhaustive. For 1924–1925, see the Deutsche La-Plata Zeitung, *Guía Germana del Río de la Plata: Adressbuch Deutschsprechender* (1924–1925) 2: 62–63, 84–88, 126.

22. *Nachrichtenblatt RA* 1, no. 11 (October 1919): 179–180.

23. *Der Bund* 2, no. 7 (July 1919).

24. *Der Bund* 2, no. 12 (December 1919).

25. *La Prensa*, 7 February 1920.

26. *AT*, 31 December 1919. Summarized in *Nachrichtenblatt RA* 2, no. 9 (May 1920): 289–299; and *Auslandsdeutsche* 3, no. 6 (March 1920).

27. G. H. K., in *Der Bund* 2, no. 3 (March 1919); VzSgE, *Jahresbericht 1923*; *NDZ*, 14 February 1927.

28. *Der Bund* 2, no. 12 (December 1919); 8, no. 4 (April 1925); VzSgE, *Jahresbericht 1919*; *Nachrichtenblatt RA* 1, no. 9 (September 1919).

29. *Langosteros* were minor officials of the Ministry of Agriculture appointed to control the locust pest (*langosta*). Many were corrupt and enriched themselves through their power to set quotas for exterminated locusts and to impose summary fines for noncompliance.

30. *NDZ*, 21 February 1927.

31. *Nachrichtenblatt RA* 1, no. 10 (October 1919); 1, no. 11 (October 1919); 7, no. 12 (June 1925).

32. *Nachrichtenblatt RA* 1, no. 5 (July 1919); 2, no. 4 (February 1920).

33. *Nachrichtenblatt RA* 2, no. 9 (May 1920), citing from the *Nieuwe Rotterdamsche Courant*, 18 March 1920. Also ibid. 1, no. 9 (September 1919); Bernhard Stichel, "Einwanderung: Konjunktur und Arbeitsmarkt," *Der Bund* 3, no. 6 (June 1920): 85–88.

34. *NDZ* 2, no. 26 (February 1921).

35. *NDZ* 1, no. 1 (September 1919). Also ibid. 1, nos. 31–34 (March–April 1920).

36. K. von Zitzgewitz, "Die Aussichten für die deutschen Einwanderer

in Argentinien," *Bundeskalender 1926* des DVA, p. 76. Also *Nachrichten-blatt RA* 9, no. 4 (February 1927), for estimates of start-up capital needed.

37. Cited in *Auslandsdeutsche* 2, no. 10 (October 1919).

38. *Nachrichtenblatt RA* 1, no. 9 (September 1919).

39. *NDZ* 1, no. 2 (September 1919).

40. *Problem*, pp. 6–7.

41. *Nachrichtenblatt RA* 1, no. 10 (October 1919).

42. *Nachrichtenblatt RA* 3, no. 18 (September 1921); 3, no. 24 (December 1921).

43. Argentina, Dirección General de Inmigración, *Memorias* (or *Informes*), 1923 through 1932; Argentina, Ministerio de Agricultura, *Resumen estadístico del movimiento migratorio de la República Argentina, años 1857–1924*; Walter Willcox and I. Ferenczi, eds., *International Migrations*, 1: 121, 544; Carl C. Taylor, *Rural Life in Argentina*, p. 97; "Immigration and Settlement in Brazil, Argentina, and Uruguay," *International Labor Review* 35, no. 1 (February 1937): 215–247; 35, no. 2 (March 1937): 352–383; *Der Bund* 6, no. 3 (March 1923); *Nachrichtenblatt RA* 5, no. 8 (May 1923); 9, no. 14 (July 1929); 14, no. 19 (September 1932). Numerous anomalies appear, especially when German data are compared to those from Argentine sources.

44. In 1923, for example, 427 Germans were deported, the highest number for all nationalities recorded. Of these, 312 had jumped ship, and another 78 were recorded as "clandestine" or "deficient documents." *Memoria 1923*.

45. In 1924, the Reichsdeutsche numbered 11,022 of a German-speaking contingent of 15,611. In 1927, a year of high Russian-German immigration, the total German-speaking group was 167 percent of the German/Austrian total.

46. Karl Thalheim, *Das deutsche Auswanderungsproblem der Nachkriegs-zeit*, pp. 35–39. By 1924 Brazil was attracting more Germans than Argentina for the first time since the end of the war.

47. Sources cited in note 43.

48. *Jahrbuch 1938* des DVA.

49. Thalheim, *Auswanderungsproblem*, pp. 28, 29–34, 75–83; Eugene M. Kulischer, *Europe on the Move: War and Population Changes, 1917–1947*, pp. 134–135, 155–161, 182–183, 186.

50. Kurt Faber, *Dem Glücke nach durch Südamerika*, p. 15. Faber and his publisher are clearly profiting from the "Argentina-boom" he writes about. The copy in my possession is the fourth printing in the original year of publication.

51. *Nachrichtenblatt RA* 4, no. 3 (February 1922); Thalheim, *Auswanderungsproblem*, pp. 78–83. Many were probably confused also by the distinction between the gold peso of international trade and the paper peso (which equaled about 44 percent of the gold) in domestic use.

52. *NDZ*, 25 October 1926, 21 February 1927; *Der Bund* 10, no. 7 (July 1927).

53. *Nachrichtenblatt RA* 6, no. 3 (May 1924); *Der Bund* 8, no. 8 (August 1925).

54. Thalheim, *Auswanderungsproblem*, pp. 85–87.

55. Carl Solberg, "Rural Unrest and Agrarian Policy in Argentina," *Journal of Inter-American Studies and World Affairs* 8 (January 1971): 35–36; *Nachrichtenblatt RA* 1, no. 14 (December 1919); 1, no. 15 (December 1919); *NDZ*, 3 September 1923.

56. *Mitteilungen* des Deutschen Auslands-Institutes 2, no. 7 (July 1919); 2, no. 9 (September 1919); 3, no. 20 (October 1920); *Nachrichtenblatt RA* 2, no. 3 (February 1920); 3, no. 10 (May 1921).

57. Reviewed and denounced in *Auslandsdeutsche* 3, no. 6 (March 1920). I possess a copy of [Germán Lamm], *Argentinien: Die Kolonie für den deutschen Siedler: Mit 400 argentinischen Papierpesos Herr seiner eigenen Scholle*, a similar production which has been extensively annotated in an unknown hand. Lamm's inaccuracies are noted, the terms *Plagiat* and *Schwindel* appear regularly in the margins, and the annotator is in no doubt that Lamm, who poses as a simple, successful colonist, is in fact a paid hack of Norddeutsche Lloyd and López Agrelo y Casanova.

58. Wilhelm Herzog, *Im Zwischendeck nach Südamerika*, p. 73.

59. M. Griesebach, "Die deutsche Auswanderungsfrage und ihre Lösung," *Mitteilungen* des DAI 2, no. 6 (June 1919): 146–151; 2, no. 7 (July 1919): 197–202; 2, no. 8 (August 1919).

60. *NDZ*, 4 October 1926, 17 January 1927.

61. *Auslandsdeutsche* 7, no. 12 (June 1924); 9, no. 21 (November 1926); *Der Bund* 9, no. 4 (April 1926); 9, no. 7 (July 1926); *Nachrichtenblatt RA* 9, no. 19 (October 1927): 224–225; *Bundeskalender 1926 des DVA*, p. 137; *NDZ*, 12 July 1926, 28 March 1927; Wipert von Blücher, *Am Rande der Weltgeschichte: Marokko, Schweden, Argentinien*, pp. 154–155.

62. The recent study by Robert Eidt, *Pioneer Settlement in Northeast Argentina*, is generally favorable to Schwelm. Marisa Micolis, *Une communauté allemande en Argentine: El Dorado. Problèmes d'intégration socioculturelle*, gives a critical though not wholly unfavorable treatment.

63. Dirección General de Inmigración, "Memoria del año 1930" (typescript); *Memoria del año 1932*.

64. Micolis, *Communauté*, p. 21.

65. Walter Stölting, *Kampf ums Dasein in Argentinien*; Otto Degener, *Auf Glücksuche nach Südamerika*; two apparently unsolicited testimonials, one from a "big planter," one from a "small colonist" in *Nachrichtenblatt RA* 12, no. 21 (November 1930). Ernst Alemann's *Grünes Gold und rote Erde*, which found Eldorado a "model colony," was considered by some to fall in the same category.

66. *NDZ*, 13 October 1924. Other sources confirm that Stichel became Schwelm's employee, salary unspecified.

67. *Nachrichtenblatt RA* 11, no. 9 (May 1929); 11, no. 10 (May 1929).

68. Especially in the Nazi *Deutsche Zeitung: Illustrierte Wochenschrift für Südamerika*, which bore no relation to the former *NDZ*, closed in 1927. The new journal disappeared after August 1933.

69. *Nachrichtenblatt RA* 13, no. 8 (April 1931); and 14, no. 11 (December 1932); *International Labor Review* 35, no. 2 (March 1937): 353–354.

70. *NDZ*, 21 February 1927.

71. *Der Bund* 14, nos. 5/6 (May/June 1932): 40–42.

72. "Auswanderung und Heimat," *Jahrbuch 1931* des DVA, p. 35.

5. Notes on the Immigrant Experience *im Affenland*

1. F. R. Francke, "Wir Alteingesessenen—oder—Wussten Sie das schon?" *Südamerika* 3, no. 5 (March–April 1953): 538–539, 541–542.
2. Kurt Faber, "Unter Landstreichern in Argentinien," *Der Bund* 3, no. 5 (May 1920): 71.
3. Alan Bullock, *Hitler: A Study in Tyranny*, p. 504.
4. Schnabl, *Buenos-Ayres*, pp. 47, 48. Also Jonin, *Durch Süd-Amerika*, 1, for similar reactions to the physical aspect of Buenos Aires in the 1880s.
5. Ewers, *Mit meinen Augen: Fahrten durch die lateinische Welt*, pp. 285–290.
6. Goldschmidt, *Argentinien*, p. 21.
7. *Vivo* is not adequately translated as "hustler" or "man on the make," for the *criollo* term conveys approval as well as warning.
8. Schnabl, *Buenos-Ayres*, pp. 54–58, 63–66.
9. Carl Beck-Bernard, *Argentinien*, p. 150.
10. *Nachrichtenblatt RA* 2, no. 13 (1920): 434; *Auslandsdeutsche* 13, no. 17 (September 1930): 609; Hans Schmidt, *Die Jagd nach der Arbeit in Argentinien*, pp. 29, 38, 39; Karl Lohausen, *Führer durch Buenos Aires*.
11. Goldschmidt, *Argentinien*, pp. 21–22.
12. *Auslandsdeutsche* 14, no. 19 (October 1931): 608.
13. "Auswanderung nach Argentinien?" *Mitteilungen* des DAI 2, no. 8 (August 1919): 254.
14. 4 August 1888.
15. *NDZ*, 1 November 1926.
16. "Die innere Eignung zum Siedlerberuf," *Phoenix* 5, no. 1 (1925): 13.
17. Arent, *Argentinien*, p. 152. Anecdote reprinted in *AT*, 28 September 1914.
18. There is no way to measure the incidence of use. The term appears in print as early as 1908 (Ewers, *Augen*, p. 290) and as late as 1953 (Francke, "Alteingesessenen," p. 540). The *NDZ* (12 April 1923) noted that disillusioned comrades used it commonly. Ernst Alemann chides the Germans for using the term so often, especially as things have gone so well for them in Argentina.
19. Goldschmidt, *Argentinien*, pp. 153–154.
20. *Buenos-Ayres*, p. 150.
21. Ibid., pp. 159–160.
22. Dirección de Inmigración, *Memoria, 1923* (for retrospective totals); *internado* data from subsequent *Memorias* and *Informes* through 1932, omitting 1931.
23. *Nachrichtenblatt RA* 3, no. 4 (February 1921): 150.
24. Information published at regular intervals in the *Zeitschrift* des DWV.
25. Argentinischer Verein Deutscher Ingeneure, *Jahresbericht 1924*.
26. *NZ/BA* 2d ser., no. 9 (December 1922).
27. M. Riester, "Zur Auswanderung nach Argentinien," *Auslandsdeutsche* 6, no. 20 (October 1923): 561.
28. Walter Stölting, *Kampf ums Dasein in Argentinien*, pp. 56–57, citing an unnamed Volksbund official.
29. Daireaux, *La vie*, 1: 157–163, for a classic description of declassed immigrants.

30. 29 June 1923.

31. Max Rhenius, *Michel auf Neuland: Abenteuerliches aus Argentinien und Paraguay*. In Rhenius' sketches, the backwoods confidence man is a stock type.

32. "Deutsche Lehrer in Argentinien," *Jahrbuch 1938* des DVA; *Freie Presse, Deutschtum*, p. 42; Max Wilfert, "Die deutsche Auslandsschule in Südamerika und der Krieg," *Zeitschrift* des DWV 3, no. 5 (1917): 250–257.

33. "Als Erntearbeiter in Argentinien," *Der Bund* 4, no. 1 (January 1921): 1–2. See also F. S., "Mein erstes Jahr in Argentinien," *Der Bund* 5, no. 5 (May 1922): 53–56; E. Brugger, "Auf Arbeitssuche in der Ernte," *Der Bund* 15, no. 4 (April 1933): 107–108.

34. "Aussichten," p. 76.

35. Lists published monthly in *Der Bund*; Gross printed names from *Poste Restante* in NZ/BA irregularly; *Jahresberichte 1923, 1924, 1925* of VzSgE; consulate advertisement for forty persons in *NDZ*, 14 March 1927.

36. Pastor Bühler, "Zur Kolonisation in den argentinischen Misionen," *Auslandsdeutsche* 6, no. 6 (July 1923): 380–381; *Evangelisches Gemeinde-blatt für die La-Plata Staaten* 1 (1919); *Nachrichtenblatt RA* 2, no. 21 (November 1920): 750–751.

37. *Nachrichtenblatt RA* 2, no. 21 (November 1920): 750–751.

38. "Lage des deutschen Einwanderers in Argentinien," *Nachrichtenblatt RA* 11, no. 1 (January 1929): 6–7.

39. *Nachrichtenblatt RA* 2, no. 7 (April 1920): 237; 2, no. 21 (November 1920): 751.

40. Goldschmidt, *Argentinien*, pp. 107–113.

41. Stölting, *Kampf ums Dasein*, p. 233.

42. Theodor Alemann, *Zukunft des Deutschtums*, pp. 26–27.

43. Schnabl, *Buenos-Ayres*, pp. 141–144.

44. von Scheele-Willich, "Innere Eignung."

45. Keiper, *Der Deutsche in Argentinien*, pp. 40–41.

6. Political Conflict, 1919–1929

1. Thalheim, *Auswanderungsproblem*, pp. 106–107; "Argentinien," "Buenos Aires," in C. Petersen et al., *Handwörterbuch des Grenz- und Auslandsdeutschtums*, 1: 136, 605; *Mitteilungen* des DAI 2, no. 7 (July 1919).

2. *NDZ*, 24 September 1923.

3. Verein Vorwärts, *50-jährige Gründungsfeier*.

4. *NDZ* 3, no. 1 (September 1921): ff. Lindemann's remarks reported in *NDZ*, 12 December 1921.

5. Alemann, *Zukunft des Deutschtums*, pp. 110–111.

6. *NDZ* 3, no. 4 (October 1921): 11. See also *NDZ* 1, no. 3 (September 1919); 1, nos. 35–39 (April–May 1921); 19 January 1925.

7. *Auslandsdeutsche* 5, no. 21 (November 1922): 617–618.

8. NZ/BA 2d ser., no. 18 (August 1923).

9. J. Schaefer, *Deutsche Militärhilfe*, p. 90, on von dem Bussche-Haddenhausen; *AT*, 6 March 1924 (Theodor Alemann's front page editorial). Captain Vogel, one of the murderers of Rosa Luxemburg, is alleged to

have found sanctuary in Argentina after his escape from jail (Herzog, *Zwischendeck*, p. 134).

10. For Ramos' later career see Marysa Navarro Gerassi, "Argentine Nationalism of the Right," *Studies in Comparative International Development* 1, no. 12 (1965): 181.

11. Moller lists Kretzschmar, von Thauvenay, and Faupel among the fifteen officers who returned to Europe in August 1914: Reichs-Marineamt: file cited, Moller to Staatssekretär RMA, 11 June 1916. Others listed by von der Becke, "Von Utz Schmidl," pp. 117–128.

12. Fritz T. Epstein, "Argentinien und das deutsche Heer: Ein Beitrag zur Geschichte europäischer militärischer Einflüsse auf Südamerika," in M. Göhring and A. Scharff, eds., *Geschichtliche Kräfte und Entscheidungen: Festschrift Otto Becker*, pp. 291–292; G. P. Atkins and L. V. Thompson, "German Military Influence in Argentina," *Journal of Latin American Studies* 4, no. 2 (November 1972): 259–269.

13. Manfred Merkes, *Die deutsche Politik im spanischen Bürgerkrieg, 1936–1939*, pp. 193–194. Hugh Thomas and Gabriel Jackson follow Merkes in their standard histories.

14. *Nachrichtenblatt RA* 2, no. 23 (December 1920): 828–829; 4, no. 24 (December 1922): 657. Moller himself was absent on an extended stay in Germany during this period. It was probably on this trip that Moller transmitted funds collected in Buenos Aires to secret anti-Weimar organizations in Germany.

15. Herzog, *Zwischendeck*, p. 52; VzSgE, *Jahresbericht, 1921*.

16. *NDZ*, 10 March 1924.

17. *NDZ*, 9 August 1926.

18. *Der Bund* 12, no. 6 (June 1930).

19. *Auslandsdeutsche* 12, no. 6 (March 1929): 176.

20. *NDZ*, 27 February 1922. Also *AT*, 9 February 1920; *Der Bund* 10, no. 8 (August 1927): 98–99, for data on the *Vereinsvorstände*.

21. In 1922 the *DLPZ* claimed 10,000 at the Sociedad Rural; *AT* and *NDZ* conceded a maximum of 3,000. In 1925 *La Nación* estimated 1,500; the Monarchists claimed 7,000.

22. *Auslandsdeutsche* 5, no. 23 (December 1922): 676; 6, no. 1 (January 1923): 16; *NDZ*, 7 September 1922; *Die Deutsche Wacht* 1, no. 1 (2 October 1922) (the *Kriegerverein's* statement); *NZ/BA* 2d ser., no. 4 (September 1922).

23. *AT*, 6 February 1921.

24. Colin Ross, "Das Problem der Heimat und das Auslandsdeutschtum," *Der Bund* 3, no. 1 (January 1920): 17–18; Ross, "La situación política y económica en Alemania," *La Prensa*, 27 January, 2, 3, 8, and 16 February 1920; Ross, "Deutsche wider Deutsche," *AT*, 15 March 1920; Ross, "Was wird? Deutschlands Gegenwart und Zukunft," *AT*, 17 March 1920.

25. *AT*, 17 March 1920; *NDZ* 1, no. 29 (March 1920).

26. *NDZ* 1, no. 29 (March 1920).

27. *NDZ* 3, no. 2 (September 1920); Ernst Alemann, "Im Kampf," 2: 7.

28. Johannes Franze, "Glanzvoller Aufstieg der deutschen Musik in Argentinien," *Mitteilungen* des IfA, special edition cited, pp. 145–148; Franze, "Richard Strauss in Buenos Aires," *Südamerika* 10, no. 2 (1959): 86–88.

29. Raúl Beruti, "Institución Cultural Argentino-Germana," *Mitteilungen* des IfA, special edition cited, pp. 160–161.

30. *Auslandsdeutsche* 4, no. 13 (July 1921): 403, announcement of Nicolai's appointment with notes on his wartime activities. *NDZ*, 24 April 1922, *ff.*; *Auslandsdeutsche* 5, no. 16 (August 1922): 469. Goldschmidt, *Argentinien*, pp. 9–20, 85–97.

31. Herzog, *Zwischendeck*. Also *NDZ*, 2 October 1923; *AT*, 23 September 1923, *ff.*

32. *NDZ*, 30 March and 6 April 1925.

33. *NDZ*, 26 January and 18 May 1922; *NZ/BA* 2d ser., no. 2 (August 1922). Oyhanarte had been a vocal congressional opponent of a *ruptura* with Germany in September 1917. He visited Germany in 1921 and was in close contact with the Central League for the Promotion of Economic Interests in Berlin (*Lateinamerika (A)* no. 20 [August 1921]: 604–605).

34. *NDZ*, 28 February 1927.

35. See Alemann's second revised and enlarged edition of *Zukunft des Deutschtums*, pp. 108–113.

36. Alvarez del Vayo was also German correspondent of *La Nación* of Buenos Aires and *El Mercurio* of Santiago. He would later serve as foreign minister of the Spanish Republic during the civil war.

37. *AT*, 3 November 1923, *ff.*

38. *NDZ*, 19 July 1923; *AT*, 28 February, 2, 4, and 11 March 1924.

39. *AT*, 28 February 1924. One of the minor curiosities of the affair was the fact that Moller was Ernst Alemann's uncle by marriage.

40. Bussemeyer, *Fünfzig Jahre Argentinisches Tageblatt*, p. 71.

41. *AT*, 28 February through 31 March 1924.

42. *NDZ*, 10 and 31 March 1924.

43. *AT*, 16 March 1924; Bussemeyer, *Fünfzig Jahre Argentinisches Tageblatt*, pp. 73–76.

44. Emil Hayn shed crocodile tears for the "honest" Alemann: "Gründung." The entire affair is glossed lightly in the later general histories of Keiper, and Lütge, Hoffmann, Körner, and is ignored by Schmidt.

45. *Auslandsdeutsche* 12, no. 7 (April 1929): 208.

46. Verein Vorwärts, *Mitteilungsblatt*, no. 4 (April 1929), and the club's *50-jährige Gründungsfeier*, pp. 15 *ff.*

47. Verein Vorwärts, *Mitteilungsblatt*, 1 September 1929.

7. The Social Crisis of the Middle Class, 1918–1933

1. Dorfman, *Industria argentina*, p. 170. Dorfman's base year 1933 = 100. Cost of living was below 100 from 1913 through 1915, rose above 100 in 1916, reached its apogee (172.3) in 1920, and slowly declined thereafter.

2. *Nachrichtenblatt RA* 4, no. 18 (September 1922): 547.

3. P. F. H. writing in *Der Bund* 6, no. 5 (May 1923): 57.

4. Dirección de Inmigración, *Memorias* or *Informes*, 1923 through 1930, 1932.

5. "Pionierarbeit," p. 51.

6. *NDZ*, 7 June 1923.

7. *NDZ* 1, no. 32 (April 1920); 17 September 1923; Verein Vorwärts,

Mitteilungen, no. 2 (February 1929); *Nachrichtenblatt RA* 3, no. 10 (May 1921): 389–390. In 1921 the painters' union had sixty members, the metal workers', fifty.

8. *NDZ*, 24 September 1923, 11 and 18 February 1924.

9. *NDZ* 2, no. 13 (November 1920).

10. *NDZ* 1, no. 1 (2 September 1919); 1, no. 36 (8 May 1920); 1, no. 40 (June 1920).

11. W. Aust, "Cuadro de los gastos de los servicios de 'Extensión Social' año 1930" (typescript); Spezial Archiv der deutschen Wirtschaft [Berlin], 4104/39-SA I 909/1, 1–8.

12. *NDZ*, 29 May/1 June 1922.

13. *NDZ* 7, no. 41 (June 1920); 1, no. 44 (July 1920); *AT*, 28 February–31 March 1924.

14. *Nachrichtenblatt RA* 4, no. 1 (January 1922): 28.

15. Ibid. 3, no. 24 (December 1921): 948.

16. Ibid.

17. A. Ritter von der Osten, "Erlebnisse eines deutschen Kaufmannes in Argentinien," *Auslandsdeutsche* 11, no. 20 (October 1928): 636–637.

18. *Nachrichtenblatt RA* 15, no. 10 (May 1933): 116.

19. *NDZ*, 1 November 1926: "the German immigrant has existential requirements too high for Argentine conditions; discontent is bound up in this. For a room, bed, chair, and nail to hang his clothes on he must spend the better part of his earnings."

20. See editor's remarks, *Der Bund* 8, no. 8 (August 1925).

21. "Deutsches Leben in Südamerika," *Der Bund* 8, nos. 1/3 (March 1925): 7–11; 8, no. 4 (April 1925): 24–26.

22. Thalheim, *Auswanderungsproblem*, pp. 106–107.

23. *Auslandsdeutsche* 8, no. 18 (September 1925): 538–539.

24. Blücher, *Rande*, pp. 146–147.

25. Petersen et al., *Handwörterbuch* 1: 122–143, 605.

26. Ibid., pp. 129–130.

27. Ibid., p. 127.

28. *Auslandsdeutsche* 11, no. 12 (June 1928): 397; *NZ/BA* 2d ser., no. 9 (December 1922).

29. Hayn, "Pionierarbeit."

30. *Der Bund* 6, no. 5 (May 1923): 58.

31. In 1920 the *Vereinsvorstände* claimed that the delegates represented five to six thousand members. The *NDZ* replied that, because of many multiple memberships, about forty leaders and some five to six hundred active *Vereinsmeier* would be more realistic (2, no. 9 [November 1920]).

32. Argentinischer Verein Deutscher Ingenieure, Buenos Aires *Jahresberichte, 1921* through *1930*.

33. Ruderverein Teutonia, Buenos Aires, *Fünfzig Jahre Ruderverein "Teutonia," 1890–1940*, pp. 23, 24, 29, 35–37, 39–40.

34. The *Jahresberichte* for 1932–1933 and 1933–1934 are missing from the Institut für Auslandsbeziehungen collection.

35. Deutscher Klub Buenos Aires, *Jahresbericht*, 1 November 1935–31 October 1936.

36. Herzog, *Zwischendeck*, p. 86.

37. Martin Arndt, "Die wirtschaftliche Grundlage der deutschen Schu-

len," *Der Bund* 15, no. 2 (February 1933): 44; Kühn, *Grundriss der Kulturgeographie von Argentinien*, p. 165.

38. By 1936, of the 34,706 European-born persons living in Belgrano, 13,055 were Spaniards, 11,429 were Italians, 2,912 were Germans, and 934 were Austrians (*Cuarto Censo General, 1936, de la Municipalidad de la Ciudad de Buenos Aires*, 2).

39. "Buenos Aires," in Petersen *et al.*, *Handwörterbuch* 1: 605; M. Riester, "Entwicklung einer Banater Schwaben-Kolonie in Piñeyro," *Auslandsdeutsche* 12, no. 19 (October 1929): 642–643.

40. Deutscher Schulverein Villa Ballester, *Jahrbuch 1945: Über Land und Meer nach Ballester*: an uneven collection of memoirs by men who had seen much of the world before settling in Villa Ballester.

8. Assimilation and the School Question, 1918–1933

1. "Die deutsche Kolonie in Montevideo," *Zeitschrift* des DWV 5, no. 5 (1919): 344–348.

2. This commonplace has recently received a narrow empirical confirmation in Francis Korn, "Algunos aspectos de la asimilación de inmigrantes en Buenos Aires," *América Latina* 8, no. 2 (April–June 1965): 77–96.

3. Standard treatment is Gino Germani, "La clase media en la Argentina, con especial referencia a sus sectores urbanos," *Materiales para el estudio de la clase media en la América Latina*, 1: 1–33, and subsequent writings. The emergence of a *criollo* middle class, and some of the probable consequences for the Buenos Aires Germans, was noted early in the postwar decade by Stichel, "Einwanderung"; and *Nachrichtenblatt RA* 2, no. 18 (September 1921).

4. On the Auslands-Institut during the 1920s and early 1930s, see Sander A. Diamond, *The Nazi Movement in the United States*, pp. 42–54.

5. According to the *Cuarto Censo General, 1936*, there were more than two unmarried Reichsdeutsche (including naturalized) males residing in Buenos Aires to every female: 4009/1901 (3: 190).

6. *Der Bund* 13, no. 10 (October 1931): 121.

7. "Buenos Aires," 1: 605.

8. *Cuarto Censo General*, 4: 370–371. The same census showed 6,841 families whose head had been born in Germany (4: 367). There were 934 naturalized German males in the city who had been married at one time or another (3: 190). This would explain part of the discrepancy, but it is difficult to believe that upward of 1,500 families were headed by women.

9. Keiper, "Deutschtum," pp. 99–100.

10. *Cuarto Censo General*, 4: 370–371. 3,659 families were headed by persons born in Austria (3: 192). The same comments apply as in note 8.

11. 3: 190, 192.

12. Religion was a major difference between the two collectivities. 31 percent of German men and 33 percent of women declared themselves Catholics; among Austrians the figure was 72 percent for both sexes. Yet in Catholic Argentina this does not appear to have had significant consequences—except to expand the pool of "other foreign" women from which

the Austrians could choose mates. The census data do not break down households by religion.

13. Survey carried out by Wilhelm Lütge; corrected results published in the *Jahrbuch 1938* des DVA. As "racial" criteria were applied, German-speaking Jews were not included.

14. *Censo General de . . . la Ciudad de Buenos Aires (Octubre 1909)*, 1: xliv; *Cuarto Censo General, 1936*, 4: 387.

15. *Freie Presse, Mai-Festschrift*, pp. 162–164; *AT*, October 1914 and March 1920 for school advertising supplements; 19 August and 7 November 1918 on the Cangallo School; Gabert, *Bildungswesen*, p. 8; Schmidt, *Geschichte*, pp. 239, 241; W. Rohmeder, "Die Verteilung der deutschen Schulen in Buenos Aires," *Die Deutsche Schule im Auslande* (Sonderheft *Argentinien*) 24, no. 10 (October 1932): 310–311.

16. Keiper, "Die Belgranoschule in Buenos Aires," in Schmidt and Boelitz, eds., *Aus deutscher Bildungsarbeit*, 1: 393.

17. Ibid., pp. 386–394; Blücher, *Rande*, p. 149.

18. *AT*, 7 November 1918.

19. *NDZ*, 29 November 1926, 18 April 1927.

20. *NDZ*, 29 November 1926.

21. *Freie Presse, Mai-Festschrift*, pp. 162–164; *Auslandsdeutsche* 16, nos. 16/17 (August/September 1933): 431.

22. *Auslandsdeutsche* 8, no. 20 (October 1925): 588; "Deutschsprachige Kultureinrichtungen in Argentinien," *Jahrbuch 1932* des DVA, pp. 121–124.

23. *Mitteilungen* des Allgemeinen Verbandes deutscher Lehrer in den La Plata Staaten (Supplement to *Zeitschrift* des DWV 4, no. 1 [1918]).

24. *AT*, 26 February 1920.

25. "Belgranoschule," p. 391.

26. *AT*, 1 January 1924.

27. *Der Bund* 2, no. 4 (April 1919): 55–56.

28. "Zur Organisation des deutschen Schulwesens in Buenos Aires," *DLPZ*, 23 November 1919.

29. *Reformvorschläge für die deutschen Schulen in Buenos Aires*, excerpted in *Auslandsdeutsche* 3, no. 2 (January 1920): 48–49.

30. *NZ/BA* 2d ser., no. 18 (August 1923).

31. *Lesebuch für die deutschen Schulen in Südamerika 6. bis 8. Schuljahr*; quoted by August Siewers (then director of the Barracas School) in *Zeitschrift* des DWV 4, no. 1 (1918): 131–132.

32. Obituary, *Zeitschrift für Kulturaustausch* [Stuttgart] 12, no. 4 (1962): 371; Herbert Koch, "Wilhelm Keiper zur Erinnerung aus Anlass seines 100. Geburtstages," ibid. 18, no. 4 (1968): 320–321.

33. "Die deutschen Schulen in Argentinien zwischen den beiden Weltkriegen," *Der Deutsche Lehrer im Auslande* [Munich] 4, no. 3 (1957): 61–62.

34. *NDZ* 1, no. 2 (September 1919): 9–10.

35. Blücher, *Rande*, pp. 149–150; Max Wilfert, "Die deutschen Schulen am La Plata," *Bundeskalender 1925* des DVA, pp. 37–46.

36. "Die deutsche Kolonie im Jahre 1931," *Jahrbuch 1932* des DVA, p. 130; Arndt, "Wirtschaftliche Grundlage," pp. 44–45; Keiper, "Vom deutsch-

en Schulwesen in Argentinien," *Jahrbuch 1936* des DVA, pp. 49–55; Keiper, "Die deutschen Schulen," p. 61.

37. "Die deutsche Auslandsschule in Südamerika und der Krieg," *Zeitschrift* des DWV 3, no. 3 (1917): 147–148; 3, no. 5 (1917): 250.

38. *Zeitschrift* des DWV 3, no. 5 (1917): 250 *ff*.

39. Ibid., p. 149.

40. *Der Bund* 10, no. 4 (April 1927): 27–28.

41. W. Rohmeder, "Wirtschaftliche Lage der deutschen Lehrer in Argentinien," *Die Deutsche Schule im Auslande* (Sonderheft *Argentinien*) 24, no. 10 (October 1932): 320–321; M. Vaillant, "Deutsche Lehrerfragen in Argentinien," ibid., pp. 318–320.

42. Keiper, "Deutsche Lehrer in Argentinien."

43. "Verteilung," pp. 311–312.

44. "Die inneren Fragen des deutschen Schulwesens in Argentinien," in Schmidt and Boelitz, eds., *Aus deutscher Bildungsarbeit*, 2: 382.

45. "Neuorientierung des deutschen Schulwesens in Buenos Aires und Umgegend," *Jahrbuch 1933* des DVA, p. 66.

46. Ibid., pp. 64–65.

47. "Inneren Fragen"; "Das deutsche Schulwesen in Argentinien," *Die Deutsche Schule im Auslande* (Sonderheft *Argentinien*) 24, no. 10 (October 1932): 305.

48. "Kultureinrichtungen"; "Deutsche Vereine," *Der Bund* 18, no. 2 (1936): 18.

49. Keiper, "Deutsche Lehrer in Argentinien."

50. Erich Elsner, *Chronik der deutschen Kolonie Rosarios*, pp. 66–67.

51. *Freie Presse, Mai-Festschrift*, p. 210.

52. The German community of Santa Fe had been declared to be in decline as early as 1921: "mostly old people . . . no future." *Nachrichtenblatt RA* 2, no. 5 (1921): 188.

53. *Grundriss*, p. 165.

54. *Der Bund* 10, no. 8 (August 1927): 98–99.

55. *Auslandsdeutsche* 12, no. 6 (March 1929): 176.

9. Cultural Despair, Perceptions of Nazism, and the *Gleichschaltung* of 1933

1. Lütge, Hoffmann, Körner, *Geschichte*, p. 308.

2. On *Deutsche Blätter* (from 1926 on), see K. J. R. Arndt and M. E. Olson, *The German Language Press of the Americas: History and Bibliography*, 2: 48 (entry 043).

3. See Juan José Sebreli, *La cuestión judía en la Argentina*.

4. Interviews, Rabbi Schlesinger and Ing. Klein (founding president, in 1935, of the *Delegación de Asociaciones Israelitas Argentinas*), Buenos Aires, 1968. Both maintained that German-speaking Jews in Buenos Aires had considered themselves German until 1933. They then reevaluated their position and sought common cause with the Eastern European Jews.

5. *Phoenix* 6, no. 4 (July 1926): 257–288; *Phoenix* 6, no. 5 (September 1926): 317–340. On 24 March 1933 Rauenbusch lectured on "National So-

cialism as World View" in the drawingroom of the *Deutsche La-Plata Zeitung* (*Auslandsdeutsche* 16, nos. 10/11 [May/June 1933]: 276).

6. *Der Bund* 9, no. 5 (May 1926): 38–41.

7. *NZ/BA* 2d ser., 24 (January 1924).

8. Dr. A. Buckeley, "Auswanderung," pp. 35–36.

9. "Die Frau in der Kolonie und ihr Verhältnis zur neuen sozialen Ordnung: Ein Weckruf," *AT*, 4 April 1920.

10. *Tragik*, pp. 121, 134. Harold-Hatzold denounced the community's anti-Semitism (p. 132) as well as the crimes being carried out in Germany that year (1933) in the name of Christianity (p. 128).

11. *NDZ*, 18 October 1926, 14 February 1927.

12. *Auslandsdeutsche* 13, no. 17 (September 1930): 609.

13. Hesse was born in Wittlich in 1885 and died in Buenos Aires in 1952. He was attached to the staff of the German Hospital at least as early as 1916. See P. Fechter, *Geschichte der deutschen Literatur*, pp. 628–630.

14. Told by Karl Wilhelm Körner, who knew Hesse well during the latter's retirement in Buenos Aires.

15. "Kampf ums Deutschtum!" pp. 33–34.

16. Klaus Kannapin, "Zur Politik der Nazis in Argentinien von 1933 bis 1943," in *Der Deutsche Faschismus in Lateinamerika, 1933–1941*, pp. 85–86.

17. *DWG, Bericht 1931.*

18. "Die deutsche Kolonie im Jahre 1932," *Jahrbuch 1932 des DVA*; Petersen *et al.*, *Handwörterbuch*, 1: 605.

19. Kannapin, "Politik," p. 86; *Der Bund* 15, no. 1 (1933).

20. *Deutscher Handlungsgehilfen-Verband am La Plata* 5, no. 37 (December 1933–February 1934).

21. *Der Bund* 15, no. 4 (1933); "Die deutsche Kolonie im Jahre 1933," *Jahrbuch 1934 des DVA.*

22. The 1921 and 1942 versions are entitled *Meine Jagd nach dem Glück in Argentinien und Paraguay*; the 1938 version was called *Die Jagd nach der Arbeit in Argentinien.*

23. All five are available in the library of the Institut für Auslandsbeziehungen, Stuttgart.

24. *NZ/BA* 3d ser., no. 3 (July 1934); no. 4 (August 1934); no. 5 (September 1934). Italics in original. It is surprising that he makes no mention of the Roehm purge of July 1934.

Bibliography

Basic Sources

In 1917 Joseph Winiger, in preparing his "Beiträge zur Geschichte des Deutschtums in den La-Plata Staaten," complained of the German-Argentines' destructiveness toward their historical materials; matters have not improved since. The losses between 1945 and 1951, when the Argentine government closed the German language associations, were especially severe. Even today there is no German-Argentine historical society nor any central repository. The important private library of Karl Wilhelm Körner was dispersed on his death in December 1968; however, the Richard Staudt Collection was transmitted to the Biblioteca Nacional the following year. See Acknowledgments for other major repositories.

Newspapers and Periodicals

The immigrant press is the starting point for any serious study. See Karl J. R. Arndt and May E. Olson, *The German Language Press of the Americas: History and Bibliography*, vol. 2 (Munich: Verlag Dokumentation, 1972), for publication data and location of holdings of *Argentinisches Tageblatt*, 1906, 1908, 1914–1933; *Deutsche La-Plata Zeitung*, 1914–1933 (specific events); *Buenos Aires Handels-Zeitung*, 1888–1924; *Vorwärts*, 1886–1897; *Neue Deutsche Zeitung*, 1919–1926; *Deutsche Zeitung*, 1927, 1933. Also *Der Bauernbund*, 1927–1930; *Der Bund*, 1917–1933; *Deutsche Blätter*, 1926; *Evangelisches Gemeindeblatt*, 1903–1933 (scattered numbers); *Lasso*, 1933–1940; *Mitteilungsblatt* der Landesgruppe Argentinien der NSDAP, 1932–1935; *Mitteilungsblatt* des Vereins Vorwärts, 1929–1933; *Nachrichtenblatt* der Ortsgruppe Buenos Aires des Deutschnationalen Handlungsgehilfen Verbandes, 1930–1931/*Der DHV am La Plata*, 1931–1935/*Der Deutsche in Argentinien*, 1935–1945 (scattered numbers); *Die Neue Zeit*, 1918–1919, 1922–1924, 1934; *Südamerika*, 1949–1959; *Unser Deutschland*, 1918; *Die Wacht*, 1918–1919/*Die Deutsche Wacht*, 1922–1923; *Zeitschrift für Argentinische Volks- und Landeskunde*, 1911–1915/ *Zeitschrift* des Deutschen Wissenschaftlichen Vereins Buenos Aires, 1915–1921/*Phoenix*, 1921–1939.

Addressbooks, Yearbooks

Argentinischer Volkskalender, 1927–1931. Buenos Aires: Argentinisches Tageblatt, 1927–1931.

Bachmann, Ernst. *Kunz' Jahrbuch und Adress-Kalender der deutschen Kolonie in Buenos Aires*. 1. Jahrgang 1884. Buenos Aires: Hugo Kunz, 1884.

Bundeskalender [after 1928 *Jahrbuch*] des Deutschen Volksbundes für Argentinien, 1925–1945. Buenos Aires: DVA, 1926–1945.

Deutsch-Argentinisches Adressbuch, 1916–1926, omitting 1919. Buenos Aires: Verlag der Zeitschrift des Deutschen Wissenschaftlichen Vereins, 1916–1926.
Deutsch-Argentinisches Jahrbuch "Der Kondor." 2. Jahrgang 1909. Buenos Aires, Wilhelm Cappus, 1909.
Deutscher Kalender für die La-Plata Staaten auf das Jahr 1899. Buenos Aires: Deutsche Buchhandlung G. van Woerden et Cie., 1899.
Deutscher La-Plata Kalender für das Jahr 1873. Buenos Aires: Ruhland und Reinhardt, 1873.
Diana, Justo E. [Argentine Consul in Berlin]. *Argentinisches Jahrbuch 1928.* Berlin: Selbstverlag des Verfassers, 1928.
Deutsche La Plata Zeitung, *Guía Germana del Río de la Plata: Adressbuch Deutschsprechender*, Tomo 2, 1924/1925. Buenos Aires: DLPZ, 1925.
Exposiciones Internacionales Buenos Aires 1910: Catálogo oficial de las secciones alemanas. Berlin: Georg Stilke, n.d.
Foerster's Illustrierter Familien-Kalender für die Deutschen der La-Plata Staaten, 1916–1931. Buenos Aires: Foerster, 1916–1931.
Other volumes in the Kunz, *"Kondor,"* and *Guía Germana* series have not been located, nor has Ernst Nolte's *Fremdenführer und Deutsches Adressbuch*, at least three numbers of which appeared between 1879 and 1883.

Voluntary Associations

The records (*Jahresberichte, Festschriften* on anniversaries, occasional *Nachrichtenblätter*) of the voluntary associations are extremely valuable sources of data, but few series are intact. See Institut für Auslandsbeziehungen [Stuttgart], *Mitteilungen* 11, nos. 2/3 (April/September 1961) (Sonderheft *Argentinien: Beitrag Deutschlands zur 150-Jahrfeier der Unabhängigkeit Argentiniens*), pp. 208–211, for the institute's holdings, which form the best single collection. The Friedrich-Ebert-Stiftung (Bonn/Bad Godesberg) has obtained the Verein Vorwärts materials. The German booksellers in Buenos Aires can be of great service. The associations are Argentinischer Verein Deutscher Ingenieure; Deutsche Handelskammer (since 1951: Cámara de Comercio Argentino-Alemana); Deutsche Wohltätigkeits-Gesellschaft; Deutscher Bauernbund; Deutscher Handlungsgehilfen Verband am La Plata; Deutscher Krankenverein; Deutscher Reitverein; Deutscher Schulverband Buenos Aires; Deutscher Turnverein (after 1908: Deutscher Klub); Deutscher Volksbund für Argentinien; Deutscher Wissenschaftlicher Verein; Deutsches Hospital; Deutsches Seemannsheim; Evangelische Gemeinde; Evangelisch-Lutherische Kirche in Argentinien; Federación de Asociaciones Argentino-Alemanas (post-1951); Landesgruppe Argentinien der NSDAP; Ruderverein Teutonia, Verein zum Schutze germanischer Einwanderer (V. zur Förderung g. E. ca. 1904); Verein Vorwärts (Club Alemán Adelante).

Archive

Bundesarchiv-Militärarchiv (Freiburg i.B.): Reichs-Marineamt: Admiralstab der Marine (F5092); Zentralabteilung (F7515 PG 69085).

Argentine Government Publications

(a) Immigration: Dirección General de Inmigración, *Memorias* or *Informes*, 1876, 1878, 1888–1900, 1902, 1907–1909, 1912–1915, 1923–1930, 1932; Ministerio de Agricultura, *Resumen estadístico del movimiento migratorio de la República Argentina, años 1857–1924* (Buenos Aires, 1925).
(b) Censuses: *Primer censo de la República Argentina, 1869*. (Buenos Aires: 1872); *Segundo censo de la República Argentina, 1895*. 3 vols. (Buenos Aires: 1898); *Tercer censo nacional levantado . . . 1914*. 10 vols. (Buenos Aires: 1916–1919); *Censo general de . . . la ciudad de Buenos Aires, 1887*. 2 vols. (Buenos Aires: 1889); *Censo general de . . . la ciudad de Buenos Aires . . . 1904* (Buenos Aires: 1906); *Censo general de . . . la ciudad de Buenos Aires . . . 1909*. 3 vols. (Buenos Aires: 1910); Municipalidad de la ciudad de Buenos Aires, *Cuarto censo general, 1936*. 4 vols. (Buenos Aires: 1940); *Censo escolar nacional correspondiente a fines de 1883 y principios de 1884*. 3 vols. (Buenos Aires: 1885); *Censo general de educación, 1909* (Buenos Aires: 1909).

Secondary Sources

Contemporary

Alemann, Ernst. *Grünes Gold und rote Erde*. Buenos Aires: Sonderdruck des Argentinischen Tageblattes, 1926.
———. "Im Kampf um die Freiheit: Erinnerungen aus fünf Jahrzehnten," *Argentinisches Tageblatt* (special supplement: *75 Jahre Argentinisches Tageblatt*). 2d section, 29 April 1964.
Alemann, Theodor. "Erlebnisse," *Argentinisches Tageblatt*, 31 December 1922/1 January 1923.
———. *Die Zukunft des Deutschtums in Amerika*. Buenos Aires: Beutelspacher, 1917; 2d rev. ed. Stuttgart: Ausland- und Heimat Verlag, 1923.
Arent, A. *Argentinien: Ein Land der Zukunft: Jubiläumsschrift zur Hundertjahrfeier der Begründung der Republik Argentinien*. Leipzig: Naumhof, 1910.
———. ["Ein deutscher Offizier"]. *Ein Land der Zukunft: Ein Beitrag zur näheren Kenntnis Argentiniens*. Munich: Südamerika Verlag, n.d.
Argentinisches Tageblatt (special supplement: *Festausgabe zum 25. Mai 1960*), 25 May 1960.
———. (special supplement: *75 Jahre Argentinisches Tageblatt*), 29 April 1964.
———. (special supplement: *Jubiläumsausgabe zur Nummer 25,000*), 9 December 1965.
Arndt, Martin. "Die wirtschaftliche Grundlage der deutschen Schulen," *Der Bund* 15, no. 2 (February 1933): 44–45.
Aust, W. [ex-Director of Extensión Social, CHADE]. Mss. in private library of K. W. Körner, Buenos Aires, including "Cuadro de los gastos de los servicios de 'Extensión Social,' año 1930," Spezial Archiv der deutschen Wirtschaft [Berlin], 4104/39-SA I 909/1, 1–8. Also pamphlets on CHADE.

Bagel, Felix [F. Alba]. *Auswanderung nach Argentinien*. Berlin: 1919.

Bähr, Erich. "Deutsche Technik am La Plata," *Mitteilungen* des Institutes für Auslandsbeziehungen 11, nos. 2/3 (April/September 1961; special edition: *Argentinien*): 162–165.

Beck-Bernard, Carl. *Argentinien*. Leipzig: Weltpost-Verlag, 1883.

Becke, General Carlos von der. "Von Utz Schmidl bis von der Goltz," *Freie Presse* (special supplement: *Mai-Festschrift 1960*), 25 May 1960, pp. 117–128.

Beruti, Raúl. "Institución Cultural Argentino-Germana," *Mitteilungen* des Institutes für Auslandsbeziehungen 11, nos. 2/3 (April/September 1961; special edition: *Argentinien*): 160–161.

Blücher, Wipert von. *Am Rande der Weltgeschichte: Marokko, Schweden, Argentinien*. Wiesbaden: Limes-Verlag, 1958.

Brugger, E. "Auf Arbeitsuche in der Ernte," *Der Bund* 15, no. 4 (1933): 107–108.

Buckeley, A. "Auswanderung und Heimat," *Jahrbuch 1931* des Deutschen Volksbundes für Argentinien (Buenos Aires: DVA, 1932), p. 35.

Bühler, Pastor. "Zur Kolonisation in den argentinischen Misionen," *Der Auslandsdeutsche* 6, no. 6 (July 1923): 379–381.

Bussche-Haddenhausen, Hilmar von dem. "Der Deutsch-Argentinische Zentralverband, seine Entstehung und bisherige Tätigkeit," *Phoenix* 1, nos. 5/6 (February 1922): 65–68.

Bussemeyer, Peter. *Fünfzig Jahre Argentinisches Tageblatt: Werden und Aufstieg einer auslandsdeutschen Zeitung*. Buenos Aires: Argentinisches Tageblatt, 1939.

Cámara de Comercio Argentino-Alemana, 1966. *Cámara de Comercio Argentino-Alemana, 1916–1966*. Buenos Aires, 1966. Includes Eduardo Alemann, "La co-operación argentino-alemana en el terreno industrial," pp. 72–86; Karl Klingenfuss, "Handel und Wandel," pp. 87–104.

Cappus, Wilhelm. "Zur Geschichte der Deutschen in Argentinien," *Zeitschrift für Argentinische Volks- und Landeskunde* 5, no. 2 (1915): 116–123; 5, no. 4 (1915): 208–216.

Daireaux, Emile. *La vie et les moeurs à La Plata*. 2 vols. Buenos Aires: Hachette, 1888.

Degener, Otto. *Auf Glücksuche nach Südamerika*. Berlin: Safari-Verlag, ca. 1929.

Deutsche Handelskammer Buenos Aires. "Einwirkung des Krieges auf den deutschen Handel in Argentinien." Typescript, 1919.

———. *Einwirkung des Weltkrieges auf die Volkswirtschaft Argentiniens*. Buenos Aires: Imprenta Germania, 1920.

Deutsche La-Plata Zeitung. Special supplement: denunciation of Weimar Republic, 25 September 1921.

Deutscher Schulverein Villa Ballester. *Jahrbuch 1945: Über Land und Meer nach Ballester*. Buenos Aires: n.p., 1945.

Dörsing, Hugo. "Neuorientierung des deutschen Schulwesens in Buenos Aires und Umgegend," *Jahrbuch 1933* des Deutschen Volksbundes für Argentinien (Buenos Aires: DVA, 1934), pp. 59–67.

———. *Reformvorschläge für die deutschen Schulen in Buenos Aires*. Buenos Aires: n.p., 1919.

Drascher, Warhold. "Deutsches Leben in Südamerika," *Der Bund* 8, nos. 1/3 (March 1925): 7–11; 8, no. 4 (April 1925): 24–26.

Duerst, Peter. *Erlebnisse und Erfahrungen: 40 Jahre im Dienste der Volksbildung in Argentinien (1872–1912).* Leipzig: Herausgegeben vom Deutschen Lehrerverein Buenos Aires, 1913.

Eckener, Hugo. *Im Zeppelin über Länder und Meere: Erlebnisse und Erinnerungen.* Flensburg: Wolff, 1949.

Elsner, Erich. *Chronik der deutschen Kolonie Rosarios.* Buenos Aires: Imprenta Mercur, 1932.

Ewers, Hanns Heinz. *Mit meinen Augen: Fahrten durch die lateinische Welt.* Munich: Georg Müller Verlag, 1919.

F. S. "Mein erstes Jahr in Argentinien," *Der Bund* 5, no. 5 (May 1922): 53–56.

Faber, Kurt. *Dem Glücke nach durch Südamerika.* Stuttgart: Verlag Robert Lutz, 1919.

———. "Unter Landstreichern in Argentinien," *Der Bund* 3, no. 5 (May 1920): 71.

Francke, F. R. "Wir Alteingesessenen—oder—Wussten Sie das schon?" *Südamerika* 3, no. 5 (March–April 1953): 538–542.

Franze, Johannes. "Glanzvoller Aufstieg der deutschen Musik in Argentinien," *Mitteilungen* des Institutes für Auslandsbeziehungen 11, nos. 2/3 (April/September 1961; special edition: *Argentinien*): 145–148.

Freie Presse. Special supplement: *Mai-Festschrift 1960,* 25 May 1960.

———. Special supplement: *Das Deutschtum in Argentinien,* December 1951.

Gabert, R. *Das deutsche Bildungswesen in Argentinien and seine Organisation.* Berlin: Reimer, 1908.

Goldschmidt, Alfons. *Argentinien.* Berlin: Ernst Rowohlt Verlag, 1923.

Goltz, Generalfeldmarschall Colmar Freiherr von der. "Reiseeindrücke aus Argentinien," Lecture, 28 January 1911, Deutsch-Argentinischer Zentralverband, Berlin. Reprinted in *Freie Presse,* 1 December 1967.

Graef, Fritz. "Der Anteil deutscher Topografen an der Forschung Argentiniens," *Jahrbuch 1938* des Deutschen Volksbundes für Argentinien (Buenos Aires: DVA, 1939), pp. 83–86.

Griesebach, M. "Die deutsche Auswanderungsfrage und ihre Lösung," *Mitteilungen* des Deutschen Auslands-Institutes 2, no. 6 (June 1919): 146–151; 2, no. 7 (July 1919): 197–202; 2, no. 8 (August 1919).

Hahn, Bolko von. "Beitrag deutscher Industrie an der Entwicklung Argentiniens," *Lasso* 3, no. 6 (December 1935).

Harold-Hatzold, Peter. *Aus zwei Jahrhunderten: Die Tragik eines Menschenlebens, nach Erlebnissen niedergeschrieben.* Buenos Aires: Selbstverlag des Verfassers, 1933.

Hayn, Emil. "Deutsche Pionierarbeit in Übersee," *Der Bund* 13, no. 6 (June 1931): 50–56.

———. "Die Entwicklung der deutschen Elektrizitätswerke in Buenos Aires," *Phoenix* 6, no. 1 (1926): 131–176.

———. "Die Gründung und die Kampfjahre des Deutschen Volksbundes für Argentinien," *Jahrbuch 1938* des Deutschen Volksbundes für Argentinien (Buenos Aires: DVA, 1939), pp. 133–135.

Herzog, Wilhelm. *Im Zwischendeck nach Südamerika*. Vienna: Malik-Verlag, 1924.

Hesse, Max René. *Morath schlägt sich durch*. Berlin: Cassirer, 1933.

────. *Morath verwirklicht einen Traum*. Berlin: Cassirer, 1933.

Hirschfeld, Günther von. *Das Problem der deutschen Handels- und Wirtschaftsinteressen in Südamerika*. Berlin: Leonhard Simion Nf, 1920.

Holleben, Baron von. "Capitales alemanes en la República Argentina," *Revista de Derecho, Historia, y Letras* 28 (September 1907): 142–145.

Holzer, Pater Johann. "Bedeutung der katholischen Seelsorge für das Deutschtum in Argentinien," *Der Auslandsdeutsche* 8, no. 16 (August 1925): 466–467.

Holzmann, Ingeniero. "Beitrag deutscher Flieger an der Entwicklung südamerikanischen Luftverkehrs," *Lasso* 3, no. 6 (December 1935).

Huber, Karl. "Auswanderung nach Argentinien?" *Mitteilungen* des Deutschen Auslands-Institutes 2, no. 8 (August 1919): 253–255.

Instituto Nacional del Profesorado Secundario [Buenos Aires]. *Memoria presentada al Señor Ministro de Justicia e Instrucción Pública . . . diciembre de 1908*. Buenos Aires: Talleres Gráficas de la Penitenciaría Nacional, 1909.

Jerusalem, Else. "Die Frau in der Kolonie und ihr Verhältnis zur neuen sozialen Ordnung: Ein Weckruf," *Argentinisches Tageblatt*, 4 April 1920.

Jesinghaus, Karl. "Zur Organisation des deutschen Schulwesens in Buenos Aires," *Deutsche La-Plata Zeitung*, 23 November 1919.

Jonin, Alexander. *Durch Süd-Amerika: Reise- und Kulturhistorische Bilder*. 1: *Die Pampa-Länder*. Translated from the Russian by M. von Petzold. Berlin: Verlag Siegfried Cronbach, 1895.

Jungenfeld, Ernst Freiherr Gedult von. *Aus den Urwäldern Paraguays zur Fahne*. Buenos Aires: Süd-Amerika Kriegsausgaben, 1917.

────. *Ein deutsches Schicksal im Urwald*. Berlin: Ullstein, 1933.

Kärger, Karl. *Landwirtschaft und Kolonisation im spanischen Amerika*. 2 vols. Leipzig: Duncker und Humbolt, 1901.

Die Katholiken deutscher Zunge in Buenos Aires: Kurzgefasste Vorgeschichte der Seelsorge für dieselben von 1865 bis 1911, nebst den ersten drei Jahresberichten der Gemeinde deutschredender Katholiken. Buenos Aires: Herausgegeben vom Gemeindevorstand, 1914.

Keiper, Wilhelm. "Die Ausbildung der höheren Lehrer in Argentinien," *Zeitschrift* des Deutschen Wissenschaftlichen Vereins 1 (1915): 334–347.

────. "Die Belgranoschule in Buenos Aires," in F. Schmidt and O. Boelitz, eds., *Aus deutscher Bildungsarbeit im Auslande*. 2: *Aussereuropa* (Langensalza: Beltz, 1928), pp. 386–394.

────. "Die deutsche Bevölkerung in Buenos Aires," *Volksforschung* 6, no. 1 (1943): 43–59; 6, no. 2 (1943); 155–167.

────. *Der Deutsche in Argentinien*. 3d ed. Langensalza: Beltz, 1938.

────. "Deutsche Lehrer in Argentinien," *Jahrbuch 1938* des Deutschen Volksbundes für Argentinien (Buenos Aires: DVA, 1939), pp. 102–108.

────. "Das deutsche Schulwesen in Argentinien," *Die Deutsche Schule im Auslande* (special edition: *Argentinien*) 24, no. 10 (October 1932): 305–309.

————. "Die deutschen Schulen in Argentinien zwischen den beiden Welt-
kriegen," *Der Deutsche Lehrer im Auslande* 4, no. 3 (1957): 61–63.
————. "Vom deutschen Schulwesen in Argentinien," *Jahrbuch 1936* des
Deutschen Volksbundes für Argentinien (Buenos Aires: DVA, 1937),
pp. 49–55.
————. "Das Deutschtum in Argentinien: Sein Werden, Wesen, und Wir-
ken." Typescript. Author's foreword dated Berlin-Charlottenburg, 22
September 1943.
————. *Das Deutschtum in Argentinien während des Weltkrieges, 1914–
1918*. Hamburg: 1942.
————. "Die inneren Fragen des deutschen Schulwesens in Argentinien,"
in F. Schmidt and O. Boelitz, eds., *Aus deutscher Bildungsarbeit im
Auslande*. 2: *Aussereuropa* (Langensalza: Beltz, 1928), pp. 369–385.
Kempski, Karl. *Argentinien*. Buenos Aires: Imprenta Mercur, 1933.
Kölliker, Alfredo, et al. *Patagonia: Resultados de las expediciones realizadas
en 1910 a 1916*. 2 vols. Buenos Aires: Deutscher Wissenschaftlicher
Verein, 1917.
Krause, Otto. *Argentiniens Wirtschaft während des Weltkrieges: Ihre Be-
deutung für die deutsche Volkswirtschaft und Auswanderung*. Berlin:
Dietrich Reimer, 1919.
Kühn, Fritz. *Grundriss der Kulturgeographie von Argentinien*. Hamburg:
Friedrichsen de Gruyter et Cie., 1933.
[Lamm, Germán]. *Argentinien: Die Kolonie für den deutschen Siedler: Mit
400 argentinischen Papierpesos Herr seiner eigenen Scholle*. Buenos
Aires: Sociedad López Agrelo y Casanova, 1925.
Lateinamerika (A):
"Argentinien und Deutschland," no. 1 (October 1919): 1–3.
"Die argentinische Industrie," nos. 2/3 (March 1920): 81–82.
"Deutschland und die öffentliche Meinung Argentiniens," no. 4 (April
1920): 153–154.
"Einwanderung und Kolonisation," no. 4 (April 1920): 169.
"Entwicklung argentinischer Industrien mit deutscher Hilfe," nos. 2/3
(March 1920): 79–81.
"Die Vereinigten Staaten und der argentinische Markt," nos. 2/3 (March
1920): 106–108.
"Die Zukunft des Baumwollbaues im Chaco argentino," nos. 2/3 (March
1920): 104–106.
Lewin, C. "Als Erntearbeiter in Argentinien," *Der Bund* 4, no. 1 (January
1921): 1–4.
Lohausen, Karl. *Führer durch Buenos Aires*. 3d ed. Buenos Aires and Ber-
lin: Verlag Kunst und Wissenschaft, 1924.
Lütge, Wilhelm, Werner Hoffmann, and Karl Wilhelm Körner. *Geschichte
des Deutschtums in Argentinien*. Herausgegeben vom Deutschen Klub
in Buenos Aires zur Feier seines 100. jährigen Bestehens. Buenos Aires:
Imprenta Mercur, 1955.
La Nación (special centennial edition), 25 May 1910.
————. (special edition, centennial of Declaration of Independence), 9
July 1916.
Napp, Richard. *1870 und 1871 Drüben und Hier: Zusammenstellung der*

wichtigsten Ereignisse des deutsch-französichen Krieges. Buenos Aires: Ruhland und Reinhart, 1871.

Nelke, Pastor Wilhelm. "Die deutsche Kolonie in Montevideo," *Zeitschrift des Deutschen Wissenschaftlichen Vereins* 5, no. 5 (1919): 343–356.

Osten, A. Ritter von der. "Erlebnisse eines deutschen Kaufmannes in Argentinien," *Der Auslandsdeutsche* 11, no. 20 (October 1928): 636–637.

Petersen, C., et al. *Handwörterbuch des Grenz- und Auslandsdeutschtums.* 3 vols. Breslau: Ferdinand Hirt, 1933–1938. "Argentinien," 1: 122–143; "Buenos Aires," 1: 605–606; "Buenos Aires Provinz," 1: 606–608.

Philipp, Emil. "Fünf Jahre Mathematikunterricht an künftige Lehrer höherer Schulen in Buenos Aires," in F. Schmidt and O. Boelitz, eds., *Aus deutscher Bildungsarbeit im Auslande.* 2: *Aussereuropa* (Langensalza: Beltz, 1928), pp. 395–400.

Reichert, Friedrich. *Auf Berges- und Lebenshöhe: Erinnerungen.* 2 vols. Buenos Aires: Editorial KAVE, 1946.

Rhenius, Max. *Michel auf Neuland: Abenteuerliches aus Argentinien und Paraguay.* Stuttgart: Ausland- und Heimat Verlag, 1921.

————. *Der Amateur-Kolonist: Nützliche Winke und Geschichten aus dem La Plata Hinterwald.* Buenos Aires: Selbstverlag des Verfassers, 1913.

Riester, M. "Zur Auswanderung nach Argentinien," *Der Auslandsdeutsche* 6, no. 20 (October 1923): 561–562.

————. "Entwicklung einer Banater Schwaben-Kolonie in Piñeyro," *Der Auslandsdeutsche* 12, no. 19 (October 1929): 642–643.

Rohmeder, Wilhelm. "Hermann Burmeister (1807–1892)," *Jahrbuch 1942 des Deutschen Volksbundes für Argentinien* (Buenos Aires: DVA, 1943), pp. 33–42.

————. "Die Verteilung der deutschen Schulen in Buenos Aires und Umgebung," *Die Deutsche Schule im Auslande* (special edition: *Argentinien*) 24, no. 10 (October 1932): 310–311.

————. "Wirtschaftliche Lage der deutschen Lehrer in Argentinien," *Die Deutsche Schule im Auslande* (special edition: *Argentinien*) 24, no. 10 (October 1932): 320–321.

Ross, Colin. "Das Problem der Heimat und das Auslandsdeutschtum," *Der Bund* 3, no. 1 (January 1920): 17–18.

————. "La situación política y económica en Alemania," *La Prensa*, 27 January, 2, 3, 8, 16 February 1920.

————. "Deutsche wider Deutsche," *Argentinisches Tageblatt*, 15 March 1920.

————. "Was wird? Deutschlands Gegenwart und Zukunft," *Argentinisches Tageblatt*, 17 March 1920.

Ruderverein Teutonia Buenos Aires. *Fünfzig Jahre Ruderverein Teutonia, 1890–1940.* Buenos Aires: C. Kepplinger, 1940.

Ruppert, Fritz. "Deutsche Gelehrtenarbeit in Argentinien," in F. Schmidt and O. Boelitz, eds., *Aus deutscher Bildungsarbeit im Auslande.* 2: *Aussereuropa* (Langensalza: Beltz, 1928), pp. 401–412.

Scheele-Willich, Cissy von. "Die innere Eignung zum Siedlerberuf," *Phoenix* 5, no. 1 (1925): 10–14.

Schmidt, Hans. *Die Jagd nach der Arbeit in Argentinien.* San Andrés: Selbstverlag des Verfassers, 1939.

————. *Meine Jagd nach dem Glück in Argentinien und Paraguay*. Leipzig: R. Voigtländer Verlag, 1921. 2d ed. Buenos Aires: Imprenta Mercur, 1942.

Schmidt, Hermann. *Geschichte der deutschen evangelischen Gemeinde Buenos Aires, 1843–1943*. Buenos Aires: Deutsche Evangelische Gemeinde, 1943.

Schnabl, Leopold. *Buenos-Ayres: Land und Leute am silbernen Strome*. Stuttgart: Levy und Müller, 1886.

Schobinger, Juan. *Inmigración y colonización suizas en la República Argentina en el siglo diécinueve*. Buenos Aires: Instituto de Cultura Suizo-Argentina, 1957.

Schulz, W. "Deutsche Geschicke und Leistungen in Argentinien," *Mitteilungen* des Institutes für Auslandsbeziehungen 11, nos. 2/3 (April/September 1961; special edition: *Argentinien*): 117–125.

Stichel, Bernhard. "Einwanderung: Konjunktur und Arbeitsmarkt," *Der Bund* 3, no. 6 (June 1920): 85–88.

Stölting, Walter. *Kampf ums Dasein in Argentinien*. Berlin: Peter J. Ostergaard Verlag, 1931.

Thalheim, Karl. *Das deutsche Auswanderungsproblem der Nachkriegszeit*. Leipzig-Crimmitschau: Rohland und Berthold, 1926.

Vaillant, M. "Deutsche Lehrerfragen in Argentinien," *Die Deutsche Schule im Auslande* (special edition: *Argentinien*) 24, no. 10 (October 1932): 318–320.

Verein Vorwärts Buenos Aires. *Festschrift zur 50-jährigen Gründungsfeier, 1882–1932*. Buenos Aires: Vorwärts, 1932. Same title for sixtieth anniversary, 1942; sixty-fifth anniversary, 1947; seventieth anniversary, 1952; seventy-fifth anniversary, 1957.

Wehner, Friedrich. "Hamburgs Beziehungen zu Iberoamerika," *Südamerika* 9, no. 1 (July–September 1958): 21–26.

Wilfert, Max. "Die deutsche Auslandsschule in Südamerika und der Krieg," *Zeitschrift* des Deutschen Wissenschaftlichen Vereins 3, no. 3 (1917): 144–150; 3, no. 4 (1917): 194–201; 3, no. 5 (1917): 249–257.

————. "Die deutschen Schulen am La Plata," *Bundeskalender 1925* des Deutschen Volksbundes für Argentinien (Buenos Aires: DVA, 1926), pp. 37–46.

————. "Deutschsprachige Kultureinrichtungen in Argentinien," *Jahrbuch 1932* des Deutschen Volksbundes für Argentinien (Buenos Aires: DVA, 1933), pp. 121–124.

Winiger, Joseph. "Beiträge zur Geschichte des Deutschtums in den La-Plata Staaten." 2 vols. Typescript dated Buenos Aires, May 1946. First published as a series of articles in *Deutsche La-Plata Zeitung* in 1917 (original file not available).

Zitzgewitz, K. von. "Die Aussichten für die deutschen Einwanderer in Argentinien," *Bundeskalender 1926* des Deutschen Volksbundes für Argentinien (Buenos Aires: DVA, 1927), pp. 75–78.

Scholarly Writings

Atkins, G. P., and L. V. Thompson. "German Military Influence in Argentina," *Journal of Latin American Studies* 4, no. 2 (November 1972): 257–274.

Bullock, Alan. *Hitler: A Study in Tyranny*. Rev. ed. Harmondsworth: Pelican, 1962.

Corbett, Sir Julian. *Naval Operations: Official History of the War*. 4 vols. London: Longmans, Green, 1921–1930.

Cúneo, D., et al. *Inmigración y nacionalidad*. Buenos Aires: Paidós, 1967.

Diamond, Sander A. *The Nazi Movement in the United States, 1924–1941*. Ithaca: Cornell University Press, 1974.

Díaz Alejandro, Carlos. *Essays on the Economic History of the Argentine Republic*. New Haven: Yale University Press, 1970.

Di Tella, Guido, and Manuel Zymelman. "El desarrollo industrial argentino durante la Primera Guerra Mundial," *Revista de Ciencias Económicas*, April–June 1959, pp. 221–224.

Dorfman, Adolfo. *Historia de la industria argentina*. Rev. ed. Buenos Aires: Solar-Hachette, 1970.

Eidt, Robert. *Pioneer Settlement in Northeast Argentina*. Madison: University of Wisconsin Press, 1971.

Epstein, Fritz. "Argentinien und das deutsche Heer: Ein Beitrag zur Geschichte europäischer militärischer Einflüsse auf Südamerika," in M. Göhring and A. Scharff, eds., *Geschichtliche Kräfte und Entscheidungen: Festschrift Otto Becker* (Wiesbaden: Franz Steiner Verlag, 1954), pp. 286–294.

Fechter, Paul. *Geschichte der deutschen Literatur*. Gütersloh: Bertelsmann, 1956.

Fischer, Peter Wilhelm. *Der Einfluss des Auslandskapitals auf die wirtschaftliche Entwicklung Argentiniens, 1880–1964*. Göttingen: Schwartz, 1970.

Franze, Johannes. "Richard Strauss in Buenos Aires," *Südamerika* 10, no. 2 (1959): 86–88.

Germani, Gino. "Asimilación de inmigrantes en el medio urbano: Notas metodológicas," *Revista Latinoamericana de Sociología* 1, no. 2 (1965): 158–177.

———. "La clase media en la Argentina, con especial referencia a sus sectores urbanos," in T. Crevenna, ed., *Materiales para el estudio de la clase media en la América Latina*. 6 vols. (Washington: Unión Panamericana, 1950), 1: 1–33.

———. *Estructura social de la Argentina*. Buenos Aires: Raigal, 1955.

———. *Política y sociedad en una época de transición de la sociedad tradicional a la sociedad de masas*. Buenos Aires: Paidós, 1968.

Germany. Marine-Archiv. *Der Krieg zur See 1914–1918: Der Kreuzerkrieg in den ausländischen Gewässern* (comp. and ed. E. Raeder). 3 vols. Berlin: 1922–1937. 1: *Das Kreuzergeschwader*, Berlin: 1922.

Hastedt, Pedro G. *Deutsche Direktinvestitionen in Lateinamerika: Ihre Entwicklung seit dem 1. Weltkrieg und ihre Bedeutung für die Industrialisierung des Subkontinents*. Göttingen: Schwartz, 1970.

"Immigration and Settlement in Brazil, Argentina, and Uruguay," *International Labor Review* 35, no. 1 (February 1937): 215–247; 35, no. 2 (March 1937): 352–383.

Kannapin, Klaus. "Die Luxburg-Affäre: Ein Beitrag zur Geschichte der Beziehungen zwischen Deutschland und Argentinien während des ersten Weltkrieges," *Wissenschaftliche Zeitschrift* der Humboldt-Universität zu Berlin 13, no. 7 (1964): 879–882.

——. "Zur Politik der Nazis in Argentinien von 1933 bis 1943," *Der Deutsche Faschismus in Lateinamerika, 1933–1941* (Berlin: Humboldt-Universität, 1966), pp. 81–102.

Katz, Friedrich. "Die deutschen Kriegsziele in Lateinamerika im ersten Weltkreig," *Wissenschaftliche Zeitschrift* der Humboldt-Universität zu Berlin 13, no. 7 (1964): 875–879.

Koblik, Steven. *Sweden: The Neutral Victor. Sweden and the Western Powers, 1917–1918. A Study of Anglo-American-Swedish Relations*. Lund: Lund Studies in International History, 1972.

Koch, Herbert. "Wilhelm Keiper zur Erinnerung aus Anlass seines 100. Geburtstages," *Zeitschrift für Kulturaustausch* 18, no. 4 (1968): 320–321.

Korn, F. "Algunos aspectos de la asimilación de inmigrantes en Buenos Aires," *América Latina* 8, no. 2 (April–June 1965): 77–96.

Kulischer, Eugene M. *Europe on the Move: War and Population Changes, 1917–1947*. New York: Columbia University Press, 1948.

Martínez, A. B., and M. Lewandowski. *The Argentine in the Twentieth Century*. London: T. F. Unwin, 1911.

Meisner, H. O. *Militärattachés und Militärbevollmächtigte in Preussen und im Deutschen Reich*. Berlin: Rütten und Loening, 1957.

Merkes, Manfred. *Die deutsche Politik im spanischen Bürgerkrieg, 1936–1939*. Bonn: Röhrscheid, 1961.

Micolis, Marisa. *Une communauté allemande en Argentine: El Dorado. Problèmes d'intégration socio-culturelle*. Québec: Centre Internationale de Recherches sur le Bilingüisme, 1973.

Navarro Gerassi, Marysa. "Argentine Nationalism of the Right," *Studies in Comparative International Development* 1, no. 12 (1965): 181–194.

Oddone, Juan Antonio. *La emigración europea al Río de la Plata: motivaciones y proceso de incorporación*. Montevideo: Ediciones de la Banda Oriental, 1966.

Pade, Werner. "Die Expansionspolitik des deutschen Imperialismus gegenüber Lateinamerika, 1918–1933," *Zeitschrift für Geschichtswissenschaft* 22, no. 6 (1974): 578–590.

Panettieri, José. *Inmigración en la Argentina*. Buenos Aires: Ediciones Macchi, 1970.

——. *Los trabajadores*. "Los Argentinos," 3. Buenos Aires: Editorial Jorge Alvarez, 1967.

Phelps, D. M. *Migration of Industry to South America*. New York: McGraw Hill, 1936.

Phelps, V. L. *The International Economic Position of Argentina*. Philadelphia: University of Pennsylvania Press, 1938.

Rippy, J. Fred. "German Investments in Argentina," *Journal of Business of the University of Chicago* 21, no. 1 (January 1948): 50–54.

——. "German Investments in Latin America," *Journal of Business of the University of Chicago* 21, no. 2 (1948): 63–64.

Schaefer, Jürgen. *Deutsche Militärhilfe an Südamerika: Militär- und Rüstungsinteressen in Argentinien, Bolivien und Chile vor 1914*. Düsseldorf: Bertelsmann, 1974.

Schiff, Warren. "The Influence of the German Armed Forces and War Industry on Argentina, 1880–1914," *Hispanic American Historical Review* 52, no. 3 (August 1972): 436–455.

Scobie, James. *Buenos Aires: Plaza to Suburb, 1870–1910.* New York: Oxford University Press, 1974.

Sebreli, Juan José. *La cuestión judía en la Argentina.* Buenos Aires: Editorial Tiempo Contemporáneo, 1968.

Solberg, Carl. "Rural Unrest and Agrarian Policy in Argentina," *Journal of Inter-American Studies and World Affairs* 8 (January 1971): 18–52.

Sommi, Luis V. *Los capitales alemanes en la Argentina.* Buenos Aires: Editorial Claridad, 1945.

Taylor, Carl. *Rural Life in Argentina.* Baton Rouge: Louisiana State University Press, 1948.

Tornquist, C. A. *El desarrollo de la República Argentina en los últimos cincuenta años.* Buenos Aires: 1919.

Tulchin, Joseph. *The Aftermath of War: World War One and United States Policy toward Latin America.* New York: New York University Press, 1971.

United States Department of Commerce. Bureau of Foreign and Domestic Commerce, *Statistics of German Trade, 1909–1913.* Washington, D.C.: Government Printing Office, 1918.

Willcox, Walter, and I. Ferenczi, eds. *International Migrations.* 2 vols. New York: National Bureau of Economic Research, 1929–1931.

Winkler, Max. *Investments of United States Capital in Latin America.* Boston: World Peace Foundation, 1928.

Zbinden, Karl. *Die schweizerische Auswanderung nach Argentinien, Uruguay, Chile und Paraguay.* Affoltern a.A. (Switzerland): Buchdruckerei Dr. J. Weiss, 1931.

Zeyen, Leo. "Deutsches Musikleben in Argentinien im Wandel eines Jahrhunderts," *Südamerika* 10, no. 1 (July–September 1959): 39–43.

Index